SCANNER MASTER

Metro D.C./Baltimore Guide

Michael Ericson, Editor

**SECOND
EDITION**

SCANNER MASTER PUBLISHING COMPANY
Post Office Box 428   Newton Highlands, Massachusetts 02161
1986

LAST MINUTE UPDATES AND CORRECTIONS

WASHINGTON, D.C.
    Metropolitan Police Department (p. 8)
    458.750M   1D: On Scene Communications (may be 458.700?)
    458.725M   2D: On Scene Communications
    458.475M   3D: On Scene Communications
    460.450R   8A: Presently used by Narcotics Task Force (Ch. B/C not in use)
    460.425R   9A: Used by Command & Supervisors (Ch. B/C not in use)
    458.700M   10D: ROPE (Repeat Offenders Task Force (Ch. A/B/C not in use)
    City Government (p. 14)
    153.980   STARPLEX (RFK Stadium - KBM921) (Armory - KDP418)
                  University of The District of Columbia (U.D.C.) (KWE379)
    155.715   D.C. General Hospital (KNCM812)
MARYLAND
    Maryland State Police (p. 18)
    494.0375   CID (listing is incorrect and should be deleted)
    Montgomery County Police (p. 47)
        Unit ID: District Units - Shift Super: (Shift) / (Sector) / 10
                  where (Sector) is A/D/G/J/M, Supervisor is a Sergeant
                  where (Sector) is B/E/H/K/N, Supervisor is MPO (rank equal to corporal)
    Prince George's County Police (p. 54)
    495.4625R   Future Expansion (listing is incorrect and should be deleted)
    155.790R   Detective Bureau & Special Operations (Input on 154.950) (KQY672)
    Prince George's County Police (p. 55)
        Radio Signals: 11 Hit & Run
                         I with Injury
                         F fatality
                        98 Eating out of Area
    Prince George's County Government (p. 59)
    155.580R   County Sheriff (Input on 154.830 NOT 158.730)
    154.830M / 155.940M Listed as former police channels: reallocated as noted on this pg.
    155.940R   Government Common / Animal Control (Input on 154.085)
    159.180R   Public Works & Highway Departments (Input on 151.055)
     45.520   Licences & Permits only
     47.620   may no longer be in use
    462.700   may no longer be in use
    Prince George's County - Municipalities (p. 59)
     46.580   College Park City Public Works (not Police Department)
    156.240   Hyattsville Public Works Department

International Standard Book Number (ISBN): 0-939430-11-8
Cover design by Roy H. Brown

                            Printed in U.S.A.

SCANNER MASTER: METRO D.C. / BALTIMORE GUIDE
TABLE OF CONTENTS

EDITOR'S INTRODUCTION

Scanner Master's Metro D.C. / Baltimore Guide, Second Edition, is an updated and revised version of our handbook which first became available nearly two years ago. The information contained in this volume represents a compilation of radio frequencies, codes and other useful information used by Municipal, County, State and Federal Agencies, as well as private businesses. Information was collected using official FCC records, data supplied by governmental agencies, reports from monitors, and actual monitoring by the author. Much of the information contained in the First Edition has been updated and reorganized based on suggestions received from you, the reader. Although every effort has been made to report accurate and complete information, we cannot be responsible for incorrect data, particularly where frequency changes are constantly occurring. Your continued correspondence identifying errors and omissions is encouraged, and will be used in future editions.

This guide has been designed for use by communications professionals, members of the news media, and interested hobbyists. We urge all individuals monitoring public service broadcasts to comply with all Municipal, County, State and Federal laws regulating the use of scanners, the divulging of contents of messages which are heard, and unauthorized response to the scene of emergencies or crimes.

This book is divided into three sections. Section 1 presents public safety listings by State. Each State is further subdivided into State Government and County listings. Within each County list are the municipalities contained therein.

Section 2, entitled "Special Allocations", includes certain quasi-businesses which require more detailed information than the straight frequency runs set out in Section 3.

Section 3 presents business frequencies grouped by the type of business. This list has been compiled to reflect a cross-section of businesses of greatest interest, ans as such is not complete. Following Section 3 is a chart showing the frequency band allocations from 25 MHz through 1300 MHz.

The inside back cover sets forth the Standard Ten Code used by most public service agencies. Where part or all of this list is used by a particular agency, reference is made to the Standard Ten Code, rather than repeating it each time.

All frequencies listed are assumed to be base to mobile (Simplex) unless otherwise indicated. The following abbreviations denote other modes of operations:

   X = unk. freq.   B = Base   M = Mobile   R = Repeater   P = Pager

Repeater inputs are listed, where known, in the VHF band. In the 450-470 MHz band input operates 5 MHz higher than receive. In the 470-512 MHz band input operates 3 MHz higher than receive. In the 806-953 MHz band input operates 45 MHz lower than receive.

The Radio Communications Monitoring Association (RCMA) is a national organization for monitor radio hobbyists. Its monthly magazine, "RCMA Newsletter", is must reading for all interested in any aspect of public service and scanner monitoring. For information, write RCMA General Manager, P.O. Box 542, Silverado, California 92676.

This Second Edition would not have been possible without the assistance and encouragement of the publisher, Richard Barnett, who has compiled much of the business section, as well as publishing the entire Scanner Master series; the updates, corrections and suggestions of readers who have contacted us since the First Edition was released; and most importantly, the many professional and volunteer members of area police and fire departments, whose help with this volume and unending service to the community should continue to serve as an example to us all.

                                        Michael Ericson
                                        Editor

DELAWARE: STATE AGENCIES

Department of Public Safety

154.665R	F1: New Castle Co. (North-Troops 1/2/6/9)	(Input 154.770)
154.755R	F2: Kent County (Central-Troop 3)	(Input 154.650)
154.665R	F3: Sussex County (South-Troops 4/5/7)	(Input 154.710)
154.695	F4: Statewide Data and Information / Car to Car	
155.475	F5: NLEEF - Nationwide Emergency Channel	
154.860	F6: SWEN - Statewide Municipal/County/State Coordination	
45.020	Highway Patrol F1: Dispatch	
44.860	Highway Patrol F2: Car to Car	
39.500	Bellefonte	

DISPATCH CENTERS:

KGA814	Bellefonte		KTA955	Lewes
WZX426	Dover		KQR469	Odessa
KGA813	Georgetown		KGF226	Rehoboth
WZZ290	Georgetown			

STATE / COUNTY MAP

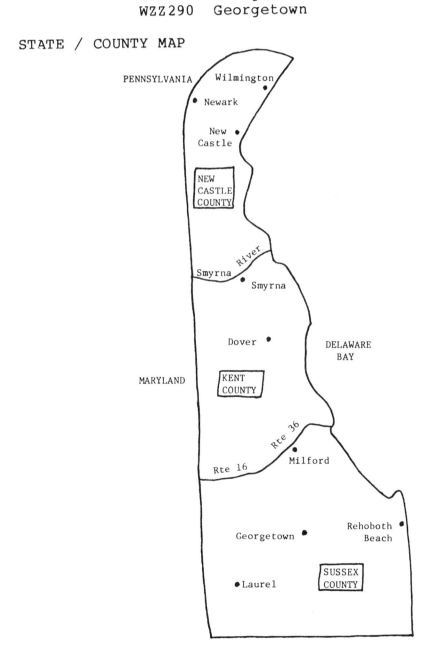

DELAWARE: STATE AGENCIES (Continued)

Department of Public Safety
TEN CODES

10-01 Under control	10-33 Parking Viol.	10-63 Advise...Loc.
10-02 Arrived	A-Disabled Car	10-64 Sp. Unit in Area
10-03 Transmit	10-34 Make copy	10-65 Attempt Warrant
10-04 Acknowledge	10-35 Confid. Info.	10-66 Radio Tower Lights
10-05 Relay	10-36 Time Check	10-67 Req. Car Washdown
10-06 Busy	10-37 Magistrate Court	10-68 Meet Officer At...
10-07 Out of Service	N-Not Open	10-69 Enroute to...
10-08 In Service	10-38 Magistrate Avail.	10-70 Report to...
10-09 Repeat	N-Not Avail.	10-71 Alert-Major Emergency
10-10 Accident	10-39 Use caution	10-72 Mobilize - Major Emergency
10-11 2-Alarm Fire	10-40 PD Needs Help	10-73 Rpt to Marshaling
10-12 Assist. HQ/FD	10-41 Check car or ped.	10-74 Supp. Committed pers.
10-13 Weather	10-42 Clear on Check	10-75 Activate Scrambler
10-14 Convoy	A-Arrest	A-Deactivate
10-15 Prisoner	R-Reprimand	10-79 Routine Transport
10-16 Pick up Prisoner	CPC-Crime Preven.	10-80 Spinal Injury
10-17 Eating	10-43 Wrecker needed	10-81 Mental Patient
10-18 Comp. ASAP	10-44 Ambulance needed	10-82 Communicable dis.
10-19 Return to...	10-45 Rescue needed	10-83 Head/Face/Neck injury
10-20 Location	10-46 Fire Truck needed	10-84 Seizure
10-21 Call by phone	10-47 Tank Truck needed	10-85 Convulsions
10-22 Disregard	10-48 Alarm at Location	10-86 Drowning
10-23 Direct Traffic	10-49 Civil Disturb.	10-87 Police Action
10-24 Req. Assistance	10-50 Contact M.E.	10-88 Overdose
10-25 E.T.A.	10-51 Call Fire Marshall	10-89 Burns
10-26 Operator's No.	10-52 Leave sector	10-90 Cardiac Arrest
A-Trf. Viol.	10-53 Road Blocked	10-91 D.O.A.
B-Crim. Viol.	10-54 Road Blocked at...	10-92 Internal Injury
10-27 Notify Agency	10-55 Pick up...	10-93 Fractured Limb
10-28 Req. Information	10-56 School Xing	10-94 Miscarriage
10-29 Wanted Checks	10-57 Bomb Threat	10-95 Emergency Maternity
N-No Wants	10-58 Trf. Light Problem	10-96 Have Oxygen Ready
W-Wants	10-59 Release OD Unit	10-97 Severe Bleeding
10-30 Doesn't Conform	10-60 Contact C.I.D.	10-98 Stroke Victim
10-31 Meet Complainant	10-61 Property Check	10-99 Heart Attack
10-32 Complainant	10-62 Clear 10-61	10-100 CLEAR AIR: EMERGENCY

Department of Transportation

47.220	F1: New Castle and Sussex Counties
47.340	F2: Kent County

DISPATCH CENTERS

Delaware City	KCV371	Dover	KGD205
Georgetown	KGE556	Georgetown	WZX933
Harrington	KGE482	Lewes	KSZ357
Middletown	KGE666	Seaford	KGE481
State Road	KGC901	Wilmington	KJY892

156.135   Delaware Turnpike - Maintenance (KJI397)

DELAWARE: STATE AGENCIES (Continued)

Statewide Fire Control

33.780	F1: Statewide Dispatch
33.820	F2: Central - Kent County (KVT766)
33.860	F2: South - Sussex County (KGC522)
33.940	F2: North - New Castle County (KGE831/WQV807)

NEW CASTLE COUNTY FIRE STATIONS

08	KGH795	Aetna	21		Mill Creek
09	KDD994	Aetna	22	KGE246	Minquadale
11	KGD394	Brandywine Hundred (N6)	23	KGD951	Minquas
12	KGH502	Christiana	24	KCH734	Odessa (N1)
13	KGB973	Claymont	25	KGD210	Talleyville (N4/6)
14	KGE745	Cranston Heights (N8)	26	KGE634	Townsend
15	KGG868	Delaware City	27	KGD511	Volunteer Hose
16	KNAG563	Elsmere	28	KSQ514	Wilmington Manor
17	KGC939	Five Points	29	KBY493	Port Penn (N14)
18		Goodwill VFD	30	KNCS212	Belvedere (N4)
19	KGE335	Hockessin (N10/11)	31	KJG921	Claymont #2
20	KGE960	Holloway Terrace	32	KGD536	Wilmington Manor #2
			--	KQS577	Delaware Air Nat

KENT COUNTY FIRE STATIONS

40	KQM649	North Bowers	49	KJY355	Frederica
41	KBN502	Camden-Wyoming	50	KBN499	Harrington
42	KGC277	Carlisle (N2)	51	KEX267	Hartley
43	KGE311	Cheswold	52	KBT569	Houston
44	KGB745	Citizens (Smyrna) (N3)	53	KCI665	Leipsic (N12)
45	KBW552	Clayton (N3)	54	KBH749	Little Creek
46	KGC524	Robbins (Dover)	55	KIZ202	Magnolia
47	KSZ256	Farmington (N2)	56	KFF350	Marydel (N13)
48	KBS717	Felton	57	KTK779	South Bowers

SUSSEX COUNTY FIRE STATIONS

70	KSX287	Bethany Beach	81	KGD977	Laurel
71	KBG932	Blades (N5)	82	KGF272	Lewes
72	KGD824	Bridgeville	83	KGD973	Millsboro
73	KTZ505	Dagsboro	84	KBN503	Millville
74	KGE889	Delmar (N7)	85	KGD941	Milton
75	KRG724	Ellendale (N1)	86	KGD461	Rehoboth Beach
76	KET202	Frankford	87	KGD942	Seaford
77	KLU380	Georgetown	88	KNBD573	Selbyville
78	KGF600	Greenwood (N1)	89	KGL636	Memorial
79	KVV638	Gumboro	90	KVA545	Roxana
80	KJS921	Indian River			

NOTES: "N" indicates license on additional frequencies as follows:

N1: Kent County Channel	N8: 460.575
N2: Sussex County Channel	N9: 453.900
N3: New Castle Co Channel	N10: Cecil Co, MD F1 (33.900)
N4: 33.680	Chester Co, PA F1 (33.900)
N5: 154.400 & 154.430	N11: Chester Co, PA F3 (33.960)
N6: 460.600 (Talleyville - WZZ980)	N12: 33.620
(Brandywine - WQY269)	N13: Caroline Co, MD F1 (33.700)
N7: Wicomico Co, MD F1 (33.980)	N14: 154.340 (KNCG405)

DELAWARE: STATE AGENCIES (Continued)

Department of Forestry Conservation
Department of Natural Resources
44.680   Administration
44.720   Enforcement Units
            Kirkwood-KSO599/Lewes-KBV871/Milford-KGE780/Georgetown-WZJ249
Department of Forestry and Agriculture
151.175   Operations (Camden-WCW565 / Redden-WCW657)
151.385   Operations (Camden-WCW565 / Redden-WCW657 / Blackbird-WCW655)
953.400   unknown use (Kirkwood-WBH543 / Milton-WBH545)
954.400   unknown use (Milton-WBH545)
957.000   unknown use (Dover-WBH544 / Lewes-WBH546)
958.000   unknown use (Dover-WBH544)

Delaware River Port Authority
460.375   Police Dispatch: North (KRX320)
            F=Ben Franklin Bridge / R=Betsy Ross Bridge
460.425   Police Dispatch: South (KRX322)
            W=Walt Whitman Bridge / B=Commodore Barry Bridge
453.425   Administration (KYB697)
156.700   Marine F14: Port Operations (KEW842)
156.120R   Bridge Maintenance (KRV276)
154.100R   Electric & Maintenance (KEX315)

State River and Bay Authority (Delaware Memorial Bridge)
155.310   Police Dispatch (New Castle - WYR675)
151.070   Bridge Maintenance (KDR414)
453.9625R   Bridge Maintenance (KDR414)

Miscellaneous State Government
35.900   Gov. Beacon Health Center (Delaware City - WXR411)
45.200   unknown use (Georgetown-KAW772)
45.240   Civil Defense Network:
            Marshallton-KCT601/Lewes-KCT602/Dover-KCT603/Delaware City-KCT604
47.620P   Bissell Hospital (Wilmington - KUQ744)
151.010R   Toll Bridge Commission (KXL263) (Input on 158.985)
151.805   University of Delaware (Newark)
151.925   University of Delaware / Wesley College (Dover)
153.995M   Unknown use (KA70289)
154.600M   University of Delaware
155.100   State Offices (Wilmington-WXT835 / Dover-KQP602)
155.400   Delaware State Hospital (New Castle - KFT454)
157.450   Statewide Safety
166.950   National Park Service: Delaware Water Gap Nat. Reservation
453.525R   Unknown use: New Castle (WXR380) / Georgetown (WXR381)
453.625R   State Colleges and Universities
            Bridgeville-KSU374/Dover-KSU375/Smyrna-KTZ416/Newark-KVG759/Lewes-KZE748
453.950R   Unknown use: Dover (WXR379)
122.900   State Aircraft - Statewide use (KTQ4) (also 122.925)
121.500   State Aircraft - Dover (WZA9) (also 123.050)
121.600   Civil Air Patrol (Statewide - KF5803)
162.550   NOAA Weather Broadcasts (Lewes)

DELAWARE: KENT COUNTY (County Seat: Dover)

Fire Department (KVT766)
33.780	F1: Statewide Dispatch
33.820	F2: County Fireground
	Med Channels 1-8 / Call 1-2 (WXM594)
	NOTE: Fire Stations included under State listings

County Government
453.375R	County Common Operations (KZE577)

Municipalities
155.250R	Clayton City Police (KWQ583) (Input on 156.030)
155.310R	Dover City Police: Dispatch (KGA871) (Input on 155.970)
159.150	Dover City Police: Car to Car
453.325R	Dover City Government (KWT752)
48.020	Dover City Utilities (KGD466)
155.250R	Milford City Police (KGB227) (Input on 156.030)
155.775	Milford City Government (KQO340)
154.455	Milford City Utilities (WGN429-30)
155.250R	Smyrna City Police (KIZ487) (Input on 156.030)
155.025	Smyrna City Government (KNAZ316)

DELAWARE: SUSSEX COUNTY (County Seat: Georgetown)

County Police (KNER815)
154.995R	Dispatch (Input on 155.985)
155.880	Car to Car

Fire Department (KGC522)
33.780	F1: Statewide Dispatch
33.860	F2: County Fireground
	Med Channels 1-8 / Call 1-2 (WXB793-6)
	NOTE: Fire Stations included under State listings

County Government
45.240	State Civil Defense Link (WRU990)
47.420	Emergency Operations Center (KNCE425)
47.620	Emergency Operations Center (WSL894)
122.800	County Air Operations (KZL8)

Municipalities
154.800R	Bethany Beach Police (WXR398) (Input on 155.910)
155.010R	Dewey Beach Police (KNFX763) (Input on 155.850)
155.040	Fenwick Island City Government (KNIK967)
155.010R	Laurel City Police (KUL759) (Input on 155.850)
155.040	Laurel City Government (KEG863)
155.010	Lewes City Police (KGB663)
155.955	Lewes City Government (KTE412)
154.965	Millsboro City Government (WQG920)
155.130R	Milton City Police (KQT975) (Input on 156.090)
155.250R	Rehoboth Beach Police (KGD552) (Input on 156.030)
155.820	Rehoboth Beach City Government (KNAZ315)
155.250R	Seaford City Police (KGX973) (Input on 156.030)
155.715	Seaford City Government (KBR372)
155.250R	Selbyville City Police (KUO906) (Input on 156.030)

<u>DELAWARE:</u>   <u>NEW CASTLE COUNTY</u>   (County Seat: Wilmington)

<u>County Police</u> (KNAU522)   (Old System-KGF268)
158.805R   F1: North Dispatch   39.860 F1: North
158.805M   F2: North Car to Car   39.540 F2: South
155.115R   F3: South Dispatch   39.700M F3: Car to Car
155.115M   F4: South Car to Car
155.490   F5: Detectives (KNAU536)
154.860   F6: SWEN (Statewide Intersystem)
155.475   F7: NLEEF (Nationwide Intersystem)
            Input to F1 & F3: 153.740M / 153.800M
            NOTE: For Radio Codes, see Scanner Master Greater Phili Guide

<u>Fire Department</u> (WQV807/KGE831)
 33.780   F1: Statewide Dispatch
 33.940   F2: County Fireground
155.235   Ambulance & Rescue Dispatch (WXF898)
            Med 3 (Prim) / Med 2 (Sec) / Med 6 (Alt) (WXF898)
            NOTE Fire Stations included under State listings

<u>County Government</u>
 37.620   Delmarva Power & Light (Wilmington) (also 37.760)
 45.160   County Government (KBJ979)
 47.620   Special Emergency (WEX649)
 47.780   Artesian Water Company (Wilmington)
154.115   County Government (KQU202)
154.540   County Board of Education (WXW691-2)
155.175   C Data Service Ctr: School Board Security (WXF899)
155.220   County Medical Society (Wilmington-KSZ364)
155.235   C Data Service Ctr: School Board Safety (WXF898/WXF900)
451.3625R   Artesian Water Company (Newark)
856.4375R   Future allocation(also 857.4375R/858.4375R/859.4375R/860.4375)

<u>Municipalities</u>
155.175   Claymont City Schools: Security (KXX320)
155.010R   Elsemere City Police (KAY931) (Input on 155.535)
155.745   Elsemere City Government (WQH723)
155.775   Middletown City Government (WRB477)
155.250R   Newark City Police F1: Dispatch (KGE351) (Input on 156.030)
154.755   Newark City Police F2: State Police (Kent County Dispatch)
156.030M   Newark City Police F3: Car to Car
154.860   Newark City Police F4: SWEN (Statewide Intersystem)
154.040   Newark City Government (KAZ662)
173.210   Newark City Utilities (WGS902)
154.800   New Castle City Police (KZB327)
173.3125   New Castle City Utilities (WGR633)
155.310   Wilmington City Police F1: Link to Delaware Memorial Bridge
155.130R   Wilmington City Police --- Dispatch (KGA819)(Input on 156.090)
155.610   Wilmington City Police --- Operations (KGA819)
155.640   Wilmington City Police --- Operations (KGA819)
154.965R   Wilmington Fire Department F1: Dispatch (KDL981)
155.055R   Wilmington Fire Department F2: Fireground (KDL981)
155.055M   Wilmington Fire Department F3: Fireground (KDL981)
153.935M   Wilmington Fire Dept: Input (also 155.935M / 155.985M)
155.925   Wilmington City Government (WXF791-2)
155.280   Wilmington Ambulances & Medical Center (SKL869-72)
462.625   Wilmington City Housing Authority (KAC8169)
856.7625R   Wilmington (also 857.7625R/858.7625R/859.7625R/860.7625R)

WASHINGTON, D.C.: CITY AGENCIES

Metropolitan Police Department

460.350R	1A:	District 1 Dispatch (KLG604)
460.400R	1B:	Southeast Tactical (KLG613)
460.400M	1C:	Simplex Car to Car
458.xxxM	1D:	On Scene Communications
460.250R	2A:	District 2 Dispatch (KLG610)
460.100R	2B:	Northwest Tactical (KLG605)
460.100M	2C:	Simplex Car to Car
458.xxxM	2D:	On Scene Communications
460.025R	3A:	District 3 Dispatch (KLG617)
460.100R	3B:	Northwest Tactical (KLG605)
460.100M	3C:	Simplex Car to Car
458.xxxM	3D:	On Scene Communications
460.500R	4A:	District 4 Dispatch (KLG614)
460.100R	4B:	Northwest Tactical (KLG605)
460.100M	4C:	Simplex Car to Car
458.xxxM	4D:	On Scene Communications
460.200R	5A:	District 5 Dispatch (KLG616)
460.100R	5B:	Northwest Tactical (KLG605)
460.100M	5C:	Simplex Car to Car
458.xxxM	5D:	On Scene Communications
460.150R	6A:	District 6 Dispatch (KLG609)
460.400R	6B:	Southeast Tactical (KLG613)
460.400M	6C:	Simplex Car to Car
458.xxxM	6D:	On Scene Communications
460.475R	7A:	District 7 Dispatch (KLG603)
460.400R	7B:	Southeast Tactical (KLG613)
460.400M	7C:	Simplex Car to Car
458.xxxM	7D:	On Scene Communications
460.450R	8A:	District 8 Dispatch (KLG607)
460.400R	8B:	Southeast Tactical (KLG613)
460.400M	8C:	Simplex Car to Car
458.xxxM	8D:	On Scene Communications
460.425R	9A:	District & HQ Officials (KLG606)
460.425R	9B:	District & HQ Officials (KLG606)
460.425R	9C:	District & HQ Officials (KLG606)
458.350M	9D:	On Scene Communications
	10A:	Future allocation
	10B:	Future allocation
	10C:	Future allocation
458.700M	10D:	On Scene Communications
460.275R	11A:	Special Operations Division (KLG611)
460.275R	11B:	Special Operations Division (KLG611)
460.275M	11C:	Simplex car to car
465.000M	11D:	Special Events/Hostages
460.325R	12A:	Citywide / Emergencies (KLG615)
460.325R	12B:	Citywide / Emergencies (KLG615)
460.325R	12C:	Citywide / Emergencies (KLG615)
460.325R	12D:	Citywide / Emergencies (KLG615)

Between 11pm-7am dispatchers simulcast 1A/12A 2A/3A 4A/5A 6A/7A
"Station Channel" refers to District Tactical Frequency

WASHINGTON, D.C.: CITY AGENCIES (Continued)

Metropolitan Police Department (Continued)
Miscellaneous Channels

159.150R	VHF simulcast F12: Citywide (Input on 155.250)	
154.890	Portable Extender F11: Special Operations Division	
158.790R	TAC-1: Undercover Operations (KRJ859) (Input on 156.030)	
158.850R	TAC-2: Undercover Operations (KLG608) (Input on 156.090)	
159.030P	Citywide Pager & Broadcasts (KBZ474)	
453.550R	"P-MARS" Mutual Aid (KLG612/WAF874)	

Harbor Division Maritime Channels

156.600	M12: Port Operations/USCG (KEB311/KEB316)	
156.800	M16: Distress/Calling (KEB311/KEB316)	
156.425	M68: Non-Commercial (KUF703)	
156.650	M72: Non-Commercial (KEB311/KEB316)	
157.025	M80: Commercial (KUF703)	
157.075	M81: Maritime Government/USCG (KUF703)	

Old Police Allocations - Still allocated but not in use (WHP83)

154.680	
154.860	KLG605
154.920	KLG616
155.310	KLG613
155.415	KLG614

TEN CODES (only ones officially used)

10-01	Unable to Copy	10-33	Officer in Trouble
10-04	Acknowledgment (2 man)	10-89	Bomb Threat
10-08	In Service	10-99	Acknowledgment (1 man)
10-30	WALES Hit (Wanted)		

UNIT IDENTIFICATION: Citywide Cruisers (D = District Number)

0xx	HQ Senior Officials	35x	Sex Squad	65x	Executive Escort
11	Dep Chief-Operations	6x	Sector Cruisers	6x	SOD Units
2D	District Commanders	4xx	Traffic Division	7x	Bomb Squad (EOD)
3x	VIP Security	07	Hack Inspector	9D	District Canine
1xx	HQ Senior Officials	3x	Alcohol Cruisers	7xx	Miscellaneous
2xx	District Officials	5xx	Miscellaneous Units	0x	Medical Examiner
00-19	Lieutenants	2D	Dist Youth Division	1D-7D	Dist Detectives
20-99	Sergeants	30-59	HQ Vice & Narcotics	8xx	HQ Special Units
3xx	HQ Detectives	6x	Federal D.E.A.	0x	Harbor Patrol
0x	Command/Supervisors	7x	HQ Vice & Narcotics	9Dx	Dist Evidence Tech
1x	Homicide Squad	9D	District Canine	TAC-xx	Undercover Units
2x	Robbery Squad	6xx	Special Operations	JUNEAU	Helicopters (1-7)
3x	Check & Fraud	0x	SOD Officials	MOTORS	Motorcycles
4x	Burglary Squad	10-49	SOD Units	RADIO-xxx:	SOD/Trf/HQ/Foot

SPECIAL OPERATIONS DIVISION

Headquarters:	N. Capitol & K Streets
Tactical HQ:	Georgia & Madison, NW
Helicopter:	National Airport
Dep Chief-SOD:	Cruiser 11
SOD Officials:	Cruisers 600-609
SOD Units:	Cruisers 610-699
ROPE Unit:	Cruiser 635
Exec Escort:	Cruisers 650-659
Bomb Squad:	Cruisers 670-679
Harbor Patrol:	Units 801-810

POLICE HEADQUARTERS
Indiana Avenue & C St, NW

YOUTH DIVISION HEADQUARTERS
North Capitol & K Streets

TRAINING SCHOOL
Route 295 & Chesapeake, SE

IMPOUND LOT
Route 295 & D.C. Line

WASHINGTON, D.C.: CITY AGENCIES (Continued)

Metropolitan Police Department: DISTRICT LOCATIONS & UNIT IDENTIFICATION

DISTRICT 1
Headquarters:	4th & E Streets, SW
Sub-District 1D1:	4th & E Streets, SE
Patrol Units:	Scout Cars 011-032
Patrol Wagons	Wagons 033-034
Commander:	Cruiser 21
Lieutenants:	Cruisers 200-203
Sergeants:	Cruisers 220-229
Youth Division:	Cruiser 521
Canine Officers:	Cruisers 591/691
Detectives:	Cruisers 710-719
Evidence Tech:	Cruisers 910-919
District Station:	Radio 1000
Special Assign:	Radio 1xxx
Motor Scooters:	1Dx

DISTRICT 2
Headquarters:	23rd & L Streets, NW
Sub-District 2D1:	33rd & P Streets, NW
Sub-District 2D2:	42nd & Albemarle, NW
Patrol Units:	Scout Cars 063-084
Patrol Wagons:	Wagons 061-062
Commander:	Cruiser 22
Lieutenants:	Cruisers 204-207
Sergeants:	Cruisers 230-239
Youth Division:	Cruiser 522
Canine Officers:	Cruisers 592/692
Detectives:	Cruisers 720-729
Evidence Tech:	Cruiser 920-929
District Station:	Radio 2000
Special Assign:	Radio 2xxx
Motor Scooters:	2Dx

DISTRICT 3
Headquarters:	16th & U Streets, NW
Sub-District 3D1:	6th & N.Y. Ave., NW
Patrol Units:	Scout Cars 085-104
Patrol Wagons:	Wagons 105-106
Commander:	Cruiser 23
Lieutenants:	Cruisers 208-210
Sergeants:	Cruisers 240-249
Youth Division:	Cruiser 523
Canine Officers:	Cruisers 593/693
Detectives:	Cruisers 730-739
Evidence Tech:	Cruisers 930-939
District Station:	Radio 3000
Special Assign:	Radio 3xxx
Motor Scooters:	3Dx

DISTRICT 4
Headquarters:	9th & Quackenbos, NW
Sub-District 4D1:	Morton & Sherman, NW
Patrol Units:	Scout Cars 119-137
Patrol Wagons:	Wagons 116-117
Commander:	Cruiser 24
Lieutenants:	Cruisers 211-213
Sergeants:	Cruisers 250-259

DISTRICT 4 (Cont)
Youth Division:	Cruiser 524
Canine Officers:	Cruisers 594/694
Detectives:	Cruisers 740-749
Evidence Tech:	Cruisers 940-949
District Station:	Radio 4000
Special Assign:	Radio 4xxx
Motor Scooters:	4Dx

DISTRICT 5
Headquarters:	7th & Girard Streets, NE
Sub-District 5D1:	F & Maryland Streets, NE
Patrol Units:	Scout Cars 138-157
Patrol Wagons:	Wagons 158-159
Commander:	Cruiser 25
Lieutenants:	Cruisers 214-216
Sergeants:	Cruisers 260-269
Youth Division:	Cruiser 525
Canine Officers:	Cruisers 595/695
Detectives:	Cruisers 750-759
Evidence Tech:	Cruisers 950-959
District Station:	Radio 5000
Special Assign:	Radio 5xxx
Motor Scooters:	5Dx

DISTRICT 6
Headquarters:	42nd & Benning Roads, NE
Patrol Units:	Scout Cars 40-55
Patrol Wagons:	Wagons 56-57
Commander:	Cruiser 26
Lieutenants:	Cruisers 217-219
Sergeants:	Cruisers 270-279
Youth Division:	Cruiser 526
Canine Officers:	Cruisers 596/696
Detectives:	Cruisers 760-769
Evidence Tech:	Cruisers 960-969
District Station:	Radio 6000
Special Assign:	Radio 6xxx
Motor Scooters:	6Dx

DISTRICT 7
Headquarters:	7th & Mississippi, SE
Patrol Cars:	Scout Cars 171-189
Patrol Wagons:	Wagons 190-191
Commander:	Cruiser 27
Lieutenants:	Cruisers 217-219
Sergeants:	Cruisers 290-299
Youth Division:	Cruiser 527
Canine Officers:	Cruisers 597/697
Detectives:	Cruisers 770-779
Evidence Tech:	Cruisers 970-979
District Station:	Radio 7000
Special Assign:	Radio 7xxx
Motor Scooters:	7Dx

DISTRICT 8
Future Capitol Hill Area Station

WASHINGTON, D.C.: CITY AGENCIES (Continued)

Metropolitan Police Department: DISTRICT MAP

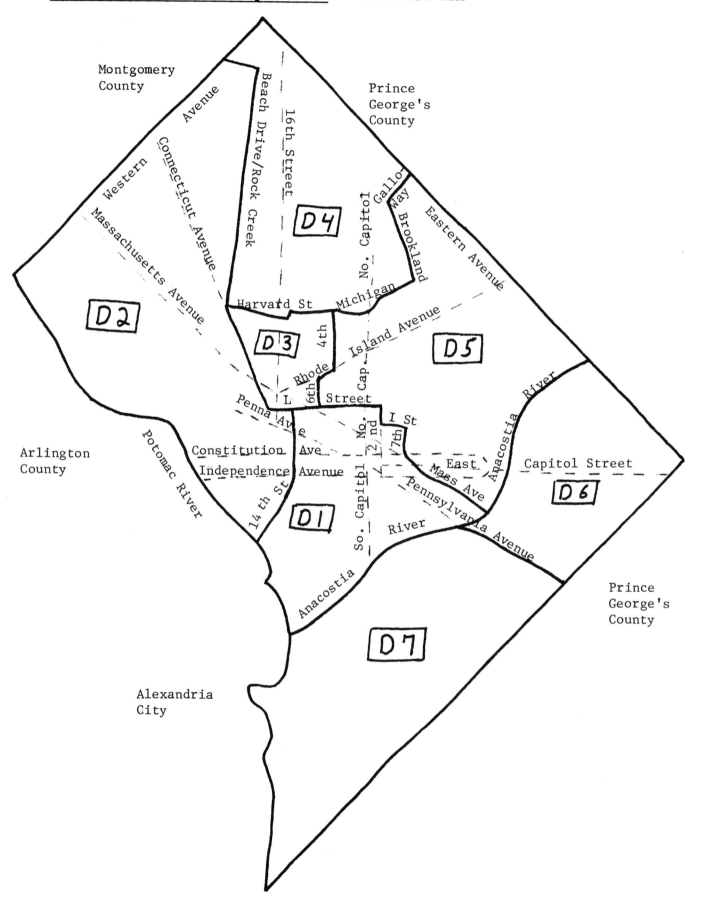

WASHINGTON, D.C.: CITY AGENCIES (Continued)

Washington Metropolitan Area Police Mutual Aid Radio System

453.550R   "P-MARS"

The Washington Metropolitan Area has set up a mutual aid radio system whereby bases and mobil units from several of the jurisdictions may communicate with each other. Base stations will communicate directly through the P-MARS frequency. Mobil units will be patched through the P-MARS frequency permitting a unit from any of the jurisdictions to communicate on their own frequency through the P-MARS to the other jurisdiction's frequency. For example, if a District 2 Officer from D.C. wished to communicate with an Officer from Montgomery County-Bethesda District, he would speak on his normal channel of 460.250, through the P-MARS frequency, and would be heard on 494.8625, the Montgomery County Channel. The same would be true for the response from the Montgomery County Officer to the D.C. Officer, only the process would be reversed. Approximately three times each day this system conducts a roll call with all base stations in the area participating. The following departments are licensed to operate on this system:

Alexandria City PD	KLY674	MDW Fort McNair	WAR440
Arlington County PD	WAF586	MP Fort Belvoir	AAC485
Armed Forces Police	WAR200	Metropolitan PD (DC)	WAF874
Fairfax City PD	WAC340	Montgomery County PD	WAF867
Fairfax County PD	WAC339	Prince George's County PD	KUX236
Falls Church City PD	WAC341	Prince William County PD	WAC346
Herndon City PD	KRS401	U.S. Park Police	KGB797
Loudon County Sheriff	WAC343	U.S. Secret Service	W.F.O.
Manassas City PD	WAC344	U.S. Secret Service	U.D.
Manassas Park PD	KWM842	U.S. Capitol Police	
MD State PD (Coll Pk)	KSU469	Vienna City PD	WAC347
MD State PD (R'ville)	KGE796	Virginia State PD (Alex)	WAC420

Fire Department   (KGA611)

154.190R	F1:	Dispatch & Simplex Fireground (Input on 154.400)
154.235	F2:	Fireground
154.280	F3:	Metro Area Mutual Aid
154.205	F4:	Chief & Fire Marshall Pager / Alternate Fireground
154.295		Allocated for future use
33.060		Ambulance Dispatch (KGA842)
155.160		Ambulance-Hospital Communications (KTH397)
155.340		Ambulance-Hospital Communications (KTH397)
		Med Channels 1-10 (KAA775)

Trunked system allocated to DC Fire (KB23372 - Mobils only)
   NOTE: There are no present plans to switch over to this system.

816.0875	817.0875	818.0875	819.0875	820.0875
816.3375	817.3375	818.3375	819.3375	820.3375
816.5875	817.5875	818.5875	819.5875	820.5875
816.8375	817.8375	818.8375	819.8375	820.8375

WASHINGTON, D.C.: CITY AGENCIES (Continued)

Fire Department (continued)

CO.	ADDRESS	ENG	TRK	MED	RS	AMB	BFC	TAU
01	2225 M Street, N.W...............	01	2	11			2	2
02	500 F Street, N.W................	02	1			7		
03	439 New Jersey Ave., N.W........	03				15		
04	2531 Sherman Ave., N.W..........	04			2	19		
05	3412 Dent Place, N.W............	05	5					
06	1300 New Jersey Ave., N.W.......	06	4		1	5	1	
07	1101 Half Street, N.W...........	07						
08	1520 C Street, S.E..............	08		9		16		
09	1617 U Street, N.W..............	09	9					
10	1342 Florida Ave., N.E..........	10	13					
11	3420 14th Street, N.W...........	11	6	1				
12	1626 N. Capitol Street..........	12				17		
13	450 6th Street, S.W.............	13	10			6		1
14	4801 North Capitol Street.......	14		18		4		
15	2101 14th Street, S.E...........	15	16		3	12	3	
16	1018 13th Street, N.W...........	16	3			14	6	
17	1227 Monroe Street, N.E.........	17						
18	414 8th Street, S.E.............	18	7			7		
19	2813 Penna. Ave., S.E...........	19						
20	4300 Wisconsin Ave., N.W........	20	12			8		
21	1763 Lanier Place, N.W..........	21				2		
22	5760 Georgia Ave., N.W..........	22	11					
23	2119 G Street, N.W..............	23						
24	3702 Georgia Ave., N.W..........	24				4		
25	3203 M. L. King Ave., S.E.......	25	8					
26	1340 Rhode Is. Ave., N.E........	26	15					
27	4201 Minnesota Ave., N.E........	27						
28	3522 Connecticut Ave.,N.W.......	28	14				5	
29	4811 MacArthur Blvd., N.W.......	29						
30	50 49th Street, N.E.............	30	17			10	8	
31	4930 Connecticut Ave.,N.W.......	31			4			
32	2425 Irving Street, S.E.........	32		3		13		
	550 Maine Avenue, S.W. (Potomac River): Fire Boat							

KEY: ENG=Engine Company / TRK=Truck / MED=Medic / RS=Rescue Squad /
AMB=Ambulance / BFC=Batallion Fire Chief / TAU=Twin Engine Unit

Special Units: Co 2: Ambulance Supervisor / Deputy Fire Chief
Co 4: Air Compressor   Co 9: Searchlight Wagon
Co 13: Foam & Dry Chem Truck / MB-5 Airport Crash
Co 24: Salvage Wagon   Co 27: Gasoline Tank Truck

NOTE: D.C. Fire uses no Ten Codes - Ambulances use these Hospital Codes:
01 Greater Southeast Community Hospital   08 George Washington University Hospital
02 Children's Hospital   09 Hadley Memorial Hospital
03 Columbia Hospital for Women   10 Providence Hospital
04 Doctor's Hospital   11 Capitol Hill Hospital
05 Howard University Hospital   12 Sibley Memorial Hospital
06 D.C. General Hospital   13 Washington Hospital Center
07 Georgetown University Hospital   15 Veteran's Administration Hospital

WASHINGTON, D.C.: CITY AGENCIES (Continued)

Fire Department (Continued)
Ambulance Hospital Codes
   CODE RED: Hospital Re-Route
   CODE ORANGE: Emergency Room Re-Route (Emergency Room Full)
   CODE YELLOW: Critical Care Re-Route (No Critical Care Beds)
   CODE WHITE: Critical Care Beds Only (No Ward Beds)
   CODE BLUE: Hospital Re-Route (No Beds Available)

City Government

Department of Environmental Services
   37.100   Trash Collection & Street Cleaning (KSO610/1/2)
   37.940   Highway Repairs & Maint. (KGC609/KGG358/KGA598/KKD518)
   37.980   Sewer Department (KGA598/KGC609/KKD518)
  158.130   Water Department (KBZ463-4/KGA596)
  153.455   Water Revenue (KVY297)

Board of Education
  153.740   Building Security (KUJ512)
  153.755   Buses & Maintenance (KUJ512)
  153.815   Buses & Maintenance (KUJ512)
  151.715   Miscellaneous Jr. & Sr. High School Operations
  816.7875   Public Schools
  820.7875   Public Schools

Division of Parking Enforcement
  495.4625R   F1: Ticket Writers (KMA675)
  495.4375R   F2: Cranes (Tow Trucks) (KMA675)
  453.875R   F3: Booting & Motor Pool (KLK746/KSV783)

Department of Transportation
  453.450R   Signal Shop "643" (KVV390)
  453.750R   Trees Department & Repair Division "942" (KVV390)
  951.000   Automatic Traffic Signals (WEG855)
  952.500   Automatic Traffic Signals (WEG855)

Miscellaneous
  453.525R   General Services Admin: Special Police (KTT830/WZX920)
   45.560   Civil Defense/Emergency Preparedness) KAT769/KAT780/KCS500
   45.600   Civil Defense/Emergency Preparedness) KFM419/KLR491/KCS497
   39.020   Corrections F1: Lorton, Virginia Facility (KGA792-5)
   39.080   Corrections F2: Lorton, Virginia Facility (KGA792-5)
  488.3125R   Corrections - D.C. Jail (KAW678) (Input on 491.3125)
  408.800R   Housing Authority (KZW924) (Input on 411.350)
  154.040   Human Resources/Health Dept (KFV983/KLR492/KWJ366/KWJ367)
  453.225R   Department of Recreation (KSV783)
  153.980   STARPLEX: Stadium/Armory Operations (KBM921/KDP418/KWF379)
  463.625   D.C. Chamber of Commerce: Board of Trade
  464.225   D.C. Chamber of Commerce / U.S. Chamber of Commerce
  816.9625   D.C. Housing Center
  155.715   unknown use (KNCM812)
  494.9625R   unknown use (WIE917)
  497.3375M   unknown use (WIE916)

WASHINGTON, D.C.: CITY AGENCIES (Continued)

<u>United States Government</u>

U.S. Park Police
166.725R	F1: Car to Car	(Input on 165.975)
411.625R	UF1: UHF Simulcast	(Input on 409.550)
166.925R	F2: Dispatch	(Input on 165.925)
411.725R	UF2: UHF Simulcast	(Input on 409.650)
167.075	F3: Special Operations	
166.850	F4: Alternate car to car	
411.825R	J.F.K. Center Security	(Input on 409.750)
411.925R	Visitors Center Security	(Input on 409.850)
123.050AM	Helicopters ("Eagle") to Hospital	

Park Police Districts
D1: Downtown Washington, D.C.
D2: George Washington Memorial Parkway
D3: Rock Creek Parkway
D4: Baltimore Washington Parkway
D5: Anacostia and Suitland Parkways
D6: New York City Field Office
D7: Special Operations Division
D8: San Francisco Field Office

NOTE: Units ID 3-digit number - 1st is District #.
Standard Ten Codes at back of volume are used.

National Park Service
166.950R	C & O Canal (Input on 166.350)
409.050	J.F.K. Center
169.775R	George Washington Memorial Parkway
417.975M	The Ellipse
164.725	VIP Limo service
40.070	Park Service Buses
40.210	Park Service Buses
416.125	Park Service Trains
150.725	Aquaduct Security
166.325	Allocated to Park Service - Ft. Reno
166.975	Allocated to Park Service - Ft. Reno
166.775	Allocated to Park Service - Fire Operations
166.600	Allocated to Park Service - Car to car
164.475	Allocated to Park Service - Security
172.475R	Utility F1: Zoo / Turkey Run / Miscellaneous Sites
172.750R	Utility F2: Mall Operations / George Washington Mem. Pkwy.
477.5125R	Walkie-Talkies
477.5375R	Walkie-Talkies

U.S. Capitol Police
164.800R	F1: Emergencies / Special Events
164.625R	F2: Primary Dispatch
164.600R	F5: Inside Operations

General Services Administration (KPA621)
415.200R	F1: Federal Protective Service: Dispatch
417.200M	F2: Federal Protective Service: Car to Car

WASHINGTON, D.C.: CITY AGENCIES (Continued)

United States Government (Continued)

Smithsonian Institution
165.035   F1: Smithsonian Secondary Operations
169.200   F2: Smithsonian Primary Dispatch
169.725   National Zoological Society

U.S. Postal Service
166.225   Motor Pool Maintenance
168.525   Central Transportation Control

Veteran's Administration
162.6625P   Hospital Pager
162.850   Hospital Operations
164.075   Hospital Administration (KLN477)
168.125   Hospital Operations
168.325   Hospital Security
414.325R   Veteran's Administration (KNA204) (Input on 409.325)

Cabinet Departments
169.150   Department of Agriculture
163.225   Department of Commerce
164.025   Department of Commerce
162.025   Department of Energy - Motor Pool
162.225   Department of Energy - Radio Telephones
168.000   Department of Housing and Urban Development

Legislative Branch
169.575   G.O.P. Republican Vote Pager
410.200   Government Printing Office - Security
415.450   Government Printing Office - Operations
409.400   Government Accounting Office
411.400   Library of Congress - Security
408.125   Library of Congress - Operations

Commissions and Agencies
 47.420   American National Red Cross (KGC525)
162.025   National Aeronautics & Space Administration (NASA)
162.275   Office of Administration - E.O.B.
162.550   NOAA Weather Service Broadcasts
163.275   U.S. Supreme Court: Security
165.2625   St. Elizabeth Mental Hospital: Security & Fire
165.3125P   St. Elizabeth Mental Hospital: Pager
165.750   FAA Aircraft Accident Investigators
166.175   National Transportation Safety Board (NTSB)
409.100   Office of Technology Assessments
409.200   Interstate Commerce Commission
409.400   Federal Home Loan Bank Board / U.S. Tax Court
415.900   NOAA Weather Service Broadcasts UHF Link
419.025   FAA Washington Flyer
463.875   General Secretariat of the OAS

WASHINGTON, D.C.: CITY AGENCIES (Continued)

<u>United States Government</u> (continued)
MILITARY OPERATIONS

Naval Security Station
138.750   F1: Operations & Security
138.675   F2: Operations & Security
138.650   Disaster Control
149.450   Emergency Network
150.150   Security Police
Naval District Headquarters
148.300   Fire Department: Command
148.310   Fire Department: Operations
150.110   Security: Primary
140.580   Security: Secondary
Andrews Air Force Base Naval Air Facility
122.850   Pilot to Dispatch
140.600   Pilot to Dispatch
386.800   Pilot to Dispatch
140.445   USMC Approach / Departure Control
413.375   Shore Patrol
138.720   Operations
140.100   Fire Department
Bolling Air Force Base
173.585   Fire & Crash Crews
163.485   Police Department
Fort McNair
 36.710   Military Police (Metro DC Armed Forces Police Network)
 36.630   Taxis & Security Patrols (WAR200)
 36.690   VIP Chauffeurs (WAR23)
 36.310   Base Operations (WAR442)
Walter Reed Army Hospital
165.085   Fire Department & Military Police
165.265   Hospital Operations
164.075P   Paging
148.575P   Paging
141.375   Medivac Operations
 41.000   Helicopters
 30.090P   Paging
 32.110P   Paging
Miscellaneous Military Operations
 36.710   D.C. Metro Area Armed Forces Police (Ft. McNair MP)
 36.510   D.C. Metro Area Armed Forces Base Link
 38.000   Iwo Jima National Monument
 36.910   VIP Buses & Taxis / Security Patrols (WAR400)
149.115   Military Police: Metro D.C. Network
165.035   Army Corps of Engineers
164.435   Army Corps of Engineers
140.125   Washington Navy Yard: Security
149.350   Washington Navy Yard: Operations
148.150   Civil Air Patrol: Telephones
149.925   Civil Air Patrol: Primary Operations
171.335   U.S. Coast Guard
409.2375   U.S. Coast Guard

MARYLAND: STATE AGENCIES

Maryland State Police

39.100	F1:	Statewide Intersystem
39.260	F2:	MARNS (Mutual Aid Radio Network)
39.300	F3:	Barracks I,Q
39.340	F4:	Barracks D,L,O
39.140	F5:	Barracks J
39.320	F6:	Barracks N,S
39.380	F7:	Barracks K,R,T
39.240	F8:	Barracks C,H,V
39.520	F9:	Barracks G,U
39.040	F10:	Barracks P
39.060	F11:	Barracks A,E
39.400	F12:	Barracks B,F
39.220		Marine Police
39.660		BCI (Bureau of Criminal Investigation)
44.740		Interstate Channel (Virginia/Delaware/Pennsylvania)
44.900		Interstate Channel (Virginia/Delaware/Pennsylvania)
151.040		Barracks M (Interstate 95 Patrol)
155.190		Barrack to Barrack Frequency
155.475		Nationwide Intersystem
155.730		Portable Extender Frequency
453.550R		Washington Metropolitan Intersystem (P-MARS)
460.050R		Baltimore Metropolitan Intersystem (P-MARS)
494.0375		CID (Criminal Investigation Division)

State Police Barracks

Barrack	Call	F	Counties Covered
A - Waterloo............	KGA915	11	Howard
B - Frederick..........	KGA918	12	Frederick
C - Cumberland.........	KGA910	08	Allegany,Garrett
D - Bel Air............	KGA919	04	Harford
E - Salisbury..........	KGA913	11	Wicomico
F - North East........	KGG903	12	Cecil
G - Westminster........	KGA917	09	Carroll
H - Waldorf............	KGA916	08	Charles
I - Easton.............	KGA912	03	Caroline,Dorchester,Talbot
J - Annapolis..........	KGF986	05	Anne Arundel
K - Security...........	KBC660	07	Baltimore (Southwest)
L - Forestville........	KGA654	04	Prince George's (South)
M - Perryville.........	KIL718	--	I-95 Toll Road
N - Rockville..........	KGE796	06	Montgomery
O - Hagerstown.........	KGA914	04	Washington
P - Glen Burnie........	KBT576	10	Department of Motor Vehicles
Q - College Park.......	KSU469	03	Prince George's (North)
R - Valley.............	KGN485	07	Baltimore (North)
S - Centreville........	KGB631	06	Kent,Queen Anne's
T - Leonardtown........	KGD716	07	St. Mary's
U - Prince Frederick...	KGD979	09	Calvert
V - Berlin.............	KZT386	08	Somerset,Worcester
HQ- Pikesville.........	KGB744	01	Statewide Headquarters
Marine Police........	KGE774	--	State Controlled Waterways

MARYLAND: STATE AGENCIES   (Continued)

Maryland State Police

NOTE: Maryland State Police use Standard Ten Codes on last page.

Unit Numbering
001-099   Superintendent & Administrative Vehicles
100-199   Vice & Narcotics
300-399   Truck Weight Inspectors
400-499   ASED (Inspection Stations)
500-599   Headquarters Criminal Investigations
700-799   BAT (Bus and Truck) / ACEU (Auto Safety Enforcement Unit)
900-999   Executive Protective Service

State Police Helicopters (Dispatched on MED Call 1 & 2)
      Helicopter 1:   Baltimore
      Helicopter 2:   Andrews Air Force Base
      Helicopter 3:   Frederick
      Helicopter 4:   Salisbury
      Helicopter 5:   Cumberland
      Helicopter 11:   Baltimore
      Helicopter 21:   Baltimore
      Helicopter 31:   Baltimore

Barrack Units (X = Barrack)
  X1   Barrack Commander
  X2   Barrack Deputy Commander
  X3   Barrack Sergeant
  X4+ Barrack Troopers

State Police District Map

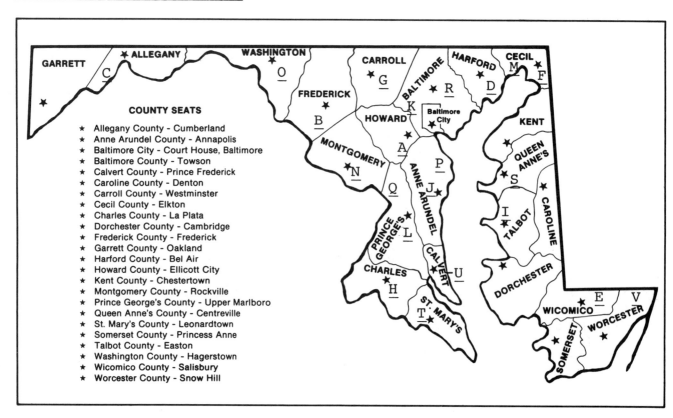

COUNTY SEATS
★ Allegany County - Cumberland
★ Anne Arundel County - Annapolis
★ Baltimore City - Court House, Baltimore
★ Baltimore County - Towson
★ Calvert County - Prince Frederick
★ Caroline County - Denton
★ Carroll County - Westminster
★ Cecil County - Elkton
★ Charles County - La Plata
★ Dorchester County - Cambridge
★ Frederick County - Frederick
★ Garrett County - Oakland
★ Harford County - Bel Air
★ Howard County - Ellicott City
★ Kent County - Chestertown
★ Montgomery County - Rockville
★ Prince George's County - Upper Marlboro
★ Queen Anne's County - Centreville
★ St. Mary's County - Leonardtown
★ Somerset County - Princess Anne
★ Talbot County - Easton
★ Washington County - Hagerstown
★ Wicomico County - Salisbury
★ Worcester County - Snow Hill

MARYLAND: STATE AGENCIES (Continued)

Department of Transportation

Toll Facilities Administration
453.100R	F1:	Baltimore Harbor Tunnel / Key Bridge (KGH607)
453.575R	F2:	Lane Memorial ("Bay") Bridge (KGH606/8)
453.975R	F3:	Nice Bridge (Potomac) / Susquehanna River (KGH609)

Unit Identification
001-009 Administration
100-199 Harbor Maintenance
200-299 Key Bridge Maintenance
400-499 J.F.K. Maintenance
600-699 Police

State Highway Administration
47.320	F1:	Statewide / District 6
47.260	F2:	Districts 5,7
47.400	F3:	Districts 1,3,4
47.140	F4:	District 2
156.045		unknown use (North East - KFG73)
458.050		unknown use (Clearspring - KGU90 / Hancock - WGT83)

Headquarters Unit Identification
001 Administrator		100-199 Engineers
002 Deputy Administrator		200-299 Construction
004 Dir. of Administration		300-399 Equipment
010 Dir. Civil Defense		400-499 Survey
040 Communications Chief		500-599 Traffic
060 Transportation Secretary		600-699 Laboratory
080 Asst. Transp. Secretary		700-799 Landscape
		800-899 Maintenance
		900-999 Bridge Maintenance

District Unit Identification (X=Dist. / Y=County)
X000 Dist. Engineer	XY00 Resident Engineer
X001 Asst. Engineer-Maint.	XY01 Highway Supervisor
X002 Asst. Engineer-Constr.	XY05 Sign Crew
X004 Traffic Engineer	XY09 Shop Foreman
X009 Dist. Equipment Super.	

Ten Codes (Differences from standard on last page)
10-03 Emergency	10-63 Signal on Flash
10-10 Out of Service	10-64 Accid. w/ Signal
10-11 Official/VIP present	10-65 Rpt. message re signal
10-27 Reply to Message	10-66 Req. PD for Traffic
10-37 Name of Operator	10-67 Signal Repaired
10-40 Avail. for phone call	10-68 No Trouble found
10-58 Requesting messages	10-69 Who is Complainant
10-59 Negative	10-78 Hole in the Road
10-60 Bulb Out	10-79 Animal Carcass
10-61 Signal Stuck	10-88 Adv. home my ETA is...
10-62 Timing is Off	10-89 ...is calling you

MARYLAND: STATE AGENCIES (Continued)

Department of Transportation (continued)

State Highway Administration Radio Signals
```
        01 Call office by phone      09 Auto Accident
           I - Immediately              I - With Injuries
        03 Report to Office          14 Radar Set up
```

State Highway Administration Districts (* indicates District HQ)

District 1		District 4 (Cont.)	
Dorchester	Cambridge (KGG836)	Baltimore Co.	Pikesville (KGG932)
Somerset	Princess Anne (KGG837)		*Central Lab. (WQK336)
Wicomico	*Salisbury (KGG850)		Kingsville (KGG832)
District 2			Glyndon (KGG847)
Caroline	Denton(KGG849)		Hereford (KBQ266)
Cecil	Nottingham (KJV407)	Harford	Churchville (KGG848)
	Cecilton (KJU883)		Darlington (KZK265)
	Elkton (KGG851)	District 5	
Kent	*Chestertown (WQK875)	Anne Arundel	*Best Gate (KBQ265)
	Massey (KBO796)		Glen Burnie (KNCE825)
Queen Anne's	Centreville (KGG833)	Calvert	Pr. Frederick (KGG854)
	Stevensville (KJU882)	Charles	La Plata (KGG838)
Talbot	Easton (KGG834)	St. Mary's	Leonardtown (KGG840)
District 3		District 6	
Montgomery	Gaithersburg (KGG933)	Allegany	Cumberland (KGG931)
	Kensington (KBO794)	Garrett	Oakland (KGG843)
Prince George's	Laurel (KGG852)		Frostburg (KBO795)
	*Greenbelt (WQK875)	Washington	Clear Spring (KGG841)
	Southern Lab. (WQK875)		Hagerstown (KDV716)
	Upper Marlboro (KGG853)	District 7	
District 4		Carroll	Westminster (KGG845)
Baltimore City	Baltimore (KGG844)	Frederick	Thurmont (KGQ253)
Baltimore Co.	Towson (KNFX740)		Frederick (KGG842)
	Catonsville (KGG846)	Howard	Dayton (KCY220)
	Golden Ring (KXA263)		

Baltimore Mass Transit Administration (KTL460/KUV613)
```
494.3375R   F1: Buses
494.4375R   F2: Buses
494.6125R   F3: Buses
494.6375R   F4: Buses
494.7625R       Security - F1: Primary
494.8125R       Security - F2: Secondary
494.9625R       Supervisors - F1
495.0375R       Supervisors - F2
494.4625        Unknown use
```

Maryland Port Authority
```
154.055     Baltimore Harbor: Port Authority (KGP634/KZC678-82/KZE691-2)
154.725     Baltimore Harbor: Port Authority Police (KZB391)
428.000     Dundalk - Port Administration ("WMH")
500.000     Dundalk - Port Administration ("WMH")
```

MARYLAND: STATE AGENCIES   (Continued)

Department of Natural Resources
Cooperative Forestry Program
151.460   F1: Forestry - Eastern/Western Divisions
151.325   F2: Parks   - Eastern/Western Divisions
151.145R   F3: Statewide- Forestry/Parks Repeater
151.355   F4: Forestry - Central Division
151.415   F5: Parks   - Central Division
151.250   F6: Forestry - Southern Division
151.310   F7: Parks   - Southern Division
159.450   State Parks - Point to Point
159.285   Mid Atlantic States Forest Fire Network

Western Div.	Eastern Div.	Southern Div.	Central Div.
Allegany	Caroline	Anne Arundel	Baltimore
Frederick	Dorchester	Calvert	Carroll
Garrett	Somerset	Charles	Cecil
Washington	Talbot	Howard	Harford
	Wicomico	Montgomery	Kent
	Worcester	Prince George's	Queen Anne's
		St. Mary's	

NOTE: DNR uses standard Ten Codes found on last page.
      Units ID by project/region No. plus individ. unit ID.

Fish and Game Administration
151.205R   Statewide Repeater (Input on 159.240)
             Annapolis(KGY281) / Cumberland(WZJ319) / Easton(KGF868) /
             Elkton(KLU311) / Flintstone(KDE201) / Frederick(KFF357) /
             Frostburg(WZJ320) / Oakland(KFX287) /
             Owings Mills (KGE486) / Salisbury (KFX286)

Bureau of Mines, Environmental Services, Water Resources
  31.340   F1: Inter-Office Administration
  31.460   F2: Natural Resources common channel
             Ellicott City(KGA539) / Madonna*(KGA548) / Midland(KGA546)
             Milburn Land*(KGE516) / North East(KGA553) /
             NR Baltimore(KGA538) / NW Frederick(KGA556) /
             Owings Mills(KGE486) / Pikesville*(KGE324) / Snow Hill
             (NOTE: * indicates stations operating only on F1)

New Game Commission
  31.580   Game Wardens
  31.860   Game Wardens

Miscellaneous - Unknown use
  31.900   Stevensville (KNFC874)
151.475

MARYLAND: STATE AGENCIES   (Continued)

Statewide Emergency Medical Services Plan

462.950 / 467.950	Call 1 (AKA Med-9)	
462.975 / 467.975	Call 2 (AKA Med-10)	
463.000 / 468.000	MED-1	463.100 / 468.100 MED-5
463.025 / 468.025	MED-2	463.125 / 468.125 MED-6
463.050 / 468.050	MED-3	463.150 / 468.150 MED-7
463.075 / 468.075	MED-4	463.175 / 468.175 MED-8

127.300Hz	Tone Code A (listed by counties below)
146.200Hz	Tone Code B (listed by counties below)
167.900Hz	Tone Code C (listed by counties below)

Primary (& Secondary) MED Channel Allocations: By County

7(1/5/8)	Allegany(A)	5(3/7/8)	Dorchester(C)	6(1/3/8)	Queen Anne's(C)
4(8)	Anne Arundel	6(2/4/8)	Frederick(B)	4(1/2/8)	St. Mary's(B)
2(3/4/7/8)	Baltimore City	3(4/7/8)	Garrett(B)	1(3/7/8)	Talbot(A)
4(8)	Baltimore	4(8)	Harford	1(2/6/8)	Washington(C)
3(4/5/8)	Calvert(A)	4(8)	Howard	2(1/6/8)	Wicomico(B)
4(8)	Carroll	6(1/3/8)	Kent(C)	4(2/6/8)	Worcester(A)
5(3/7/8)	Cecil(B)	2/5(1/6/8)	Montgomery(A)		
8(1/5/7)	Charles(C)	1(5/7/8)	Prince George's(B)		

NOTE: All Counties have Call 1 & 2 except Baltimore City (only Call 1)

County Call Signs are included in County listings. State Call signs are:

KXB740 Crownsville	KXB745 Mt. Airy	KXB749 Ellicott City
KXB742 Baltimore	KXB746 Westminster	KXB750 Aberdeen
KXB743 Owings Mills	KXB747 Harve De Grace	KXB751 Rosedale
KXB744 Manchester	KXB748 Madonna	

Marine Channel Allocation

The following nationwide allocations are used by State, Local, and Federal Governments, on the various bays, rivers, and Atlantic Ocean:

156.300	F06:	Intership Safety
156.350	F07:	Maritime Limited Coast
156.600	F12:	Port Operations
156.650	F13:	Navagational
156.700	F14:	Port Operations
156.800	F16:	Distress
156.050	F21:	Maritime Government
157.100	F22:	(22A) Maritime Government (switch from F16)
157.150	F23:	Maritime Government
157.250	F25:	Ship to Shore
157.300	F26:	Ship to Shore
157.400	F28:	Ship to Shore
157.075	F81:	Maritime Government (Oil Clean Up Operations)
157.175	F83:	Maritime Government (Auxiliary)

State of Maryland Marine Stations: Annapolis (KZA871-2/KSK348) / Anne Arundel (KAJ667) / Baltimore City (KYU696/WQB495) / Honga (KYU695) / Cambridge (KZA873) / Edgewater (KZA870) / Kent Narrows (KXE254) / Ocean City (KYU698) / Salisbury (KYU697/KZA869) / Tilghman Is. (KZA868)

MARYLAND: STATE AGENCIES   (Continued)

Maryland State Government

State Department of Justice
453.350R   F1: Annapolis (WRB476)
453.550R   F2: Annapolis (WRB476)
453.400R   F3: Annapolis (WRB476)

Civil Defense Network
 44.740   Civil Defense / State Police Interstate Network
 44.900   Civil Defense / State Police Interstate Network
 47.500   Statewide Civil Defense Network: County Intersystem
              Civil Defense Communications Areas
              1 Western Maryland   3 Eastern Maryland
              2 Baltimore Metro Area   4 Southern Maryland

Department of Corrections
153.860   Hagerstown (KKC633) / Jessup (KKC634) /
              Midland (KTI719) / Towson (KLE764)
153.965   Hagerstown (KKC633) / Jessup (KKC634)
153.980   Hagerstown (WZX569) / Owings Mills (KNBW239)
453.475   Correctional Training Center (Hagerstown)

Department of Health and Mental Hygiene
 33.100   Springfield State Hospital (KSS995)
152.0075   Springfield State Hospital (KUQ883)
 39.580   Crownsville State Hospital - Security (WXT870)
155.265   Salisbury State Hospital (KYO531)
155.265   Spring Grove State Hospital (Catonsville)

State Colleges and Universities
155.025   Frederick State College (KWM740)
              Midland State College (KTI719)
              University of MD: Eastern Shore (Princess Anne-KLM638)
              University of MD: College Park Campus-Physical Plant(KDT392)
              Frostburg State College
              Reisterstown State College
151.955   Western Maryland College (Westminster)
155.550R   Catonsville State College: Police (KIL428)
153.875B   Towson State University (Mobils on 158.820)
 39.120   St. Mary's College - Security (KKV479)
494.9125R   University of MD: Baltimore Campus - Security (KNS222)
495.2375R   University of MD: Baltimore Campus - Security (KNS244)
453.575R   University of MD: College Park Campus - Security (KXV427)
463.1125   University of MD: La Plata Campus

Statewide Fire and Safety Networks
154.280   Fire Mutual Aid Network
155.340   Hospital - Ambulance EMS Network
460.525R   Allocated on Eastern Shore for Safety Network

MARYLAND: STATE AGENCIES   (Continued)

Maryland State Government

Department of General Services
155.775   Capitol Buildings (Catonsville) (KQU307)
               Capitol Buildings (Annapolis) (KLR324)
               Capitol Buildings (Baltimore) (KXF289)
               Department of Agriculture (Annapolis)
155.025   National Aquarium of Baltimore (KJZ924)
155.100   National Aquarium of Baltimore

Licensed to Maryland State Government - Use Unknown
 37.260   Alloc to MSP - license may have lapsed (Salisbury-KTA967)
 39.200   Alloc to MSP - Coleman/Dares Beach/Stevensville (KGE774)
153.740M   Mobils only (KA79071)
154.800R   Parkville (KGC981) (Input on 156.210)
155.055   Baltimore (KJZ924)
155.085   Baltimore (KAA296)
155.205   Catonsville (WQD249)
155.715   Towson (KLE764)
155.850M   allocated to State Police (KA28581/KA82856)
156.210M   allocated to State Police (KGC981)
158.805   Baltimore (WSL880)
158.745   Burtonsville (KNCS597)
453.4625M   allocated to State Police (Mobils only - KB32400)
453.9875M   allocated to State Police (Mobils only - KB41599)

NOTE:The following "split" frequencies have recently been allocated to the Maryland
     State Police - uses have yet to be confirmed. Transmitters are located at the
     following locations: Dares Beach / Oakland / Owings Mill / Salisbury /
     Stevensville / Still Pond / Town Hill. Call Signs are KNGB244-9. Those
     frequencies marked with an "*" are not licensed at Owings Mill and Salisbury.
     The single mobile frequency may be an input to one or more of the repeater
     frequencies.

151.1825R
151.2275R
151.2725R
151.2875R
151.3775R*
151.3925R*
151.4075R*
156.0525M   (KB28861)

United States Government
 34.180   U.S. Wildlife Department - Surveillence & Enforcement Units
 34.830   U.S. Wildlife Department - Surveillence & Enforcement Units
166.950R   National Park Service - Statewide Ops (Input on 166.350)
169.400   Interior Department (Gibbs Pond)
170.050   Interior Department (Gibbs Pond)
171.725   Interior Department (Round Mdw)
172.525   Interior Department (Round Mdw)
150.285   U.S. Air Force
406.5625   U.S. Coast Guard (Anplsbyb)

MARYLAND: ALLEGANY COUNTY   (County Seat: Cumberland)

County Sheriff (KDG881)
39.180   Dispatch / Coordination with Garrett & Washington Counties
451.825R   Mobil Repeater Frequency

Fire Department (KTG669)
33.780   F1: Dispatch
33.680   F2: Fireground
46.140   Alert Pager (WXF883)
153.830   Portables
               MED Channel 7 (Alt-1/5/8) (KAB226)
      VOLUNTEER FIRE COMPANIES
      KJB855 Baltimore Pike (Cumberland)   *+KGD459 Frostburg #1
     +KUE646 Barton Hose #1   KTK612 Lanaconing
      KXZ894 Bloomington   +KGJ642 La Vale
      KC5867 Borden Shaft (Cumberland)   WYV218 Luke
     +KJN810 Bowling Green (Cumberland)   *WSX943 McCoole
    +KNEU518 Bowmans Addition (Cumberland)   +KC5895 Midland
      KUB997 Community (Creapstown)   KE4342 Mt. Savage
     +KWJ361 Corriganville   KV2116 Oldtown
      KUS551 District 16 (Cumberland)   WQU329 Orleans (Little Orleans)
      WRA652 East Garrett County (Finzel)   +KOP912 Potomac #2 (Westernport)
      NOTE: * = licensed only on F1 / + = licensed on 153.830 (portable)

County Government
154.980R   Health Department-Primary (KVD574) (Input on 156.000)
155.280   Health Department-Secondary (KVF504)
155.115R   Highway Department (KVD573) (Input on 155.715)

Municipalities
453.675R   Bloomington: Upper Potomac River Commission (WQD697)
155.430R   Cumberland City Police (KGA886) (Input on 154.815)
33.880   Cumberland City Fire Department (KGD446)
453.100R   Cumberland City Fire Department (KSE713)
158.820   Cumberland City Department of Public Works (KAW513)
154.025   Cumberland City Government (WQA760)
72.680   Cumberland City Government (WBT779)
159.150   Frostburg City Police (KJD307)
158.805   Frostburg City Government (KUV581)
39.180M   Lanaconing Town Police (KA6102)
155.175   Lanaconing: George's Creek Ambulance Service (KNIB800)
33.040   La Vale Volunteer Rescue Squad (KQW333)
155.205   La Vale Volunteer Rescue Squad (KNFJ222)
154.100   Luke City Government (KTN201)
460.575R   Westernport: Potomac Volunteer Fire Company #2 (KOP912)
155.205   Westernport: Tri-County Ambulance & Rescue Squad (KYB822)

State and Federal Governments
39.240   MSP-F8: Barrack C (Cumberland-KGA910)
47.320   SHA-F1: District 6
151.460   DNR-F1: Forestry (Western Division)
151.325   DNR-F2: Parks (Western Division)
155.025   State Colleges Security (Frostburg/Midland) (KTI719)
166.950R   National Park Service (Oldtown) (Input on 166.350)

MARYLAND: ANNE ARUNDEL COUNTY (County Seat: Annapolis)

County Police (KTL670)

494.3125R	F1:	Northern District
495.3375R	F2:	Eastern District
494.3625R	F3:	Western District
494.4125R	F4:	Southern District
494.5125R	F5:	Detectives
494.4625R	F6:	Teletype
460.050R		Baltimore Metro Intersystem (KGR249)

Fire Department (KGD479)

154.010	F1:	Dispatch
154.340	F2:	Response
154.175	F3:	Fireground
154.295	F4:	Fireground
154.280		Mutual Aid
153.830		Walkie Talkies
46.500		Fire Alarm "2" (V.F.D.) & Command Post
		MED Channel 4 (Alt-8)

FIRE STATIONS

1	GALESVILLE	Galesville VFD
2	EDGEWATER	Woodland Beach VFD
3	RIVA	Riva VFD
5	GAMBRILLS	Waugh Chapel Fire Station
7	CROWNSVILLE	Herald Harbor VFD
11	BALTIMORE	Orchard Beach VFD
12	SEVERNA PARK	Earleigh Heights VFD
13	PASADENA	Riviera Beach VFD
14	PASADENA	Green Haven VFD
15	PASADENA	Powhatan Beach VFD
16	GLEN BURNIE	Lombardee Beach VFD
17	ARNOLD	Arnold VFD
18	GLEN BURNIE	Marley VFD
19	ANNAPOLIS	Cape St. Claire VFD
20	PASADENA	Lake Shore VFD
21	HANOVER	Dorsey Harmans Station
23	SEVERNA PARK	Jones Station Fire Station
24	SHADYSIDE	7th Dist. Ambulance & Rescue Squad
26	GLEN BURNIE	South Glen Burnie Station
27	LAUREL	Maryland City VFD
28	ODENTON	Odenton VFD
29	JESSUP	Jessup VFD
31	BALTIMORE	Brooklyn Community VFD
32	LINTHICUM	Community Fire Company
33	GLEN BURNIE	Glen Burnie VFD
34	GLEN BURNIE	Ferndale VFD
40	ANNAPOLIS	West Annapolis Fire & Improvement Assoc.
42	DEALE	Deale Volunteer Fire & Rescue Squad
43	B.W.I.	Baltimore-Washington Airport
45	FT. MEADE	Fort George S. Meade
Battalion 1		North County
Battalion 2		Northeast County
Battalion 3		South County
Battalion 4		Northeast & Central County
Battalion 35		Annapolis City

MARYLAND: ANNE ARUNDEL COUNTY (Continued)

County Government

33.140	Board of Education
39.980	Sheriff's Office (WQD430)
45.480	Unknown use (Severna Park-KBW782)
151.085R	Highway Department (KGE844) (Input on 159.060)
153.515B	Public Works & Utilities (KGY729) (Mobils on 158.175)
153.740	Unknown input (KA48377)
154.770R	County Jail (KLU610) (Input on 156.210)
155.145	Civil Defense (KYG679/KYG682-3/KST207)
155.835R	County Executive (KVA296/KJU860/KNFC629) (Input on 153.920)
155.895	Unknown input (KR4669)
158.910	Unknown input (KA62415)
453.250R	Inspectors (KZJ47/WDQ373)
461.650	Board of Education (WRX801)
495.1625R	Unknown use (WAE695)
495.2125R	County Government Common (WAE733/KWI845)
495.2375R	Animal Control
851.7625R	Unknown use (KNFU739)

Municipalities

159.210R	Annapolis City Police F1: Dispatch (KGA921) (Input-155.910)
156.210R	Annapolis City Police F2: Car to Car (KGA921) (Input-155.655)
158.835	Annapolis City Department of Public Works (KDO300)
154.995	Crofton City Police Department (KRM914)
47.460	Easternport Volunteer Fire Department
155.430	Gibson Island City Police (KNCY906)
154.540	Gibson Island Corporation (KNCF332)
461.650	Millersville City Board of Education (WRX801)

State and Federal Governments

39.140	MSP-F5: Barrack J (Annapolis-KGF986)
39.040	MSP-F10: Barrack P - MVA (Glen Burnie-KBT576)
47.260	SHA-F2: District 5
151.250	DNR-F6: Forestry (Southern Division)
151.310	DNR-F7: Parks (Southern Division)
453.575R	Toll Facilities-F2: Bay Bridge (KGH606/8)
39.580	Crownsville State Hospital - Security (WXT870)
155.775	State Capital Security (KLR324)
453.350R	State Department of Justice F1 (WRB476)
453.550R	State Department of Justice F2 (WRB476)
453.400R	State Department of Justice F3 (WRB476)
140.460	USN Ship Research & Development Center Fire Department
139.500	USN Surface Weapons Center Fire Department
416.375	NOAA (Davidsonville)
416.475	U.S. Coast Guard (Crofton) (also 418.012)
34.430	National Park Service (Glen Burnie State Park)
169.400	National Park Service (Sandy Point State Park) (also 170.050)
163.075	G.S.A. (Curtis Bay) (also 163.175)
407.125	Curtis Bay USCG Depot (also 415.775/416.635/419.650/419.850)
148.425	Naval Academy-CHIMES: Fire Department
148.350	Naval Academy-OUTLAW: Security
149.290	Naval Academy-MASON: Maintenance
148.950	Naval Academy-MARS: Military Affiliated Radio Station
149.000	Naval Academy Fire Department (Secondary & Disaster Control)
148.240	Naval Academy Fire Department (Alternate Operations)
150.390	Naval Academy Atlantic Navy Link
148.050	Naval Academy U.S. Air Force

MARYLAND: BALTIMORE CITY

Police Department   (KGA410)

453.425R	District 1: Central
453.775R	District 2: Southeast
453.275R	District 3: East
453.525R	District 4: Northeast
453.825R	District 5: North
453.925R	District 6: Northwest
453.625R	District 7: West
453.050R	District 8: Southwest
453.675R	District 9: South
453.200R	Citywide 1: Traffic
453.300R	Citywide 2: Traffic & Special Events
453.650R	Citywide Tactical
453.975R	Special Operations Division
453.350R	Criminal Investigation Unit
453.725R	Internal Affairs Division
453.400R	Narcotics & Vice
460.050R	Baltimore Metro Intersystem
460.525R	Vehicle Repairs
460.550R	Vehicle Repairs
158.970	Portable Walkie-Talkies
154.650B	Old Dispatch Freq (also 155.190B / 155.550B / 155.610B)
155.430M	Old Dispatch Freq (also 155.670M / 155.850M / 155.970M)

DISTRICT MAP

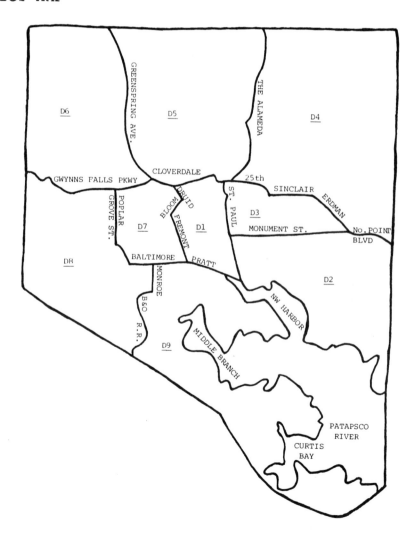

MARYLAND: BALTIMORE CITY (Continued)

Police Department
TEN CODES (Differences from standard on last page)

10-05 Failed to Acknowledge	10-39 Disabled Police Vehicle
10-11 Meet...at...	10-40 Request crime lab
10-12 Not Available	10-41 Request impound truck
10-13 Officer Needs Assistance	10-42 Request animal shelter
10-14 Wagon Run	10-43 Malfunctioning Traffic Signal
10-15 Urgent Wagon Run	A - Light Completely Out
10-16 Back up unit...	B - Red Signal Out
10-17 Call Assignment	C - Signal Sticking
10-18 Go to Assignment	D - Stop/Yield Sign Missing
10-25 Stopping Susp. Car	10-44 Req. Perm. for Foot Patrol
10-26 Go to Citywide Channel	10-45 Permission Denied
10-30 Person/Car Wanted	10-46 Permission Granted
10-32 Sufficient units	10-47 Negative
10-36 Copy Description	10-48 Positive
10-37 Request Tow Truck	10-49 Hourly Call
10-38 Request Ambulance	

Fire Department (KGC220)

154.310R	F1:	Truck Dispatch (Input on 154.445)
154.370	F2:	Fireground - 1
154.385	F3:	Fireground - 2
154.325	F4:	Fireground - 3 / Administrative / Pager
154.415	F5:	Station Dispatch (WRV649-709)
154.145	F6:	Ambulance Dispatch
153.830	F7:	Portable Units
154.280	F8:	Mutual Aid
154.070		Unknown input
154.265		New allocation - use unknown (also 154.295)
853.5875R		Allocated-future(also 853.8375R/854.0125R/854.2125R)
		MED Channel 2 (Alt-3/4/7/8)

City Government

453.850R	A:	Transit & Traffic / Mayor / Highway Department (KRB423/KWH408/KGF987/KFW249/KGE865)
453.700R	B:	Highway Dept. / Snow Plows (same call as A)
453.600R	C:	Animal Control / Parks / Sanitation (same call as A)
453.500R	D:	City Jail / Sewer Dept / Water Dept (same call as A)
494.987R	E:	Executive / Mayor's Office (KXC752)
495.112R	F:	Sheriff / Civil Defense / City Common (KXC752)
495.187R	G:	Health Department (KXC752)
495.262R	H:	Parks Department (WBG847-9)
495.287R	I:	Pyrolysis Plant (KXC752)
494.587R	J:	Rapid Transit / Board of Education (KZN998)
494.487R	K:	Rapid Transit / Board of Education (WBG850-1)
494.387R	L:	Rapid Transit / Board of Education (WBG852-4)
48.060	M:	Water Department
161.790		Civil Defense Network (also 161.250)
155.790		Supreme Bench - Court Security
462.700		District Court of Maryland - Baltimore City (KAA9757)
158.925B		City Jail Security (KBI987-94/WXT794-5) (Mobils on 156.000)
158.745B		unknown use (KNDG743) (Input on 153.800)
151.235		Watershed Section
154.115		Unknown use (KNEN217)
155.800		Unknown use (KNAA556) (also 155.880)

MARYLAND: BALTIMORE CITY (Continued)

Mass Transit Administration (KTL460/KUV613)
494.3375R	F1:	Buses
494.4375R	F2:	Buses
494.6125R	F3:	Buses
494.6375R	F4:	Buses
494.7625R		Security - F1: Primary
494.8125R		Security - F2: Secondary
494.9625R		Supervisors F1
495.0375R		Supervisors F2
494.4625		unknown use
160.395		Subway: Road Channel
161.085		Subway: Police Department
161.475		Subway: Yard Channel
161.565		Subway: Maintenance

University of Maryland
494.912R	Baltimore City Campus - Security (KNS222)
495.237R	Baltimore City Campus - Security (KNS244)
155.400	Baltimore City Campus - Safety (MIEMSS)
452.975R	Baltimore City Campus - Safety (MIEMSS)

Maryland Port Authority
154.055	Baltimore Harbor - Port Authority (KGP634/KZC678-82/KZE691-2)
154.725	Baltimore Harbor - Port Police (KZB391)

Miscellaneous Maryland State Government
155.025	National Aquarium of Baltimore (KJZ924)
155.100	National Aquarium of Baltimore
155.775	Department of General Service - State Buildings (KFX289)
155.055	unknown use (KJZ924)
155.085	unknown use (KAA296)
158.805	unknown use (WSL880)

United States Government - Cabinet Departments
171.525	Department of Agriculture (also 415.300)
166.150	Department of Commerce
171.340	Department of Health & Human Services (also 407.975/415.625)
163.750	Department of Labor

U.S. Agencies & Commissions
166.950R	National Park Service: Ft. McHenry Monument (Input on 166.350)
162.400	NOAA Weather Broadcasts
163.4375	Army Corps of Engineers
163.075	General Services Administration (also 167.060/413.875/419.175)
40.450	Veterans Administration (also 163.050/164.990)
172.175	Federal Aviation Administration (also 172.300)
148.410	U.S. Navy MARS - Military Affiliated Radio System
148.375	U.S. Navy MARS - Military Affiliated Radio System
148.950	U.S. Navy MARS - Military Affiliated Radio System

MARYLAND: BALTIMORE COUNTY (County Seat: Towson)

Police Department

39.420	A:	Precinct 3 (Northwest)
39.440	B:	Precincts 12,13 (Southeast)
39.560	C:	Countywide Emergency & Administration
39.620	D:	Precincts 1,2 (West)
39.720	E:	Precincts 6,7 (North)
39.840	F:	Precinct 11 (East)
39.960	G:	Precincts 8,9 (Northeast)
39.780	H:	Countywide Car to Car
39.920		County Auxiliary Police Department
155.970		Portables (KA3636)
156.150		Portables (KA3636)
158.910		Portables (KA3636)
158.970		Portables (KA3636)
155.670		unknown use (KOM740)
460.050R		Baltimore Metro Intersystem (KRL339)
852.9125R		Allocated for future use
853.0125R		Allocated for future use
853.2125R		Allocated for future use
853.4125R		Allocated for future use
956.100		unknown use (Towson-KCT74)

Police Precincts

1 Wilkins (KGA890)	9 Fullerton (KGA893)
2 Woodlawn (WBW809)	10 Whitemarsh (Future station)
3 Garrison (KGA892)	11 Essex (KGA888)
6 Towson (KBP322)	12 Dundalk (KGA895)
7 Cockeysville (KGA339)	13 Edgemere (KBZ405)
8 Parkville (KGC983)	

Unit Identification

1xx Traffic Units	4xx Western Patrol
2xx Central Patrol	5xx Detectives
200-50 Dist. 6	6xx Spare Cars / Chaplains
251-70 Dist. 8	7xx K-9 / Tac Units
271-80 Dist. 9	9xx Sheriff / Fire Investigators
3xx Eastern Patrol	
300-40 Dist 11	
341-60 Dist 12	

Disposition Codes   Supplement standard 10 codes

01 Report
02 Report - Incident unfounded
03 Report - Incident handled by other agency
04 Report - Incident unverified
05 No Report - Incident unfounded
06 No Report - Incident handled by other agency
07 No Report - Incident unverified
08 No Report - Incident adjusted
09 No Accident Report - MVA Forms Issued (Public Property)
10 No Accident Report - MVA Forms Issued (Private Property)

MARYLAND: BALTIMORE COUNTY (Continued)

Fire Department (KGC337)

46.460	F1:	Fire Dispatch
46.280	F2:	Ambulance Dispatch
46.520	F3:	East Fireground (East of York Road)
46.560	F4:	West Fireground (West of York Road)
46.160	F5:	Future use
33.420		V.F.D. Alert
153.830		Portables
154.280		Mutual Aid
		MED Channel 4 (Alt-8) (KXB752)

Box & Station Numbers
01 Towson (Eng 1,101/Trk 1)
02 Pikesville
03 Woodlawn
04 Catonsville (Eng 4-41)
05 Halethorpe (Eng 5/Trk 5)
06 Dundalk (Eng 6-61)
07 Essex (Eng 7-71)
08 Fullerton (Eng 8/Trk 8)
09 Edgemere
10 Parkville
11 Hillendale
12 Middle River
13 Westview (Eng 13/Trk 13)
14 Brooklandville
15 Eastview (Eng 15/Trk 15)
16 Golden Ring
17 Texas (Eng 17/Trk 17)
18 Randallstown (Eng 18/Trk 18)
19 Garrison

Radio Codes
01 Nothing Showing
02 Smoke Showing
03 Working Fire
04 Possible Additional
   Alarms Needed
05 Standard Operation-
   No Lights or Siren
06 Pre Fire Plan
10 Civil Disturbance

Radio Signals
30 False Alarm

Volunteer Fire Stations

155		Coffee Wagon
156		Coffee Wagon
200	KGC629	Cowenton
210	KGC667	Community-Bowleys Quarters (Note 1/5)
220	KGC669	Middle River
230	KGC633	Middleborough
240	KGC605	Rockaway Beach
250	KGC604	Hyde Park (Note 4)
260	KGC710	North Point-Edgemere (Note 1)
270	KGC699	Wise Avenue-Dundalk (Note 2)
280	KGC607	Rosedale (Note 4)
290	KGC701	Providence (Note 2)
300	KGC707	Lutherville (Note 1)
310	KGC580	Owings Mills (Note 3/4)
320	KCT272	Pikesville (Note 1)
330	KGC632	Woodlawn
340	KSW953	Violetville
350	KGC673	Arbutus (Note 1/5)
360	KGC608	Lansdowne (Note 4)
370	KGC711	English Council
380	KGG829	Long Green
390	KGD780	Cockeysville
400	KGC702	Glyndon (Note 3)
410	KGC634	Reisterstown (Note 1)
420	KGC700	Boring
430	KGC606	Arcadia (Note 5/6)
440	KGC672	Hereford
450	KGD221	Maryland Line
460	KGC668	Liberty Road-Randallstown
470	KGD288	Jacksonville
480	KGE460	Kingsville
490		Butler
500	KBQ751	Chestnut Ridge
520		Middle River Amb/Rescue (Note 1)
535		Hereford Ambulance

Note 1 Rescue/Floodlight
Note 2 Floodlight only
Note 3 Truck
Note 4 Licensed on VFD Alert Channel
Note 5 Licensed on Portable Channel
Note 6 Licensed on Carroll Co. F1: Dispatch
Note - Stations w/ call signs licensed on F1

MARYLAND: BALTIMORE COUNTY (Continued)

County Government

33.060	Sanitation Department / Highway Department (KGD280)
33.100	Licenses and Permits
45.120	unknown use (Baldwin-KDG294)
45.440	Utility Department Inspections (KLX804)
45.720	Highway Department (KGD280)
46.000	Board of Education (WQY267)
151.235B	Parks & Recreation Department (WGH326) (Mobils on 159.300)
153.755	unknown input (KZ3852)
158.775	unknown use (KDC593)
854.4125R	Public Works: Allocated for future use
854.5875R	Public Works: Allocated for future use
854.7375R	Public Works: Allocated for future use
955.900	unknown use (Towson-WIA454)
959.500	unknown use (Lutherville-KCT75)
959.700	unknown use (Lutherville-KCT75)

Allocated to County Government for future use (KNIA877)

856.2125R	856.4625R	856.7125R	856.9625R
857.2125R	857.4625R	857.7125R	857.9625R
858.2125R	858.4625R	858.7125R	858.9625R
859.2125R	859.4625R	859.7125R	859.9625R
860.2125R	860.4625R	860.7125R	860.9625R

State and Federal Governments

39.380	MSP-F7: Barrack K (Security-KBC660)
39.380	MSP-F7: Barrack R (Valley-KGN485)
47.400	SHA-F3: District 4
151.355	DNR-F4: Forestry (Central Division)
151.415	DNR-F5: Parks (Central Division)
453.100R	Toll Facilities F1: Harbor Tunnel (KGH607)
153.860	Department of Corrections (Towson-KLE764)
153.875B	Towson State University (Mobils on 158.820)
154.800R	unknown use (Parkville-KGC981) (Input on 156.210)
155.025	Reisterstown State College
155.205	Safety (Catonsville-WQD249)
155.265	Spring Grove State Hospital (Catonsville)
155.550	Catonsville State University (KIL428)
155.715	unknown use (Towson-KLE764)
155.775	State Buildings (Catonsville-KQU307)
460.525R	Eastern Shore Safety Net (KXB743)
428.000	Port Administration (Dundalk-WMH)
500.000	Port Administration (Dundalk-WMH)
166.950R	National Park Service (Hampton) (Input on 166.350)
40.800	U.S. Navy - Baltimore Harbor (also 149.070/150.075)
148.695	Fort Holabird Army Minimum Security Prison (also 139.150)
162.590	Fort Howard Veterans Administration (also 164.500/164.990)
163.075	General Services Administration (Middle River)
413.875	G.S.A. (Woodlawn) (also 419.175/419.600)

MARYLAND: CALVERT COUNTY   (County Seat: Prince Frederick)

County Police
39.520	Dispatch (Maryland State Police F9: Prince Frederick)

Fire Department   (KCO372)
33.820	F1: Dispatch
33.600	F2: Emergency and Disaster Net / Fireground
154.280	Mutual Aid
	Med Channel 3 (Alt-4/5/8) (WZY460/KAB218)

FIRE STATIONS
Co. 1: Chesapeake Beach (8500 Block Bayside Road)
Co. 2: Prince Frederick Dtwn. (Solomons Is. Rd. - Rte. 2/4)
RS 2: Prince Frederick Dtwn. (Solomons Is. Rd. - Rte. 2/4)
Co. 3: Newtown (13000 Block Solomons Island Road- Rte. 2/4)
RS 4: Prince Frederick Dtwn. (Solomons Is. Rd. - Rte. 2/4)
Co. 5: Dunkirk (10100 Block Maryland Boulevard)
Co. 6: Huntingtown (4000 Block Solomons Is. Rd. - Rte. 2/4)
U.S. : United States Naval Reservation

VOLUNTEER FIRE COMPANIES
KFN556 Solomons VFD & Rescue
KGD267 Mechanicsville VFD (St. Mary's County)
KGE674 North Beach VFD (also on 46.280 / 46.480)

County Government
154.025	WYD934
154.055	WZJ497
154.085	WZJ497

State and Federal Governments
39.520	MSP-F9: Barrack U (Prince Frederick-KGD979)
47.260	SHA-F2: District 5
151.250	DNR-F6: Forestry (Southern Division)
151.310	DNR-F7: Parks (Southern Division)
169.400	National Park Service (North Beach)
170.050	National Park Service (North Beach)
163.000	U.S. Army (Chesapeake Beach)
138.620	U.S. Navy (Chesapeake Beach)
140.175	U.S. Navy (Chesapeake Beach)
140.575	U.S. Navy (Chesapeake Beach)
140.850	U.S. Navy (Chesapeake Beach)
140.925	U.S. Navy (Chesapeake Beach)
140.950	U.S. Navy (Chesapeake Beach)
141.950	U.S. Navy (Chesapeake Beach)
139.500	U.S. Navy (Solomons Island)
140.040	U.S. Navy (Solomons Island)
142.825	U.S. Navy (Solomons Island)
142.860	U.S. Navy (Solomons Island)
264.100	U.S. Navy (Solomons Island)

MARYLAND: CAROLINE COUNTY (County Seat: Denton)

<u>County Police</u> (WQX229/KWL393)
   39.580   Dispatch & Coordination with Dorchester & Talbot Counties

<u>Fire Department</u> (WSZ317)
   33.700   F1: Fire Dispatch
   33.440B   F2: Fire Chiefs (Mobils on 33.420)

                  FIRE STATIONS
                  1 KGH374 Federalsburg
                  2 KFB904 Preston
                  3 KGF677 Denton
                  3 KFB905 Denton
                  4 KBZ282 Ridgley
                  6 KBZ281 Greenboro
                  7 KFB903 Goldsboro
                  - KKL612 Queen Anne's County (Mutual Aid Network)

<u>County Government</u>
   151.010   Highway Department (KGF514)
   154.100B   County Government Common (WYF933) (Mobils on 153.740)
   159.270   Caroline Soil Conservation (WXT602)

<u>Municipalities</u>
   154.830   Federalsburg Police Department
   154.890   Federalsburg Police Department

<u>State and Federal Governments</u>
   39.300   MSP-F3: Barrack I (Easton-KGA912)
   47.140   SHA-F4: District 2
   151.460   DNR-F1: Forestry (Eastern Division)
   151.325   DNR-F2: Parks (Eastern Division)

MARYLAND: CARROLL COUNTY (County Seat: Westminster)

<u>County Sheriff</u> (KTS713)
  39.880   Dispatch (NOTE: use standard ten code on last page)

<u>Fire Department</u> (KGN512)
  33.940   F1: Dispatch
  33.920   F2: Ambulances
154.280   F3: Mutual Aid
               MED Channel 4 (Alt-8)
       FIRE COMPANIES

1	KGC648	Mt. Airy		8	KGD318	Union Bridge
2	KGC759	Hampstead		9	KGH850	Reese
3	KVJ776	Westminster		10		New Windsor
4	KGC897	Manchester (Note 1)		11	KEP695	Harney
5	KGC814	Tanneytown (Note 4)		12	KGC765	Sykesville (Note 2)
6	KFD608	Pleasant Valley		13	KNCE968	Gamber
7	KDK648	Lineboro (Note 1)		14	KJK702	Windfield (Note 1/3)
					KGC606	Arcadia-Balt Co (Note 1)

        Note 1: licensed only on F1:Dispatch
        Note 2: licensed on 153.830
        Note 3: licensed on 154.145 (KNIG402)
        Note 4: licensed on Baltimore County F1: Dispatch (46.460)

<u>County Government</u>
155.040B   Department of Public Works (KCJ973) (Mobils on 158.880)
155.055B   County Government Common (KVW204/WBN976) (Mobils on 158.955)
156.180   Highway Department (KXE547)
453.725R   Highway Department (KXE547)
155.280   County Medical Society (KGW662)
163.250   County Mecical Society (KGW662)
  33.080   County Vet Clinic (WYV266/KVN481)

<u>Municipalities</u>
154.770M   Hampstead City Police
153.740   Hampstead City Government (KGL689)
155.730   Manchester City Police
155.745   Manchester City Government (KVA200)
158.865R   Tanneytown City Government (WRL637) (Input on 158.940)
155.040R   Westminster City Police F1: Disp/DPW (KGD821) (Input-158.850)
155.070   Westminster City Police F2: Secondary (KGD821)
154.115   Westminster City Government (KIU440)
154.995   Westminster City Government (KIU440)

<u>State and Federal Governments</u>
  39.520   MSP-F9: Barrack G (Westminster-KGA917)
  47.260   SHA-F2: District 7
151.355   DNR-F4: Forestry (Central Division)
151.415   DNR-F5: Parks (Central Division)
  33.100   Springfield State Hospital (KSS995)
152.007   Springfield State Hospital (KUQ883)
151.955   Western Maryland College (Westminster)

MARYLAND: CECIL COUNTY (County Seat: Elkton)

County Sheriff
39.900	F1:	Dispatch (KLQ212/KXZ812)
39.940	F2:	Car to Car / Civil Defense (KYB760/KXZ727)
154.815		unknown use (KYB760)
955.500		unknown use (WAH716)

Fire Department (KBI858)
46.180	F1:	Dispatch
46.540	F2:	Fireground / Civil Defense
46.400	F3:	Municipal Volunteer Fire Departments
153.830		Portables
953.800		unknown use (WJA83)
		MED Channel 5 (Alt-3/7/8) (KAA863)

FIRE STATIONS
1	KGD258	Cecilton
2	KGD256	Chesapeake
3	KLG558	Elkton (Singerly Fire Co.)
4	KGD257	North East
5	KGD254	Charlestown
6	KGD255	Perryville
7	KGD341	Port Deposit (Water Witch VFD)
8	KGD262	Rising Sun (Community VFD)
9	KGG319	Hacks Point
11		Perry Point (U.S. Veterans Administration)
13	KOE278	Elkton (Singerly Fire Co.)
14	KSS919	Elkton (Singerly Fire Co.)

County Government
453.150	County Common Operations (KNIC739)

Municipalities
155.790	Elkton City Police F1: Dispatch (KGB962)
154.830	Elkton City Police F2: Car to Car (KGB962)
39.340M	Chesapeake Town Police (KO5118) (MSP F4: Harford County)
39.340M	Rising Sun Town Police (KK9511) (MSP F4: Harford County)

State and Federal Governments
39.400	MSP-F12: Barrack F (North East-KGG903)
151.040	MSP-Barrack M (Perryville-KIL718)
47.260	SHA-F4: District 2
151.355	DNR-F4: Forestry (Central Division)
151.415	DNR-F5: Parks (Central Division)
453.975R	Toll Facilities - F3: Susquehanna Bridge (KGH609)
163.750	U.S. Department of Labor (Port Deposit)
164.350	Veterans Administration (Perry Point)
164.990	Veterans Administration (Perry Point)
173.640	Veterans Administration (Perry Point)

MARYLAND: CHARLES COUNTY (County Seat: La Plata)

County Sheriff (KDU438)
```
45.640        F1
45.400        F2
46.540        F3
45.140        F4
```

Fire Department (KDV793)
```
46.420        F1: Dispatch
46.360        F2: Fireground
153.830       Portables
              MED Channel 8 (Alt-1/5/7) (KAA642/KCL843)
```

VOLUNTEER FIRE COMPANIES

WZU489	Bel Alton	KGB686	La Plata
WRG374	Benedict	KUV794	Marbury (10th District)
KRJ781	Bryans Road (Note 3)	KGD267	Mechanicsville (Note 2)
WSB895	Cobb Island (5th Dist)	KGC631	Nanjemoy (Note 1)
WRG839	Hughesville	KNGW942	Potomac Hts Fire/Rescue (Note 4)
KEL445	Indian Head Fire/Rescue	KGC622	Waldorf
KNVI938	Indian Head Fire/Rescue	WRB465	Waldorf
KNFC910	Ironsides	KA47796	Waldorf

NOTE 1: Only licensed on F1: Dispatch
NOTE 2: St. Mary's County (Mutual Aid)
NOTE 3: Also licensed on 154.220
NOTE 4: Also licensed on 46.340 (Rescue Squad)

County Government
```
173.2375      Department of Public Works (WGR520-8)
453.425R      unknown use (KNBU824)
453.725R      unknown use (KXE563/WAN528)
462.600       County Humane Society
```

Municipalities
```
39.180        Indian Head City Government (KNCU931)
46.340        Potomac Heights Rescue Squad (Indian Head)
45.620        La Plata City Police Department (KUB937)
45.440        La Plata City Government (KTH541)
```

State and Federal Governments
```
39.240        MSP-F8: Barrack H (Waldorf-KGA916)
47.260        SHA-F2: District 5
151.250       DNR-F6: Forestry (Southern Division)
151.310       DNR-F7: Parks (Southern Division)
38.450        U.S. Army (Blossom Point)
141.400       U.S. Army (Blossom Point)
142.900       U.S. Army (Blossom Point)
140.950       U.S. Navy (Blossom Point)
143.675       U.S. Navy (Blossom Point)
143.700       U.S. Navy (Blossom Point)
140.275       U.S. Navy (La Plata)
148.325       U.S. Navy (Pomonkey)
149.025       U.S. Navy (Pomonkey)
140.950       U.S. Navy (Waldorf)
138.850       U.S. Naval Ordinance Station (Indian Head)
              (also 138.940/139.425/139.475/139.525/140.840
              (158.520/158.550/158.550/158.610/158.640/168.670)
```

<u>MARYLAND: DORCHESTER COUNTY</u> (County Seat: Cambridge)

<u>County Police</u> (KZJ920)
    39.580   Dispatch & Coordination with Caroline & Talbot Counties

<u>Fire Department</u> (KJI511)
    46.060   F1: Countywide Dispatch
    46.400   F2: Municipalities
                  MED Channel 6 (Alt-1/3/8) (KBP693/KCG891)

                  VOLUNTEER FIRE DEPARTMENTS
                  KGC709   Cambridge City (Note 2)
                  KAP750   Church Creek
                  KNAG295 East New Market
                  KAP745   Eldorado & Brookville
                  KAP748   Hoopers Island (Fishing Creek)
                  KAP752   Hurlock
                  KAP749   Lakes & Straits (Wingate)
                  KAP751   Linkwood-Salem (Note 1)
                  KAP747   Lloyds
                  KAP377   Madison
                  KBA315   Neck District (Hudson)
                  WSY480   Secretary City
                  KCR288   Taylors Island
                  KAP746   Vienna (Note 1)

                  Note 1: Licensed on F1 & F2 (all others only licensed on F1)
                  Note 2: Licensed on 153.830

<u>County Government</u>
    150.995R   Highway Department (KEO255) (Input on 156.240)
    151.070R   Highway Department (KYK482) (Input on 156.075)
    158.745   County Common Operations (KNAI303)
    155.760   Sheriff's Office (KJW437)

<u>Municipalities</u>
    453.300R   Cambridge Police Department (KGB449)
     39.200   Cambridge Police (may not be in use) (KGB449)
    155.115   Cambridge City Government Common (KIB689)
    155.145   Cambridge City Highway Department (KWV839)
    154.770M   Hurlock City Police (KB33474)
    154.830M   Hurlock City Police (KB33474)

<u>State and Federal Government</u>
    39.300   MSP-F3: Barrack I (Easton-KGA912)
    47.400   SHA-F3: District 1
    151.460   DNR-F1: Forestry (Eastern Division)
    151.325   DNR-F2: Parks (Eastern Division)
    34.430   National Park Service (Cambridge)

MARYLAND: FREDERICK COUNTY (County Seat: Frederick)

Sheriff's Office (KGE374)

39.020	F1:	Primary Dispatch
39.400	F2:	Secondary / State Police Dispatch
155.490		Intersystem with Frederick City Police (KNEN799)

Fire Department

46.420	F1:	Administration & Fireground (KJL599)
46.340	F2:	Dispatch (KTP975)
154.280		Mutual Aid
		MED Channel 6 (Alt-2/4/8) (KBP685/KNFL905)

FIRE STATIONS

1	KGG530	Independent (Note 3/4)	13	WQN218	Rocky Ridge
2	KGG530	Juniors (Note 3/4)	14	KGE630	Carroll Manor-Adamstown (Note 1/3)
3	KGG530	United (Note 3/4)	15	KJL553	New Market
4	KGG530	Citizens (Note 3/4)	16	KJL587	Woodsboro
5	KAV713	Brunswick Fire	17	KJI554	Libertytown (Note 3)
6	KJI553	Emmitsburg-Vigilant (Note 1)	18	KFI622	Graceham
7	KBS485	Middletown (Note 2/3)	19		Brunswick Rescue
8	KJD879	Myersville (Note 1)	20	KTS626	Jefferson
9	KJI552	New Midway	21	KRO264	Wolfsville (Note 1)
10	KGD455	Thurmont (Note 3)	22	KSS202	Lewistown
11	KGE799	Walkersville	23	KMK313	Urbana
12	KJI557	Braddock Heights			Fort Detrick

NOTE 1: Licensed only on F1   NOTE 3: Licensed on 153.830
NOTE 2: Licensed only on F2   NOTE 4: Frederick City Fire Cos.

County Government

45.200	Board of Education (KJK609)
151.070R	County Roads (KGD667) (Input on 156.120)
153.845	County Government Common (KUP268/WXF849)
155.055	unknown use (KGS818)
460.125	Adult Detention Center

Municipalities

155.370	Brunswick City Police (KGE718/KNFF716)
494.412R	Frederick City Police F1: Dispatch (KGA247)
494.362R	Frederick City Police F2: Car to Car/Admin. (KGA247)
494.312R	Frederick City Police F3: Detectives (CID) (KGA247)
155.490	Frederick City Police - Net with Co. Sheriff (KGA247)
851.4625	Frederick City Board of Education (WYN646)
45.360	Frederick City Department of Public Works (KCS549)
156.000	Thurmont City Government & Police (KCR945-7)
155.715	Walkersville City Commissioners (KNEJ763)

State and Federal Governments

39.400	MSP-F12:Barrack B (Frederick-KGA918)
47.260	SHA-F2: Division 7
151.460	DNR-F1: Forestry (Western Division)
151.325	DNR-F2: Parks (Western Division)
155.025	Frederick State College (KWM740)
165.060	Fort Detrick: Fire Department
419.600	Fort Detrick: Department of Health & Human Services
36.050	Fort Detrick: U.S. Army (also 139.175/141.025/171.475/237.400)
142.155	U.S. Air Force MARS (Frederick) (also 143.460)
165.340	Department of Health & Human Services (Frederick)
171.725	National Park Service (Thurmont Park/Catoctin Mountains)
172.525	National Park Service (Thurmont Park)

MARYLAND: GARRETT COUNTY (County Seat: Oakland)

County Police (KYQ343)

39.180	Dispatch / Coordination with Allegany & Washington Counties
452.375R	Mobile Repeater Frequency

Fire Department (KMJ961)

33.880	F1: Dispatch
33.960	F2: Fireground
37.980	South Garrett County Rescue Squad (KZB322)
	MED Channel 3 (Alt-4/7/8) (KBP682/KNFF841-3)

VOLUNTEER FIRE COMPANIES
KXZ893   Accident
WQY615   Bittinger
KXZ894   Bloomington (Note 1)
KGD446   Cumberland (Allegany County Mutual Aid) (Note 2)
KUS551   Cumberland-Dist 16 (Allegany Co. Mutual Aid)
KNFB474 Deep Creek (McHenry)
KSS812   Deer Park
KXZ896   Deer Park
WRA652   East Garrett County (Finzel) (Note 1/2)
KXZ897   Friendsville
KNBJ601 Gorman
KTQ275   Grantsville (Note 1)
KXZ898   Kitzmiller
KTK612   Lanaconing (Allegany County Mutual Aid) (Note 1/2)
KQ7710   Oakland

NOTE 1: Licensed only on F1 (all others on F1 & F2)
NOTE 2: Licensed also on Allegany Co. F1(33.78) / F2(33.68)

County Government

155.280	County Safety (KDS971)
155.820	unknown use (KYU467)
155.955	unknown use (KIK948)
156.180	Highway Department (KGG760)
158.835	unknown use (KYU467)
37.900	County Memorial Hospital (KGF872)

State and Federal Governments

39.240	MSP-F8: Barrack C (Cumberland-KGA910 / Oakland-KDE211)
47.320	SHA-F1: District 6
151.460	DNR-F1: Forestry (Western Division)
151.325	DNR-F2: Parks (Western Division)
453.675R	Upper Potomac River Commission (Bloomington) (WQD697)

MARYLAND: HARFORD COUNTY (County Seat: Bel Air)

County Sheriff (KUV669)
```
 37.200     F1: Dispatch
 37.300     F2: County-Municipal Intersystem
 37.260     F3: Special Operations Division
 37.400         (newly allocated-use unknown)
154.785         Unknown use
```

Fire Department (KGD273)
```
 33.740     F1: Dispatch
 33.760     F2: Fireground
 33.660     F3: Alternate
154.280         Mutual Aid
460.575R    F1: Dispatch (Future)
460.600R    F2: Fireground (Future)
460.625R    F3: Alternate (Future)
460.525R        Rescue Dispatch (KXB753)
                MED Channel 4 (Alt-8) (KXB753)
```

FIRE STATIONS						UNIT IDENTIFICATION	
1	KMJ887	Level	8	KSZ977	Joppa Magnolia	11-20	Engines
2	KGE519	Aberdeen	9		Darlington	21-30	Tankers
3	KBF245	Bel Air	10		Fawn Grove	31-40	Trucks
4	KJI616	Abington	11		Edgewood Arsenal	41-50	Brush Trucks
5	KSZ798	Harve De Grace	12		Aberdeen Proving	61-70	Air Units
6	KGF671	Delta Cardiff			Grounds	91-99	Ambulances
7	KYW859	Jarrettsville	13	KNBF450	Fallston		

County Government
```
 37.940     Highway Department (KGE375)
 37.960     Highway Department (KGE375)
154.980     unknown use (Bel Air -KKQ960)
155.085B    unknown use (Abington-KIU559) (Mobils on 153.995)
```

Municipalities
```
 37.180     Aberdeen City Police Department (KIU666)
153.860     Aberdeen City Government (KLX821)
155.940     Aberdeen City Government (KQO339)
 37.220     Bel Air City Police Department (KFN443)
155.145     Bel Air City Government (KTX598)
 37.320     Harve De Grace City Police Department (WZM869)
453.825R    Harve De Grace City Police Department (WQQ336)
```

State and Federal Governments
```
 39.340     MSP-F4: Barrack D (Bel Air-KGA919)
 47.400     SHA-F3: District 4
151.355     DNR-F4: Forestry (Central Division)
151.415     DNR-F5: Parks (Central Division}
 49.800     Edgewood Arsenal Army Chemical Center
165.060     Edgewood Arsenal Army Chemical Center - Security
```

MARYLAND: HOWARD COUNTY (County Seat: Ellicott City)

County Police (KGC527)

159.090R	F1:	Dispatch (Input on 155.370)
155.595R	F2:	Data/Emergency/Special Events (Input on 154.650)
155.475	F3:	Nationwide Police Emergency Network
155.115R	F4:	Fire/Police Coordination
460.050R		Baltimore Metropolitan Intersystem
957.150		unknown use (Cooksville-WCE340)

TEN CODES (Standard 10 Codes used with the following exceptions)

10-66 Bar Check	10-82 Open Cell
10-67 Gas Pumps	10-84 Channel 2

DISPATCH CODES

1 Homicide	7 Auto Theft	14 Vandalism	21 Liquor Violation
2 Rape	9 Arson	15 Weapons Viol	23 Intoxication
3 Robbery	10 Forgery	17 Sex Offense	24 Disorderly
4 Assault	11 Fraud	18 Narcotics	29 Runaway/Missing
5 B & E	12 Embezzlement	19 Gambling/Vice	
6 Larceny	13 Stolen Property	20 Family Crimes	SIGNAL 13: EMERGENCY

Fire Department (KGG529)

154.250R	F1:	Fire Dispatch (Input on 153.770)
154.220	F2:	Fireground
154.280	F3:	Mutual Aid
155.115	F4:	Fire/Police Coordination (KYU411)
154.265M		Allocated for future use
154.295M		Allocated for future use
		MED Channel 4 (Alt-8)

FIRE STATIONS

1 ELKRIDGE	6275	Old Washington Road
2 ELLICOTT CITY	8390	Main Street
3 WEST FRIENDSHIP	12460	Friendship Road (Rte. 144)
4 LISBON	1330	Route 94
5 CLARKSVILLE	12335	Clarksville Pike (Rte. 108)
6 SAVAGE	8925	Lincoln Street
7 COLUMBIA	5815	Bannaker Road
8 ELLICOTT CITY	9601	Route 99 (Substation)
9 COLUMBIA	5950	Tamar Drive (Substation)

UNIT ID (X = Fire Station)

Unit 1	Fire Administrator
Unit 2	Deputy - Operations
Unit 3	Admin Services Ch
Unit 4	Fire Prevention Ch
Comm 1	Communications Off
Comm 99	Mobil Comm. Unit
X1/X2/X3	Fire Engines
X5/X6	Ambulances/Medics
X7/X8	Brush Trucks

County Government

37.260	Civil Defense Network (KYU411)
151.115R	Highway Department (KGG444) (Input on 156.060)
151.775	Howard Community College (KVS559)
155.820R	County Jail/Utilities/Animal Control (KYU411)
155.895R	Public Schools (KYU411)
155.925	unknown use (KYU411)
156.015M	unknown input (KYU411)
158.895M	unknown input (KYU411)

Municipalities

151.865	Columbia City Parks and Recreation (KUH483/KNFD748)
154.540	Columbia City Parks and Recreation (KSX466)

MARYLAND: HOWARD COUNTY   (Continued)

State and Federal Governments
39.060	MSP-F11: Barrack A (Waterloo-KGA915)
47.260	SHA-F2: District 7
151.250	DNR-F6: Forestry (Southern Division)
151.310	DNR-F7: Parks (Southern Division)
153.860	Department of Corrections (Jessup-KKC634)
153.965	Department of Corrections (Jessup-KKC634)
166.560	U.S. Department of Agriculture
393.855	U.S. Navy (Atlantic Net)
143.520	U.S. Navy (Scaggsville)

MARYLAND: KENT COUNTY   (County Seat: Chestertown)

County Police   (KAV414)
39.080	Primary Operations
154.830	VHF Repeater

Fire Department   (KEC763)
33.980	F1:
33.840	F2:
33.040	Kent-Queen Anne's Rescue Squad (KEC762)
	MED Channel 6 (Alt-1/3/8) (KEC489)

Fire Stations
2	KGH339	Millington
3	KGD659	Galena
4	KCL542	Kennedyville
5	KRX454	Betterton
6	KNAU478	Chestertown
7	KGD391	Rock Hall

County Government
39.980	Sanitation District (KNBB776)
154.100	County Government Common (WZM744)
154.515	Board of Education (WXZ825)
173.203	County Utilities (WCG616/WCG624-9)

Municipalities
39.340	Chestertown Police Department (KH5894)
155.055	Chestertown City Government (KNCS896)
154.515	Chestertown City Board of Education (WXZ825)
90.500	Worton Board of Education (WKHS)

State and Federal Government
39.320	MSP-F6: Barrack S (Centreville-KGB631)
47.140	SHA-F4: District 2
151.355	DNR-F4: Forestry (Central Division)
151.415	DNR-F5: Parks (Central Division)

MARYLAND: MONTGOMERY COUNTY (County Seat: Rockville)

County Police

494.7125R	F1:	D1 - Rockville	(Sectors A/B/C)	(KSE564)
494.8625R	F2:	D2 - Bethesda	(Sectors D/E)	(KXF426)
494.9125R	F3:	D3 - Silver Spring	(Sectors G/H)	(KYX558)
495.3125R	F4:	D4 - Wheaton/Glenmont	(Sectors J/K)	(KXF427)
495.3375R	F5:	D5 - Germantown	(Sectors M/N)	(KYX556)
495.3625R	F6:	Countywide - Detectives		
495.3875M	F7:	Countywide - Car to Car		
495.4125R	F8:	Countywide - Detectives (Future: Data & Information)		
494.7125M	F9:	Rockville District car to car		
494.8625M	F10:	Bethesda District car to car		
494.9125M	F11:	Silver Spring District car to car		
495.3125M	F12:	Wheaton/Glenmont District car to car		
495.3375M	F13:	Germantown District car to car		

POLICE DEPARTMENT DISTRICT AND SECTOR MAP

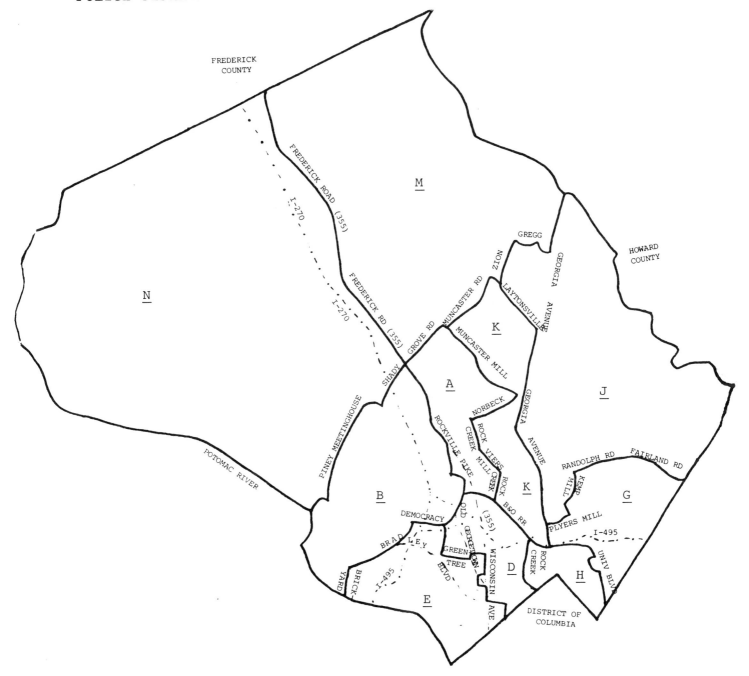

MARYLAND: MONTGOMERY COUNTY (Continued)

County Police

UNIT IDENTIFICATION: District Units (X = District Number)

Staff & Special Units   District Patrol Units

X00	Commander	Beat Unit: (Shift) / (Sector) / (Beat)
X01	Deputy Commander	Shift Super: (Shift) / (Sector) / 10
X02	Ops Lieutenant	Beat Backup: (Shift) / (Sector) / (Beat) / 1,2,etc.
X03-04	Sector Commander	Sector Backup:(Shift) / (Sector) / "Sam" / 1,2,etc.
X05-09	Admin Personnel	Shifts: Shift # refers to officer individ shift (7 shifts)
X20-39	Tac Teams	4 shifts/day: 0600-1600/1000-2000/1600-0200/2000-0600
X50-65	Traffic Units	Sectors: 2 sectors/district (Sector C: Rockville City PD)
X66-69	School Safety	Beats: Each Sector includes four beats (1-4)
X70-80	Persons/Property	
X81-90	C.I.D.	

UNIT IDENTIFICATION: Headquarters & Staff

01	Chief	16	Op Supp Cdr	35-39	R'ville Admin	60-61	FBI (Sil Spr)
02-03	Dep Chief	17-19	Bur Admin	40	SAO Liaison	62	Fire Marshal
04-06	Bureau Cdr	20	HQ Admin	41-43	Research/Plan	70-79	Int Affairs
07-09	Dep Bur Cdr	21-24	Info Svc	46	Legal Advisor	80	States Atty
10-14	Duty Cdr	30	R'ville Chief	51-53	Property Div	95-96	Medical Exam.
15	Comm Rel Cdr	31-34	R'ville Cdr	54-58	Abandoned Auto	97-99	Media Services

UNIT IDENTIFICATION: Countywide Special Units (Prefix "9")

9/A/10-20	Acad Staff	9/G/10-19	Gen Assign	9/R/10-15	Comm Rel
9/B/10-35	Prop Div	9/I/10-19	Intellig Div	9/S/10-15	School Safety
9/C/10-30	Crime Preven	9/K/10-19	Canine Div	9/T/10-18	Tac Div
9/D/10-19	Gaithersburg	9/L/10-30	Sheriff	9/U/10-20	Phone Reports
9/E/10-11	Chemist	9/M/10-15	Chevy Chase	9/V/10-15	Vice Div
9/F/10-16	ID Div	9/N/10-20	Narcotics	9/Y/10-35	Youth Div

RADIO TEN CODES (Complete Listing

10-01	Receiving poorly	10-15	Transp Prisoner	10-30	Doesn't Conform
10-02	Receiving well	10-16	Meet unit at...	10-31	Message Check
10-03	No Trans. x/ Emerg	10-19	Request Shift Cdr	10-32	No Messages
10-04	OK (1 man unit)	10-20	Location	10-40	Welfare/Status Check
10-05	On the Scene	10-21	Req Field Super	10-41	Situation under Control
10-06	Busy	10-22	Disregard	10-50	OFFICER NEEDS HELP
10-07	Out of Service	10-23	License Check	10-51	Non-Emerg Assist
10-08	In Service	10-24	Contact Desk Clerk	10-60	Wanted/Stolen Indicated
10-09	Repeat	10-25	In Contact with...	10-70	Surveillence at...
10-10	Avail at (Loc)	10-26	Report to Station	10-81	Crime in Progress
10-11	Disp to rapidly	10-27	Advise Phone Number	10-86	Call Home
10-12	Weather/Road cond	10-28	Registration Check	10-97	Reception Check
10-13	Request tow truck	10-29	Wanted/Stolen Check	10-99	OK (2 man unit)
				10-100	Riot/Large Disturbance

STATUS ACTIVITY CODES

11	Traffic Court-In County	24	Crim Warrant Svc/Arrest	34	School Safety Activity
12	Non Trf. Court-In County	25	Tnsp other Co Agency	51	Detail (Non Traffic)
13	Crossing Detail	26	Susp Sit/Car/Person	52	Prearranged Trf Detail
15	Take 10 Prog (Foot beat)	27	Investig-Prelim/Followup	53	Trf Problem (On Patrol)
16	Routine Business check	28	ID Field Investigation	54	Traffic Stop
19	Serving Summons	29	Canine Activity	55	Radar Detail
21	Serving Trf Warrant	31	Transport - Co. Police	91	Super/Admin Duty
22	Assist other unit	32	Out of County-Bus/Inv/Ct.	92	Eating Meal
23	Traffic Escort	33	Vehicle Maintenance/Gas	99	Miscellaneous Activity

MARYLAND: MONTGOMERY COUNTY (Continued)

County Police

EVENT CLEARANCE CODES

0100 HOMICIDE
  11 Firearm
  12 Sharp Instrument
  13 Blunt Instrument
  14 Fist/Hands
  15 Other
  16 By Police Officer
  20 Negligent Manslaughter

0200 RAPE
  11 By Force
  12 Attempt-Force

0300 ROBBERY
  1x Firearm
  2x Knife/Cutting
  3x Dangerous Weapon
  4x Strong Arm
  1 Hwy/Rd/Alley
  2 Business(x3/4/6)
  3 Gas/Svc Station
  4 Chain Store
  5 Residential
  6 Bank/S&L/CrUnion
  7 Other

0400 AGGREVATED ASSAULT
  1x Firearm
  2x Cut/Stab
  3x Dangerous Weapon
  4x Beat-Serious Injury
      1 On Citizen
      2 On Police Officer
      3 On Spouse

0500 BURGLARY
  1x Forcible Entry
  2x No Force
  3x Forcible Attempt
  1 Residential-Night
  2 Residential-Day
  3 Residential-Unkn
  4 Commercial-Night
  5 Commercial-Day
  6 Commercial-Unkn
  7 School-Night
  8 School-Day
  9 School-Unkn

0600 LARCENY
  1x $200 or over
  2x $50 - $199
  3x Under $50/Attempt
  1 Pick Pocket
  2 Purse Snatch
  3 Shoplifting
  4 From Auto
  5 Auto Part
  6 Bicycle
  7 Building (X3/8)
  8 Coin Operated Machine
  9 Other Larceny

0700 AUTO THEFT
  11 Auto
  12 Buses / Trucks
  13 Other Motor Vehicle

0800 ASSAULT
  1x Assault & Battery
  2x Simple Assault
  1 On Citizen
  2 On Police Officer
  3 On Spouse

0900 ARSON
  11 Successful Arson
  12 Arson Attempt

1000 FORGERY/COUNTERFEIT
  11 Credit Cards
  12 Checks
  13 All Other

1100 BAD CHECKS
  1x $300 or More
  2x Less than $300
  1 Merchandise
  2 Labor/Services
  3 Stop Payment
  4 Others

1200 EMBEZZLEMENT/THEFT
  1x $300 or More
  2x Less than $300
  1 Embezzlement
  2 Larceny after Trust
  3 Confidence Games
  4 Others

1300 STOLEN PROPERTY
  11 Possess/Buy/Receive

1400 VANDALISM
  11 Dwelling
  12 Vehicle
  13 Business
  14 School
  15 Church/Temple
  16 Constr Site
  17 Other

1500 WEAPONS
  11 Concealed
  12 Possession
  13 Discharging
  14 Other

1600 PROSTITUTION/VICE
  11 Disorderly House
  12 Solicit/Pander
  13 Prostitution-Other
  14 Prostitution-Attempt

1700 SEX OFFENSES
  11 Sex Assault
  12 Indecent Exposure
  13 Indecent Phone Call
  14 Peeping Tom
  15 Unnat/Perverted-Force
  16 4th Degree Sex Offense
  17 Incest
  18 All other Sex Offenses

1800 CONTROLLED DANGEROUS SUBST
  1x Possession
  2x Selling
  3x Using
  4x Manufacturing
  5x Forged Prescription
  6x Possession of Implement
  1 Opium & Derivatives
  2 Synthetic
  3 Marijuana/Hashish
  4 Barbiturates/Amphetamines
  5 Hallucinogenic
  6 Harmful Inhalant
  7 Cocaine & Derivatives
  8 All other CDS

MARYLAND: MONTGOMERY COUNTY (Continued)

County Police

EVENT CLEARANCE CODES (continued)

1900 GAMBLING
11 Numbers/Lottery
12 Horse Racing
13 Crap/Cards
14 Other

2000 FAMILY OFFENSES
11 Desertion/Non-Support
12 Child Neglect
13 Child Abuse
14 Other/Child Snatching

2100 JUVENILE OFFENSES
11 Runaway
12 Out of Control
13 Loitering under 18
14 Other

2200 LIQUOR LAW VIOLATIONS
11 Selling w/o license
12 Furnishing minor
13 Possession-under 18
14 Untaxed liquor viol
15 Hours Sale violation
16 Drinking in public

2300 CONTRIBUTING
11 Liquor to minor
12 Other (X Liquor/sex)

2400 DISORDERLY CONDUCT
11 Unlawful assembly
12 Disorderly house(Xsex)
13 Disorderly conduct

2500 VAGRANCY
11 Vagrancy Tramp

2600 SUICIDE
1x Suicide-Successful
2x Suicide-Attempt
1 Firearm
2 Cut/Stab
3 Poison/Overdose
4 Hanging
5 Asphyxiation
6 Other

2700 OTHER OFFENSES
11 Abortion
12 Air Pollution Control
13 Animal Poisoning
14 Bigamy
15 Blackmail/Extortion
16 Bomb Threat
17 Bldg Code Viol
18 Dog/Cat Control
19 Failure to Pay
21 False Alarm
22 False Crime Report
23 Fire Code Violation
24 Fireworks
25 Escapee
26 Kidnapping
27 Littering/Dumping
28 Loitering-Over 18
29 Perjury
31 Pornography
32 Public Nuisance
33 Rental Car Viol
34 Rogue & Vagabond
35 Soliciting w/o lic
36 Taxi Cab ordinance
37 Trespassing
38 Threat/Annoy phone
39 Zoning violation
41 Bicycle/Minibike
42 Smoking ordinances
50 Fug. from Justice
51 Fug. from MD Juns.
91 All other non-traffic
92 Conspiracy

2800 TRAFFIC OFFENSES
11 Abandoned Auto
12 Driving under infl
13 Bicycle/Minibike
14 Parking Offenses
91 All other Traffic

2900 MISCELLANEOUS CALLS
1x Sudden Deaths
1 Accident Non-Traffic
2 Drowning
3 Natural
4 Undetermined
31 Animal Bite
32 Animal Complaint
33 Disabled Motor Vehicle
34 Drunk
35 Fires (not Arson)
36 Ill Person
37 Injury-Non Traffic
38 Invest/Police Info
41 Lost Property
42 Mental Transport
43 Missing Person
44 Open Window/Door
46 Rec. Prop/Montg Co
47 Rec. Prop/Others
48 Traffic Haz/Park Compl
49 Vacant House Complaint
51 Family Trouble
52 Susp Sit/Person/Car
6x Bank/S&L Alarms
7x Other Commercial Alarms
8x Residential Alarms
1 Accidental/Error
2 Malfunction
3 Weather
91 Other Misc Calls
95 Follow up earlier call

5xxx TRAFFIC ACCIDENTS
3xx Fatal
4xx Personal Injury
5xx Property Damage
1x Public Rd/St/Hwy
2x Park Lot/Garage/Pub Prop
3x Other Private Property
1 Accident
2 Hit & Run

EVENT CLEARANCE CODES: Disposition Suffix
DASH ONE   Verified/adjusted/no report or arrest
DASH TWO   Verified/report made/no arrest
DASH THREE   Verified/no report/arrest or charge made
DASH FOUR   Verified/report made/arrest or charge made
DASH FIVE   Not Verified/no report
DASH SIX   Unfounded/no report

MARYLAND: MONTGOMERY COUNTY (Continued)

Fire / Rescue Department (KGC334)

153.950M	F1:	Primary Fireground Operating Channel
154.160R	F2:	Dispatch (input on 154.710)
154.280	F3:	Mutual Aid Network
155.100	F4:	Secondary Fireground / Administration
155.340	F5:	EMS-1 - Ambulance/Hospital Communications
154.160M	F6:	Simplex Fireground
153.950R	F7:	WMATA Subway Incident Operations (Input on 154.830)
154.355		MODAT Status Communications
		MED Channels 2/5 (Alt-1/6/8) (WRX770-3/KWL414-6)
33.040		Rescue Co. 1: Bethesda-Chevy Chase Rescue Squad
462.625		Rescue Co. 2: Wheaton Rescue Squad (KAB1720/KAB3525-6)
462.650		Rescue Co. 2: Wheaton Rescue Squad (KAB1720/KAB3525-6)

FIRE STATIONS

```
 1 SILVER SPRING.......................8131 Georgia Avenue
 2 TAKOMA PARK.........................7201 Carroll Avenue
 3 ROCKVILLE...........................380 Hungerford Drive
 4 SANDY SPRING........................816 Olney-Sandy Spring Road
 5 KENSINGTON..........................10620 Connecticut Avenue
 6 BETHESDA............................6600 Wisconsin Avenue
 7 CHEVY CHASE.........................8001 Connecticut Avenue
 8 GAITHERSBURG-WASHINGTON GROVE........801 Russell Avenue
 9 HYATTSTOWN..........................25801 Frederick Road
10 CABIN JOHN..........................8201 River Road
11 GLEN ECHO...........................5920 Massachusetts Avenue
12 HILLANDALE..........................10617 New Hampshire Avenue
13 DAMASCUS............................26334 Ridge Road
14 UPPER MONTGOMERY....................19801 Beallsville Road
15 BURTONSVILLE........................15430 Old Columbia Pike
16 SILVER SPRING (Four Corners)........111 University Blvd East
17 LAYTONSVILLE........................21400 Laytonsville Road
18 KENSINGTON (Glenmont)...............12251 Georgia Avenue
19 SILVER SPRING (Montgomery Hills)....1945 Seminary Road
20 BETHESDA (Cedar Lane)...............9041 Old Georgetown Road
21 KENSINGTON (Parkland)...............12500 Veirs Mill Road
23 ROCKVILLE (Rollins Avenue)..........121 Rollins Avenue
24 HILLANDALE (Colesville).............13216 New Hampshire Avenue
25 KENSINGTON (Aspen Hill).............14111 Georgia Avenue
26 BETHESDA (Democracy)................6500 Democracy Boulevard
27 PUBLIC SERVICE TRAINING ACADEMY.....10025 Darnestown Road
28 GAITHERSBURG (Mill Creek)...........7272 Muncaster Mill Road
29 HYATTSTOWN (Germantown).............20100 Aircraft Drive
30 CABIN JOHN (Potomac)................9404 Falls Road
31 ROCKVILLE (Shady Grove).............9615 Darnestown Road
33 ROCKVILLE (Falls Road)..............11430 Falls Road
40 SANDY SPRING (Olney)................116911 Georgia Avenue
50 NATIONAL NAVAL MED CENTER...........8901 Rockville Pike-Bldg 20
51 NATIONAL INSTITUTES OF HEALTH.......9000 Rockville Pike-Bldg 12
52 NAVAL SHIP RESEARCH & DEV CTR.......Carderock MD  -Bldg 10
53 NATIONAL BUREAU OF STANDARDS........Service Drive -Bldg 303
54 WALTER REED HOSPITAL ANNEX..........Forest Glen Annex-Bldg 121
55 NAVAL SURFACE WEAPONS CENTER........White Oak MD
DMAHTC (Defense Mapping Agency)........6100 MacArthur Boulevard
RESCUE CO 1: BETHESDA-CHEVY CHASE.......5020 Battery Lane
RESCUE CO 2: WHEATON VOL RESCUE........11435 Grandview Avenue
```

MARYLAND: MONTGOMERY COUNTY (Continued)

Fire / Rescue Department
NOTE: No ten codes are used. Condition RED indicates all
       transmissions kept to a minimum during emergencies.

STATION APPARATUS (X = Station Number)

ENGINE X-1	First Due Pumper (one at all stations)
ENGINE X-2	Second Due Pumper (all stations except 1/19/20/21/25/26/27)
ENGINE X-3	Third Due Pumper (only at stations 2/3/4/6/9/13/14/16/40)
ENGINE X-4	Reserve Pumper (only at stations 3/13)
BRUSH X-5	Brush Truck (stations 3/4/8/9/10/14/15/17/21/24/28/29/30/31/33/40)
BRUSH X-6	Alternate Brush Truck (only at stations 9/13/14)
AMBULANCE X-7	Reserve Ambulance (only at Station 13)
AMBULANCE X-8	Reserve Ambulance (only at Stations 8/13/14/24/40)
AMBULANCE X-9	First Due Ambulance (all stations except 6/7/12/13/18/19/20/25/26)
	NOTE: Ambulances ID as MEDIC X-9 if paramedic on board
TRUCK-X	Only at Stations 1/2/3/5/6/8/11/18/19/20/24/25/26/27
MOBILE-X	Command Incident Car (at Stations 4/5/6/10/11/19)
	NOTE: Station 19 Mobil IDs as MOBIL-1
BOAT-X	Rescue Boats (at Stations 3/9/10/11/14/15/30)
SQUAD-X	Heavy Rescue (at Stations 3/9/15/21)
CANTEEN-X	Located at BCC Rescue Squad & Stations 4/5
TANK WAGON-X	Located at Stations 14/17 (NOTE: Station 17 has Tank Wagons 17-1/17-2
SPECIAL UNIT-X	Air Cascade (Stations 16/17) / Training & Disaster (Station 27)
TWIN ENGINE-X	Located at Station 19
UTILITY-X	Department Utility Vehicle
SET	Special Evacuation Team Vehicle (located at Station 26)
HazMat-1	Hazardous Materials Van (located at Station 7)
CHIEF X-1	Station / Volunteer Department Chief
CHIEF X-2	Station First Deputy Chief
CHIEF X-3	Station Second Deputy Chief

COUNTYWIDE UNIT IDENTIFICATION

Supervisory Staff	Fire Prevention Division	Medic/Rescue Units
1 Director	FM-01 Chief	Medic 1: BCC Rescue Squad
2 Fireboard Chairman	FM-02 Assistant Chief	Medic 2: Wheaton Rescue Squad
3 Admin Svc Chief	FM-10 Lieutenant	Medic 3: Sta. 03-Rockville
4 Prog Dev Chief	FM-11 Sergeant	Medic 4: Sta. 12-Hillandale
5 Lieutenant	FM-12 Sergeant	Medic 5: Sta. 01-Silver Spring
6 Operations Chief	FM-20 Lieutenant	Medic 6: Sta. 08-Gaithersburg
7 Fire Science Intern	FM-21 Sergeant	Medic 7: Sta. 25-Aspen Hill
8 Admin Div Staff	FM-22 Sergeant	Medic 8: Sta. 13-Damascas
10 Training Officer	FM-30 Lieutenant	Medic 9: Sta. 18-Glenmont
11 Fire Instructor	FM-31 Sergeant	
12 Rescue Instructor	FM-32 Sergeant	Rescue 10-15 BCC Rescue Squad
13 Acad Maint Tech	FM-51 Sergeant - Investig	Rescue 18-19 BCC Heavy Rescue
15 Training Staff	FM-52 Sergeant - Investig	Rescue 21-25 Wheaton Rescue
20 Commun Officer	FM-53 Sergeant - Investig	Rescue 28 Wheaton Light Rescue
21-24 EOC Shift Super	FM-60 Lieutenant - Pub Ed	Rescue 29 Wheaton Heavy Rescue
25 EOC Staff	FM-61 Sergeant - Pub Ed	Rescue 31 Medic 5 w/o paramed.
30 EMS Officer	FM-62 Sergeant - Pub Ed	Rescue 41 Located at Sta. 26
31 EMS Lieutenant		
33-36 Paramedics		

MARYLAND: MONTGOMERY COUNTY (Continued)

County Government

County Government Network (call signs in morse code)
155.100	F1: Animal Control / Building Ops. / Fire F4 / Sheriff F3
155.985	F2: Building Security & Maint / Disaster Net / Sheriff F2

Maryland National Capital Park & Planning Commission (KZK218/KIF677)
151.280R	F1: MNCPPC Park Police - Primary (Input on 151.160)
151.340	F2: MNCPPC Park Police - Secondary / Park Service

UNIT ID:

7xx Patrol Div	7xx Patrol Div	7xx Patrol Div	Shift 1:
00-09 Shift Sgt	4x Shift 1 Beat	7x Special units	2300-0700
1x Shift 1 Motor	5x Shift 2 Beat	8x Special units	Shift 2:
2x Shift 2 Motor	6x Shift 3 Beat	9x Special units	0700-1500
3x Shift 3 Motor	1-5 Beats 1-5	8xx Sp. Ops. Div.	Shift 3:
1-5 Beats 1-5	6-9 Horses/	NOTE: MNCPPC use	1500-2300
6-9 Extra units	Extra units	MCP Radio Codes	

Department of Transportation (KGC804-807)
453.950R	Highway Division F1: NORTH (East repeater-Damascas)
453.950R	Highway Division F2: NORTH (West repeater-Poolesville)
453.400R	Highway Division F3: SOUTH (East repeater-Colesville)
453.400R	Highway Division F4: SOUTH (West repeater-Seven Locks)
150.995	Highway Construction Inspectors (KGC807)
452.775R	Ride-On Bus F1: Gaithersburg Area (WQF598/KXJ281)
452.850R	Ride-On Bus F2: Silver Spring Area (WSE382/WRE227)

Miscellaneous County Operations
155.805	Board of Education Buses & Security (KBQ802)
462.625	Human Resources: Handicapped Ride-On Bus (KAA8106-7)
39.580	Montgomery College - Takoma Park Campus (KRO260)
154.540	Montgomery College - Rockville Campus (Security)
464.125	Montgomery College - R'ville (WQE355)
494.8125M	Montgomery County Detention Center (Internal Security)
464.375	Public Libraries (KNFJ606-18/WRE772)
155.520	County Sheriff F1: Dispatch & Operations (KGB792/KCP560)

Municipalities
156.240	Gaithersburg City Department of Public Works (KLD682)
155.895	Kensington City Government (KQS532)
45.400	Poolesville City Commissioners (KNDG308)
495.2375M	Rockville City Police F1: Simplex car to car (KXY611)
495.2375R	Rockville City Police F2: Dispatch (KXY611)
155.745	Rockville City Gov't F1: Animal Control/Parks (KSM986)
155.760	Rockville City Gov't F2: Public Works (KGH346)
39.820	Takoma Park City Police F1: Dispatch (KGB248)
39.760	Takoma Park City Police F2: Portables (KGB248)
156.105	Takoma Park City Highway Department
854.9625R	Takoma Park City Government

State Government
39.320	MSP-F6: Barrack N (Rockville-KGE796)
47.400	SHA-F3: District 3
151.250	DNR-F6: Forestry (Southern Division)
151.310	DNR-F7: Parks (Southern Division)
158.745	unknown use (Burtonsville-KNCS597)

MARYLAND: MONTGOMERY COUNTY (Continued)

Federal Government
National Institutes of Health
411.450R	Bethesda Facility: Security
415.825R	Bethesda Facility: Fire Department
36.220R	Taxis/Maintenance (Bethesda-KID470 / Poolesville-KBJ334)
36.350	Poolesville Facility (KBJ334)
171.235	Bethesda Facility (also 409.000/415.925/416.7875/419.600)

Department of Energy - Emergency Command Center
162.025	Motor Pool
162.225	Radio Telephones
40.470	Germantown Facility (also 164.225/164.375/169.950)
236.600	Germantown Facility (410.350)
416.300	Bethesda Facility
162.050	Germantown & Bethesda Facilities (also 170.075)

National Bureau of Standards (Gaithersburg)
166.175R	Security (input on 169.025)
166.150	Security & Fire Department
164.025	Motor Pool
162.175	unknown use (also 163.225/163.000/165.560)
217.250	unknown use (410.150/410.825)

Naval Operations: National Naval Medical Center (Bethesda)
                 Naval Surface Weapons Center (White Oak)
                 Naval Ship Research & Development Center (Carderock)
140.580	Joint Security Network
142.225	Disaster Network - Primary: Magic Swimmer
142.450	Disaster Network - Secondary: Magic Swimmer
140.560	Joint Operations Network
142.500	Surface Weapons Center & Ship R&D Center
140.725	Navy Med: Security & Fire Department
140.275	Navy Med: Ambulances: "Mercy Network"
142.525	Navy Med: Maintenance
148.275P	Navy Med: Pager
296.000	Navy Med: Medivac Ambulances
164.300	Navy Med: Security (also on 162.125)
41.830	Navy Med: Administrative (low power)
148.545	Navy Med: U.S. Air Force
143.355	Navy Med: U.S. Army (also 407.325)
140.075	Navy Med (also 140.200/140.650/140.675/140.775/140.820)
142.000	Navy Med (also 267.600)
140.350	Ship R&D Center: U.S. Navy operations
138.720	Surface Weapons Center: U.S. Navy operations (also 139.500)

Miscellaneous Federal Government
41.380	Health & Human Services: Parklawn Security (also 164.300)
408.050	Public Health Service (Rockville) (also 409.000)
166.950R	National Park Service: C & O Canal (input on 166.350)
171.725	Department of the Interior: Fox Hill (also 172.525)
27.850	FEMA: Federal Emergency Management Agency (Olney-KBG643)
167.975	FEMA (Rockville & Olney) (also on 173.185)
168.525	U.S. Postal Service: Bethesda Post Office
163.375	U.S. Postal Service: Rockville Post Office (also 417.650)
34.980	NOAA--Rockville (also 36.220/38.220/164.350/166.050/170.200
163.325	Commerce Dept: Silver Spring (also 163.350/166.125/169.350)
36.990	U.S. Army (Damascus-WAR29) (also on Metro DC Net - 36.510)
164.960	220 MP Brigade Army Reserve Training Center (Gaithersburg)
164.275	NRC Office of Inspection(Bethesda)(also 167.875/411.200)
168.000	Consumer Product Safety Commission (Bethesda)

MARYLAND: PRINCE GEORGE'S COUNTY (County Seat: Upper Marlboro)

County Police (KUX236)

494.6875R	F1:	D1: Hyattsville (Sectors A/B)
494.5625R	F2:	Clinton (Sector F)
494.9375R	F3:	Countywide - Administration
495.1375R	F4:	D3: Seat Pleasant (Sectors G/H)
494.5375R	F5:	D2: Upper Marlboro (Sector D) / Bowie (Sector E)
495.0875R	F6:	D4: Oxon Hill (Sectors J/K)
494.8875R	F7:	D1: Laurel (Sector C)
494.7375R	F8:	Special Operations/Detectives
453.550R		PMARS: Washington Metropolitan Area Intersystem
155.790R		Detective Bureau (KQY672)
494.4875R		Future expansion
495.4625R		Future expansion
954.200		unknown use (Oxon Hill-WAU49)
955.400		unknown use (Bowie-WAU48)
957.800		unknown use (Seat Pleasant-WAU50)
959.000		unknown use (Seat Pleasant-WAU50)

COUNTY POLICE DISTRICT & BEAT MAP

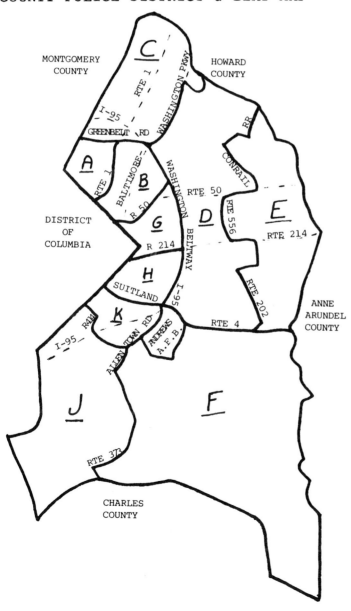

MARYLAND: PRINCE GEORGE'S COUNTY (Continued)

County Police

TEN CODES (Complete Listing)

10-01 Receive Poorly	10-14 L Alcohol	10-36 Correct Time
10-02 Receive well	M Marines	10-37 Dispatcher
10-03 Stop Transmit	N Navy	10-40 Advise Public Service
10-04 Acknowledgment	W Wide Load	10-41 No calls for you
10-05 Relay to...	10-15 Prisoner Enroute	10-42 License Check
10-06 Busy	10-20 Location	10-62 Unable to Copy
10-07 Out of Service	10-21 Request Calls	10-64 Network Free
10-08 In Service	10-22 Disregard	10-70 Statewide Message
10-09 Repeat	10-25 Contact...	10-85 ...left Station at...
10-10 Out of Service	10-27 Reply to Message	10-86 Call Home
10-11 Slow Transmit	10-28 Stolen Check	10-89 ...called Station
10-13 Weather Cond	10-29 Wanted Check	10-94 Test Transmitter
10-14 Convoy/Escort	10-30 Does not Conform	10-95 No Transmitting
A Army	10-32 Assign. Complete	10-97 Reception Check
B Bank	10-33 Go to Station	10-98 Req Sig 99 out of area
E Explosive	10-34 Local Dispatch	10-99 One Man Unit
F Funeral	10-35 Confidential Info	A Two Man Unit

RADIO SIGNALS

01 Contact Station	22 Investigate trouble	73 Disorderly Juvenile
I Immediately	23 Animal Complaint	74 Unlawful Assembly
03 Report to Station	B Animal Bite	75 Request camera
I Immediately	I Animal Injury	76 Assist Fire Dept
04 Meet Complainant	F Dead Animal	C Crowd control
05 Investigate Vehicle	26 Snow	T Traffic
06 Investigate Occupant	30 Summons Issued	77 Fi-Fa
I DWI	40 Track-ups	78 Burglar Alarm
07 Invest Susp Person	43 Cave In	79 Open Building
A Armed	44 Bomb Scare	80 Car Wash
08 Registration Info	46 Motorcycle	81 Death Report
09 Accident	47 Rape/Robbery	82 Meet officer at...
I Injury	50 Cross Burning	83 Notification at...
F Fatal	55 Eviction	84 Hold up
12 Jail Break	60 Assault Report	86 B&E In progress
13 OFFICER NEEDS ASSIST	61 Burglary Report	87 School Crossing
I Station Trouble	62 B&E House	88 Pick up mail
14 Investigate Felony	63 Larceny Report	89 Pick up property
F Felony warrant	64 Murder	90 Vehicle repairs
X Extradite	65 Sex	91 Gas
15 Unlawful assembly	66 Suicide Attempt	99 Eating
F Fight	67 Drowning	100 Cars Control Transmissions
R Riot	68 Disorderly	500 Lookout to Follow
20 Ambulance-routine	70 Drunk	
E Escort	71 Family Dispute	
I Emergency	72 Juvenile Complaint	

MARYLAND: PRINCE GEORGE'S COUNTY (Continued)

County Police

UNIT IDENTIFICATION: Beat Car Numbering
        Beat Car: (Shift) / (Sector) / Beat (1-9)
        Sergeant: (Shift) / (Sector) / 10
        Tactical: (Shift) / (Sector) / 30-49
        Shift 1: 2300-0700   Shift 3: 1500-2300
        Shift 2: 0700-1500   Shift 4: Off Duty

UNIT IDENTIFICATION: Staff & Command

01 Chief	12 Cdr-Dist 2	23 Adm Asst:Adm	52 Co Exec Aid
02 Asst-Ops	13 Cdr-Dist 3	24 OIC-Res&Dev	53 Chief Adm Officer
03 Asst-Admin	14 Cdr-Dist 4	25 OIC-Personnel	54 State's Attorney
04 Cdr-Patrol	15 Cdr-R&I	26 OIC-Central Svc	60 Catholic Chaplain
05 Cdr-Tech Svc	16 Cdr-Comm	40 Staff Off Ops	61 Protestant Chaplain
06 Cdr-BCI	17 Cdr-SOD	41 Super-Dist 1	63 Medical Examiner
07 Cdr-Admin Svc	18 Cdr-BCI Sp Enf	42 Super-Dist 2	64 Radio Repair
08 Exec Asst	19 Cdr-BCI Maj Cr	43 Super-Dist 3	65 Assoc Dir - Parks
09 Cdr-Training	20 Cdr-Property	44 Super-Dist 4	67-9 Board of Ed Security
10 Cdr-Comm Rel	21 Cdr-Insp Svc	50 Co Executive	12xx Cadets
11 Cdr-Dist 1	22 Adm Asst:Ops	51 Co Councilman	

UNIT IDENTIFICATION: Countywide Special Units

HOMICIDE & SEX ("M")		PROPERTY DIV ("P")		TACTICAL DIV ("T")		ADMIN & STAFF ("S")	
M01	Lieutenant	P01	Hyatts Lieut	T01-02	OIC-Tac Div	S02	NCO Ops Staff
M02-09	Detectives	P02-09	Hyatts Det.	T03	NCO-SOD	S04	NCO-Patrol
M10	Sergeant	P10	Hyatts Sgt.	T10	Sgt-Squad 1	S11	NCO-Dist 1
M11-19	Detectives	P11-19	Hyatts Det.	T11-19	Det-Squad 1	S12	NCO-Dist 2
M20	Sergeant	P20	Hyatts Sgt.	T20	Sgt-Squad 2	S13	NCO-Dist 3
M21-29	Detectives	P21-29	Hyatts Det.	T21-29	Det-Squad 2	S14	NCO-Dist 4
M30	Sergeant	P30	Oxon Hill Sgt	T30	Sgt-Squad 3	S20	NCO Ops Staff
EVIDENCE TECH ("O")		P31-39	Oxon Hill Det	T31-39	Det-Squad 3	S21	SAO Liaison
0/01	Sergeant	P40	Oxon Hill Sgt	T40	Sgt-Squad 4	S40	NCO-Patrol
0/02-9	Technicians	P41-59	Oxon Hill Det	T41-49	Det-Squad 4	JUVENILE DIV ("Y")	
ROBBERY DIV ("R")		P60	Ck/Fraud Sgt	T70	NCO-Auto Theft	Y01-09	Units
R01	Lieutenant	P61-64	Ck/Fraud Det	T71-73	Det-Auto Theft	Y10	Sergeant
R02-09	Detectives	SPECIAL UNITS ("SU")		T100	OIC-K9 Div	Y11-29	Units
R10	Sergeant	SU01-03	Equip Vans	T101-17	K9 Units	Y30	Hyatts Sgt
R11-19	Detectives	SU04-06	Buses	T110	Sgt-K9	Y31-49	Hyatts Units
R20	Sergeant	SU07	Gas Tanker	VICE CONTROL ("V")		Y50	Oxon Hill Sgt
R21-29	Detectives	SU09	Comm Van	V01	Lieutenant	Y51-69	Oxon Hill Det
R30	Sergeant	SU10	Light Truck	V02-04	Narc Det.	Y80	Sgt-Missing
		SU11	6-Wheel Drive			Y81-85	Det-Missing

MUNICIPALITIES USING COUNTY F1		MUNICIPALITIES USING COUNTY F4	
Colmar Manor	(201-205)	District Heights	(301-309)
Bladensburg	(210-215)	Morningside	(320-325)
Cheverly	(220-225)	Seat Pleasant	(330-335)
University Park	(226-229)	Forest Heights	(340-345)
Landover Hills	(230-235)	Fairmont Heights	(350-355)
Edmonston	(240-245)		
Mt. Rainier	(250-259)		
Hyattsville	(270-279)		
Riverdale	(280-284)		

MARYLAND: PRINCE GEORGE'S COUNTY (Continued)

<u>Fire Department</u>   (KUX242-3)
494.8375R   F1: Fire Dispatch
495.0125R   F2: Ambulance Dispatch
494.7875R   F3: Fireground-South
495.0625R   F4: Fireground-North
494.7875M   F5: Fireground-South (simplex)
495.0625M   F6: Fireground-North (simplex)
494.6625R   F7: Fire Dispatch-South County (simulcasts F1)
153.830   Portables (KGA361)
154.280   Mutual Aid (KGA361)
 46.120P   Pager (KGA361)
953.000   unknown use (District Heights-KHW75)
956.600   unknown use (Hyattsville-KHW76)
                 MED Channel 1 (Alt-5/7/8) (KAA338/KAA348/WZJ406-8)
         NOTE: County Fire Department uses no ten codes.

FIRE STATIONS

Sta	Bat	Location	Address
01	4	HYATTSVILLE	6201 Belcrest Road
02	8	COTTAGE CITY	3840 Bladensburg Road
03	4	MOUNT RAINIER	34th Street & Shephard Street
04	4	BRENTWOOD	3712 Utah Avenue
05	1	CAPITOL HEIGHTS	6201 Central Avenue
06	1	HILLSIDE	1234 Larchmont Avenue
07	8	RIVERDALE	4714 Queensbury Road
08	1	SEAT PLEASANT	50 Addison Road
09	8	BLADENSBURG	4312 Edmonston Road
10	6	LAUREL	901 Montgomery Street
11	6	BRANCHVILLE	4905 Branchville Road
12	6	COLLEGE PARK	7507 Baltimore Boulevard
13	8	RIVERDALE HEIGHTS	6101 Roanoke Road
14	6	BERWYN HEIGHTS	8811 60th Avenue
15	-	FIRE PREVENTION BUREAU	
16	-	COMMUNICATIONS DIVISION	
17	3	BOULEVARD HEIGHTS	5101 Alton Street
18	2	GLENN DALE	6910 Glenn Dale Road
19	2	BOWIE #1	13008 9th Street
20	7	MARLBORO #1	14815 Pratt Street
21	5	OXON HILL #1	7600 Livingston Road
22	1	TUXEDO-CHEVERLY	5711 Tuxedo Road
23	3	FORESTVILLE	8321 Old Marlboro Pike
24	5	ACCOKEEK	1600 Livingston Road
25	7	CLINTON	9025 Woodyard Road
26	3	DISTRICT HEIGHTS	6208 Marlboro Pike
27	3	MORNINGSIDE	6200 Suitland Road
28	2	WEST LANHAM HILLS #1	7609 Annapolis Road
29	3	SILVER HILL	6900 Old Silver Hill Road
30	8	LANDOVER HILLS	6800 Annapolis Road
31	6	BELTSVILLE #1	4911 Prince George's Avenue
32	5	ALLENTOWN ROAD #1	8097 Allentown Road
33	1	KENTLAND #1	7701 Landover Road
34	4	CHILLUM-ADELPHI #1	7833 Riggs Road
35	6	GREENBELT	125 Crescent Road
36	7	BADEN	Rte 381 & Baden-Westwood Rd
37	1	RITCHIE	6701 Ritchie-Marlboro Road

MARYLAND: PRINCE GEORGE'S COUNTY (Continued)

Fire Department

FIRE STATIONS (cont)

Sta	Bat	Location	Address
38	1	CHAPEL OAKS	5412 Sheriff Road
39	2	BOWIE #2 (Belair)	15454 Annapolis Road
40	7	BRANDYWINE	Rte 381 & Tower Road
41	6	BELTSVILLE #2 (Calverton)	4300 Powder Mill Road
42	5	OXON HILL #2 (Glassmanor)	350 March Avenue
43	2	BOWIE #3 (Pointer Ridge)	16400 Pointer Ridge Drive
44	4	CHILLUM-ADELPHI #2	6330 Riggs Road
45	7	MARLBORO #2 (Marlton)	7700 Croom Road
46	1	KENTLAND #2 (Largo)	235 Thaxton Parkway
47	5	ALLENTOWN ROAD #2 (Silesia)	10900 Fort Washington Road
48	2	WEST LANHAM HILLS #2	8301 Good Luck Road
49	-	LAUREL RESCUE SQUAD	
60	-	TECHNICAL SUPPORT / STAFF PERSONNEL	

	601-05	Fire Chiefs
	606-10	Deputy Chiefs: Special Operations
	6011-15	Deputy Chiefs: Field Operations
	6016-25	Bureau Chiefs: Fire Suppression
	6026-30	Bureau Chiefs: Support Services
	6040	Bureau Chief: Special Operations
	6050	Protestant Chaplain
	6051	Catholic Chaplain
	6052	County Attorney
	6053	Special Details Chief

Sta	Bat	Location
61	-	ADMINISTRATIVE SERVICES
62	-	SUPPORT SERVICES: Apparatus Maintenance Division
63	-	EMERGENCY MEDICAL SERVICES DIVISION
64	-	SUPPORT SERVICES: Logistics Division
65	-	SUPPORT SERVICES: Training Division
69	-	HARRY DIAMOND LABORATORY

MUTUAL AID STATIONS TO PRINCE GEORGE'S COUNTY

Co	Station Location	Co	Station Location
70	Howard County Station 6	83	Charles County Station 5
71	Howard County Station 7	84	Charles County Station 7
72	Naval Ordinance Laboratory	85	Charles County Station 8
73	Fairfax County Station 11	86	Charles County Station 9
74	Andrews Air Force Base	87	Charles County Station 11
75	Anne Arundel Co. Sta. 3	90	Montgomery County Station 1
76	Anne Arundel Co. Sta. 5	91	Montgomery County Station 2
77	Anne Arundel Co. Sta. 7	92	Montgomery County Station 12
78	Anne Arundel Co. Sta. 27	93	Montgomery County Station 15
79	Cheltenham Naval Station	94	Montgomery County Station 16
80	Charles County Station 1	95	Montgomery County Station 19
81	Charles County Station 2	96	Montgomery County Station 24
82	Charles County Station 3		

MARYLAND: PRINCE GEORGE'S COUNTY (Continued)

County Government
```
  45.520      Animal Control/Licenses & Permits (KTV805/KFM401)
  47.620      Civil Defense Network (KGG523/KXX553)
  48.380      Water Services
 151.055      Department of Public Works (KGM35/WLT22)
 151.895      County Waste Management
 153.785      Board of Education (KGG251/WLA271)
 154.085R     County Common (WBY344/WBW921/WGZ701-2) (Input on 155.940)
 154.830M     (Former Police Channel - KUG45) (also 154.950M)
 155.010      (Former Police Channel - KVA497)
 155.580R     County Sheriff (KFD590) (Input on 158.730)
                A=Supervisors / C=Civil Div / V=Transport Vans / X= Warrant Div.
 155.655      Prince George's County Community College: Security
 155.685      (Former Police Channel: Detectives - WQY670-2)
 155.880B     unknown use (KNET4879)
 158.760      Civil Defense Network (WLA22/KOC82/WBV865/KJR430)
 159.180      Highway Department (KTZ440)
 462.700      Civil Defense Link
 463.625      Prince George's County Hot-Line (KKV480)
 494.6625     County Jail (shared with Fire Department)
 496.0375     Prince George's County Community College
```
Maryland National Capital Park and Planning Commission
```
 159.315R     F1: MNCPPC Park Police Dispatch
 159.315M     F2: MNCPPC Park Police car to car
 158.940      F3: Civil Defense Network (KTV806)
 159.390      F4: MNCPPC Maintenance (KJH201)
```

50x Lieut & Staff	54x Day Shift	xx1 North of BW Pkwy
51x Lieut & Staff	55x Evening Shift	xx2 BW Pkwy to Central Ave
52x Investigators	58x Horse Patrol	xx3 Central Ave to Branch Ave
53x Midnight Shift	59x Cycles	xx4 South of Branch Ave.
		xx5-9 Extra Units

Municipalities (Note: Takoma Park listed under Montgomery County)
```
 453.150R     Berwyn Heights Police Department (KJW698)
 453.900R     Bladensburg City Police Department (KJN738)
 156.000      Bowie City Government / D.P.W. (KCN368) (also 155.955)
 153.755      Cheverly City Government (KZG271)
  33.740      Chillum-Adelphi Volunteer Fire Department (KCR899)
  33.860      Chillum-Adelphi Volunteer Fire Department (KGG372)
  46.580      College Park City Police Department (KDL953-4)
 154.815      Cottage City Police Department (KNHZ556)
 155.880      Cottage City Government (KNBB775)
 154.995      Crofton City Government (KRM914)
 155.850      District Heights Police Department (WYK604)
 453.800R     Greenbelt City Police Department (KGC674)
 154.115      Greenbelt City Government (KNEK265)
 155.130      Hyattsville Police Department (KFF284)
 453.150R     Laurel Police Department (KTP995/KVS262) (also 453.375R)
 163.250      Greater Laurel-Beltsville Rescue Squad (KRM247)
  33.020      Laurel Rescue Squad (KGD400)
  33.880      Laurel Fire Department
 154.965      Laurel Department of Public Works
 153.875      New Carrollton City Government (KNIV553)
 495.1625R    Mount Rainier Police Department (KGG322)
  33.880      Mount Rainier Volunteer Fire Department (WZJ565)
 155.565      Riverdale City Police Department (KVX705)
 154.830      Shrewsbery City Police Department (WZU70-1)
```

MARYLAND: PRINCE GEORGE'S COUNTY (Continued)

State and Federal Governments
39.300	MSP-F3: Barrack Q (College Park-KSU469)
39.340	MSP-F4: Barrack L (Forestville-KGA654)
47.400	SHA-F3: District 3
151.250	DNR-F6: Forestry (Southern Division)
151.310	DNR-F7: Parks (Southern Division)
151.655	Bowie Race Track

University of Maryland (College Park)
151.775	General use (KKE305)
151.805	General use (WXM827)
151.865	Department of Residential Life (WXK900)
151.895	General use (WYJ450)
154.540	Shuttle Bus Service/Student Union Security (KAU839)
154.570	Athletic Department (also 154.600)
155.025	Physical Plant (KDT392)
453.575R	Police Department (KXV427)
464.425	Escort Service - Evenings Only (KKM498)
464.475	Shuttle Bus Service (KUL520)
464.550	Energy Services

Beltsville National Agriculture Research Center
413.900	Center Security
164.925	General use (also 168.025/171.525)

National Intelligence Support Center (Suitland)
415.200R	GSA Federal Protective Service F1
417.200	GSA Federal Protective Service F2
36.690	U.S. Army (also 411.500)
138.650	U.S. Navy (also 139.480)
351.800	Federal Aviation Administration (also 415.550/419.8875)

U.S. Naval Comm Center (Cheltenham)
149.450	Fire Department F1
150.150	Fire Department F2
138.650	Operations (also 139.480)

Military Operations
163.440	U.S. Army: Knollwood Facility (also 164.150)
407.525	U.S. Army: Adelphi Facility
407.350	U.S. Army: Silver Hill Facility (also 411.500/414.825)
138.650	U.S. Navy: Hyattsville Facility (also 139.480)
140.100	U.S. Navy: Camp Springs Facility
303.400	U.S. Air Force: Brandywine Facility
142.155	U.S. Air Force: Silver Hill MARS (also 143.460)
165.140	U.S. Air Force: Silver Hill Facility (also 169.600/407.375)

Commissions and Agencies
167.975	FEMA (U.S. Army Facility - Hyattsville)
132.850	FAA (Clinton) (also 133.550/135.000/135.525)
411.400	Library of Congress (Landover)
166.200	Postal Service-Largo Facility (also 167.125)
164.500	Postal Service-Laurel Bulk Mail (also 172.300)
410.975	Census Bureau (Silver Hill) also 414.625)
410.500	National Environmental Sattelite Service (Suitland)
162.100	National Ocean Survey (Riverdale) (also 169.350)
410.100	Commerce Department
409.025	Department of Health & Human Services (Silver Hill)
166.950R	National Park Service (Landover) (Input on 166.350)
165.925	National Park Service (Greenbelt) (also 171.725)

MARYLAND: QUEEN ANNE'S COUNTY (County Seat: Centreville)

County Operations
County Sheriff (KNIH472)
39.500   Dispatch & Coordination with Delaware State Police
Fire Department (WZV465)
46.080   F1: Dispatch
46.160   F2: Fireground
46.140   F3: Municipal Volunteer Fire Departments
33.040   Queen Anne's - Kent Rescue Squad (KEV440)
154.280   Statewide Mutual Aid Network
          MED Channel 6 (Alt-1/2/8) (WSV959)
       NOTE: County also licensed to Dispatch on following:
          Caroline Co F1 (33.700) / Talbot Co F1 (33.900)
          Kent Co F1 (33.980) / Kent Co, Delaware F1 (33.820)
       FIRE STATIONS

1		Kent Island	5	KGF426	Church Hill
2	KDQ303	Grasonville	6	KGD980	Sudlersville
3	KGF738	Queenstown	7	KCL483	Crumpton
4	KZE708	Goodwill VFD	8	KGL532	Queen Anne
		(Centreville)	9		Romancoke

County Government
153.740   County Government Common (KNBB769)
151.130R   Highway Maintenance (KJG926) (Input on 156.135)

State and Federal Governments
39.320   MSP-F6: Barrack S (Centreville-KGB631)
47.140   SHA-F4: District 2
151.355   DNR-F4: Forestry (Central Division)
151.415   DNR-F5: Parks (Central Division)
453.575R   Toll Facilities Admin. F2: Bay Bridge (KGH606/8)
149.775   U.S. Army (Matapeake) (also on 150.465 / 163.435 / 413.5625)
138.525   U.S. Navy (Kent Island) (also on 138.550)

MARYLAND: SOMERSET COUNTY (County Seat: Princess Anne)

Fire Department (KNIL557)
46.240   F1: Countywide Dispatch & Civil Defense Network
46.180   F2: Municipal Dispatch & Operations

FIRE STATIONS	F1 Call	F2 Call	FIRE STATIONS	F1 Call	F2 Call
Ewell	KNJX776	KNIR782	Princess Anne	KNJX780	KAZ880
Marion Station	KNJX777	KNHP365	Deal Island	KNJX781	KRM333
Tylertown	KNJX778	KNIW978	Crisfield	KNJX782	KNIB669
Princess Anne	KNJX779	KAZ880	Mt. Vernon	-------	KNJC269

Municipalities, State and Federal Governments
153.860   Crisfield City Government (WZM913)
39.200   Princess Anne City Police (WZT996)
156.105R   Princess Anne Highway Department (KBI843) (Input on 151.100)
173.2025M   Princess Anne Board of Education (KZ6006)
39.240   MSP-F8: Barrack V (Berlin-KZT386)
47.400   SHA-F3: District 1
151.460   DNR-F1: Forestry (Eastern Division)
151.325   DNR-F2: Parks (Eastern Division)
155.025   University of MD - Eastern Shore Campus (Princess Anne)
162.400   NOAA Weather Broadcasts (Eden) (also 162.475)

MARYLAND: ST. MARY'S COUNTY (County Seat: Leonardtown)

County Operations
County Sheriff (KYB852)
 39.460   F1: Primary Dispatch
 39.700   F2: Secondary Operations
155.370M   Mobil Extenders
155.475   NLEEF: Nationwide Intersystem
Fire Department (KGD270)
 33.720   F1: Dispatch
 33.940   F2: Fireground
                MED Channel 4 (Alt-1/2/8) (KAA499/KNAU426)
             FIRE STATIONS
             01 KGB468 Leonardtown   06 KGD266 Second District/Valley Lee
             02 KGD267 Mechanicsville*   07 KGF588 Hollywood
             03 KGB388 Bay Dist/Lexington Pk 08 Harry Lundeberg Seamanship School
             04 KGD268 Ridge   13 Patuxent Naval Air Station
             05 KGD269 Seventh Dist/Avenue 14 Webster Field
             * Also licensed on Charles Co F1/F2 and on Calvert Co F1/F2
County Government
154.980   County Government Common (KUB926)

State and Federal Governments
 39.380   MSP-F7: Barrack T (Leonardtown-KGD716)
 47.260   SHA-F2: District 5
151.250   DNR-F6: Forestry (Southern Division)
151.310   DNR-F7: Parks (Southern Division)
 39.120   St. Mary's College Security (KKV479)
163.325   Department of Commerce (Point Lookout)
163.440   U.S. Army (Helen)

MARYLAND: TALBOT COUNTY (County Seat: Easton)

County Operations
County Police (KYO346)
 39.580   Dispatch & Coordination with Caroline & Dorchester Counties
Fire Department
 33.900   F1: County Dispatch (KRG767)
 33.640   F2: Fireground and Chiefs
                MED Channel 1 (Alt-3/7/8) (KAA413/WRX755)
             FIRE STATIONS
             20 KGE367 Oxford   60 KGC552 Easton
             30 KGE369 Trappe   70   Tillghman Island
             40 KGE370 St. Michael 80 KGE368 Queen Anne
             50 KGE372 Cordova
County Government
155.085M   Soil Conservation District (KA93518)

Municipalities, State and Federal Governments
154.950   Easton Police Department (KGB464)
 39.300   MSP-F3: Barrack I (Easton-KGA912)
 47.140   SHA-F4: District 2
151.460   DNR-F1: Forestry (Eastern Division)
151.325   DNR-F2: Parks (Eastern Division)
163.325   Commerce Department (Tillghman Island) (also 163.350)
410.575   Commerce Department (Trappe)
142.155   U.S. Air Force MARS (Easton) (also 143.460)

MARYLAND: WASHINGTON COUNTY (County Seat: Hagerstown)

County Police (KYI857)
39.180   Dispatch and Coordination with Allegany & Garrett Counties

Fire Department (KGC676)
33.860	F1	
33.840	F2	
33.800	F3	[County & Stations below with * licensed on this channel]
154.280		Mutual Aid
453.150R		Future use (KNEX271)
		MED Channel 1 (Alt-2/6/8) (KDX246/WZB630)

FIRE STATIONS (all stations licensed on F1 & F2)

KGH441	Boonsboro	KNBU823	Halfway	KXM965	Mt. Etna
KXM958	Clear Spring	KGD671	Hancock	KNHR510	Potomac Valley*
KXM959	Fairplay	KXM964	Leitersburg	KXM967	Sharpsburgh
KXM960	Funkstown	KVA341	Longmeadow (Hagers)	KXM968	Smithburg
KXA455	Hagerstown City FD*	KNHR576	Longmeadow (Hagers)	KXM969	Williamsport
KCM961	Hagerstown	KXQ945	Maugansville	WRA411	Williamsport
KXM962	Hagerstown	KGH441	Maugansville		

County Government
37.940	Highway Department (KNFB471-3/KGH213/KLK473)
37.980	Community Rescue Commission (also 147.300)
151.130R	Highway Department (KGH213) (Input on 156.015)
153.485	Water Department (KGF820)
154.995	unknown use (KNCB983)
155.160	Civil Defense Network (KEY840)
155.280	Rescue & Health Departments (KDX246/KWI762/KWM633-5)
155.295	County Safety Network (KXG898)
155.400	County Hospital (KWI762)
158.220	Sanitation District
954.500	unknown use (WCE921)
958.100	unknown use (WCE922)

Municipalities
155.790	Hagerstown Police Department F1: Dispatch (KGA870)
155.745	Hagerstown Police Department F2: Alternate (KZO480)
151.895	Hagerstown Water Department
152.630	Hagerstown Telephone Company
153.530	Hagerstown City Lights Department
155.205	Hagerstown Community Rescue Company
155.820	Hagerstown Department of Public Works (KFZ738)

State and Federal Governments
39.340	MSP-F4: Barrack O (Hagerstown-KAG914)
47.320	SHA-F1: District 6
151.460	DNR-F1: Forestry (Western Division)
151.325	DNR-F2: Parks (Western Division)
153.860	DOC-Hagerstown (KKC633) (also on 153.965)
153.980	DOC-Hagerstown (WZX569)
453.475	DOC-Correctional Training Center (Hagerstown)
149.865	Fort Ritchie Cascade-Security-"Base 240"(also 150.435)
139.175	Fort Ritchie Cascade - U.S. Army(also 143.355/148.600)
149.600	Fort Ritchie Cascade - U.S. Army(also 149.850/237.400)
241.000	Fort Ritchie Cascade - National Guard
166.950R	Nat.Pk.Svc. - Antietam/Hancock/Fairview Mt. (Input-166.350)
162.475	NOAA Weather Broadcasts (Fairview Mountain)

MARYLAND: WICOMICO COUNTY   (County Seat: Salisbury)

County Sheriff   (KIT655)
39.640   Dispatch

Fire Department   (KFB943-9)
33.980   F1: Dispatch
33.800   F2: Fireground
33.480   F3: Fireground
154.325   Signaling, Set off Sirens, Verify, etc
              MED Channel 2 (Alt-1/6/8) (KBP582/WYH543)
              FIRE STATIONS
              KXA373 Allen   KFB944 Pittsville
              KFB946 Bivalve   KFB947 Powellville
              KFB943 Fruitland   KGA530 Salisbury City FD
              KFB948 Hebron   KFB941 Sharptown
              KFB949 Mardella   KFB945 Willards
              KKB942 Parsonburg

County Government
151.040R   Highway Department (KJS952) (Input on 156.060)
155.040P   County Pager
155.805   County Youth & Civic Centers
464.975   Board of Education (KGA935)
457.975   Board of Education (WCR248)
461.775   County Humane Society

Municipalities
39.400   Delmar City Police Department (KKL986)
158.820   Delmar City Government (KIU550)
155.925   Fruitland City Government (KNBV363)
155.940   Fruitland City Government (KNBV363)
460.075R   Salisbury City Police Department (KGA935)
39.820   Salisbury City Police (may no longer be in use)
155.925B   Salisbury City City Government (KNCU532) (Mobils on 158.865)
48.300   Salisbury: Delmarva Power and Light (also 48.240)

State and Federal Governments
39.060   MSP-F11:Barrack E (Salisbury-KGA913)
44.740   MSP-Interstate with Delaware & Virginia State Police
47.400   SHA-F3: District 1
151.460   DNR-F1: Forestry (Eastern Division)
151.325   DNR-F2: Parks (Eastern Division)
37.260   State Government - may no longer be in use (KTA967)
154.515   Salisbury State College - Security
155.025   Salisbury State College - Maintenance
155.775   Salisbury State College - Security
155.265   Deers Head Center / Holly Center (KYO531)
162.475   NOAA Weather Service Broadcasts (Salisbury)
163.440   U.S. Army (Salisbury)

MARYLAND: WORCESTER COUNTY (County Seat: Snow Hill)

County Police (KZM891)
39.100   Dispatch (Maryland State Police F1)

Fire Department (KFN576)
46.380   F1: Dispatch
46.440   F2: Fireground
            MED Channel 4 (Alt-2/6/8) (KAA424/KKG739/WRA252/WRD860
            FIRE STATIONS
            100 KGC264 Pocomoke
            200 KFN489 Stockton
            300 KFN590 Girdletree
            400 KCX991 Snow Hill
            500 KFN488 Newark
            600 KGG248 Berlin*
            700 KCK784 Ocean City* (also KGF710 / KXI891-2)
            800 KEO259 Showell
            900 KDB521 Bishopville
            1100 KGW471 Ocean Pines (also KNIR580)
                     * indicates also licensed on 46.400

County Government
62.975   County Safety (WRA252)
155.085   Sanitation District (KQS544)
155.115   County Common (KXV587)
156.120   Highway Department (KJF767)
452.975   unknown use (WCR248)

Municipalities
46.580   Berlin City Police Department (KTZ523)
46.400   Fire Department (KGG248)
45.440   Pocomoke City Police Department (KQW386)
Ocean City
460.150R   Police Department F1: Dispatch (KGC657)
460.325R   Police Department F2: Car to Car (KGC657)
155.370   Police Department Walkie-Talkies (KGC657)
39.480   Police Department Car to Car (low power)
46.320   Fire Department F1: Ambulance Dispatch
46.380   Fire Department F2: County Fire Dispatch
46.400   Fire Department F3: Fireground (KRF341)
46.360   Fire Department F4: Fireground (KRF341)
154.025B   unknown use (KSU640) (Mobils on 158.955)
154.040R   unknown use (KTC895)
155.220   Beach Patrol (KUE565)
158.895   unknown use (KNCZ346)
452.650   Boardwalk Trams (WZX480)

State and Federal Governments
39.240   MSP-F8: Barrack V (Berlin-KZT386)
47.400   SHA-F3: District 1
151.460   DNR-F1: Forestry (Eastern Division)
151.325   DNR-F2: Parks (Eastern Division)
169.400   Nat.Pk.Svc.-Snow Hill/Pub.Landing/Assatiague(also 170.050)

VIRGINIA: COMMONWEALTH AGENCIES

Department of State Police

159.000B	F1:	Div.1 - Richmond-Southwest	(KIC365)	(Mobils-154.935)
158.985B	F2:	Div.1 - Richmond-Northeast	(KIC365)	(Mobils-154.905)
159.165B	F3:	Div.2 - Culpepper	(KIC367)	(Mobils-155.445)
159.135B	F4:	Div.7 - Alexandria	(KNAA586)	(Mobils-155.460)
159.135B	F5:	Div.3 - Appomattox-North	(KIB701)	(Mobils-155.460)
159.165B	F6:	Div.3 - Appomattox-South	(KIB701)	(Mobils-155.445)
159.165B	F7:	Div.4 - Wytheville-West	(KIC368)	(Mobils-155.445)
159.000B	F8:	Div.4 - Wytheville-East	(KIC368)	(Mobils-154.935)
159.165B	F9:	Div.5 - Chesapeake-No.East	(KIC410)	(Mobils-155.445)
159.135B	F10:	Div.5 - Chesapeake-So.West	(KIC410)	(Mobils-155.460)
158.985B	F11:	Div.6 - Salem-South	(KID667)	(Mobils-154.905)
159.000B	F12:	Div.6 - Salem-North	(KID667)	(Mobils-154.935)
159.135B	F13:	Div.5 - Chesapeake-E.Shore	(KIC825)	(Mobils-155.460)
154.695M	F14:	TAC-1 Statewide Car to Car		
154.665M		TAC-2 Statewide Tactical Channel		
453.350		Portable Extender Frequency		
453.550		P-MARS: Washington,D.C. Area Mutual Aid		
453.800		T-CAP: Tidewater Mutual Aid Network		
39.500		SIRS-1: Statewide Sheriff Emergency Network		
39.540		SIRS-2: Statewide Sheriff Utility Channel/Town Disp		
42.860B		Training Division (Mobils on 42.680) (Old D1:Richmond)		
42.880B		Training Division (Mobils on 42.700) (Old D2:Culpepper)		
42.920		Training Division (Old Car to Car)		
39.300		Training Division		

TEN CODES (Standard except following:)

10-10	Negative	10-31	Pickup...
10-11	...on duty	10-32	...units needed
10-14	Message	10-34	Time check
10-15	Message Delivered	10-35 through 10-39 Reserved	
10-16	Reply to Message	10-40	Bomb threat
10-17	En Route	10-43	Suspicious Vehicle
10-18	Urgent	10-44	Suspicious Person
10-19	In Contact with...	10-45	Stoping Suspicious Vehicle
10-26	E.T.A.	10-47	Chase
10-30	Use Caution	10-48	Wanted Indicated

RADIO SIGNALS

02	Contact HQ by Teletype I-Immediately	18	Plane Crash
		21	FCC Call Sign
13	Officer Needs Assistance I-Station Needs Assist.	22	Signal Check
		25	Turn on Mobil Relay
16	Radar with Chase Car	26	Turn off Mobil Relay
17	Vehicle Mounted Radar	31	Switch to Surveillence Freq

VIRGINIA: COMMONWEALTH AGENCIES (Continued)

Department of State Police (continued)

STATE POLICE DIVISIONS (* denotes Division Headquarters)

Div	Area	Location	Div	Area	Location	Div	Area	Location
1SW	1	Ashland	3N	16	Harrisonburg	5E	31	Melfa
1NE	2	Warsaw	3N	17	Stauton	5NE	32	*Chesapeake
1NE	3	West Point	3N	18	Charlottesville	5NE	33	Gloucester
1SW	4	Mineral	3N	19	Burkingham	5SW	34	Franklin
2	5	Fredericksburg	3S	20	Lynchburg	5SW	35	Emporia
1SW	6	*Richmond	3S	21	*Appomattox	5SW	36	Waverly
1SW	7	Petersburg	3S	22	South Hill	5NE	37	Williamsburg
1SW	8	Rich-Peters Pike	3S	23	South Boston	6N	38	Clifton Forge
7	9	Springfield	4E	24	Pulaski	6N	39	Lexington
7	10	Leesburg	4E	25	Galax	6S	40	*Salem
7	11	Indep. Hall	4E	26	*Wytheville	6S	41	Bedford
2	12	Warrenton	4W	27	Briston	6S	42	Martinsville
2	13	Winchester	4W	28	Claypool Hill	6S	43	Danville
2	14	Lurray	4W	29	Vansant	1NE	44	Port Royal
2	15	*Culpepper	4W	30	Norton	7	45	*Alexandria

STATE POLICE DIVISION MAP

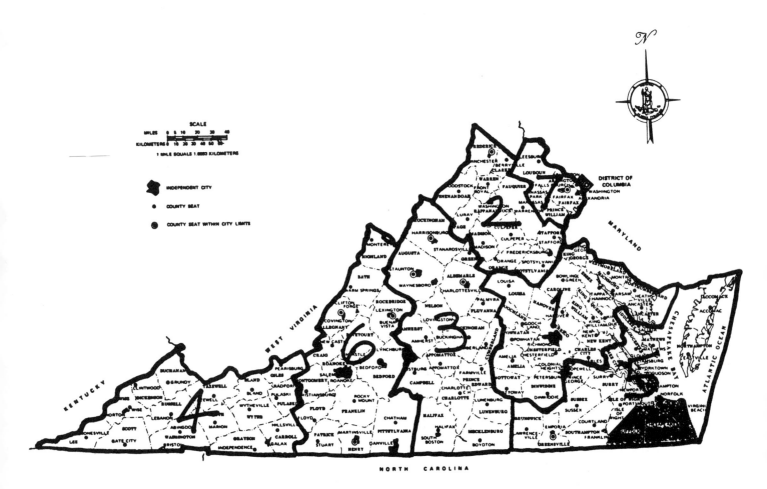

VIRGINIA: COMMONWEALTH AGENCIES (Continued)

State Police Districts and Areas listed by Counties

Accomack......Dist 5/Area 31	Louisa...........Dist 1/Area 04
Albemarle.....Dist 3/Area 18	Lunenburg........Dist 3/Area 22
Alleghany.....Dist 6/Area 38	Madison..........Dist 2/Area 15
Amelia........Dist 1/Area 07	Mathews..........Dist 5/Area 33
Amherst.......Dist 3/Area 20	Mecklenburg......Dist 3/Area 22
Appomattox....Dist 3/Area 21	Middlesex........Dist 5/Area 33
Arlington.....Dist 7/Area 09	Montgomery.......Dist 6/Area 40
Augusta.......Dist 3/Area 17	Nelson...........Dist 3/Area 18
Bath..........Dist 6/Area 38	New Kent.........Dist 1/Area 03
Bedford.......Dist 6/Area 41	Northampton......Dist 5/Area 31
Bland.........Dist 4/Area 24	Northumberland...Dist 1/Area 02
Botetourt.....Dist 6/Area 39	Nottoway.........Dist 1/Area 07
Brunswick.....Dist 5/Area 35	Orange...........Dist 2/Area 15
Buchanan......Dist 4/Area 29	Page.............Dist 2/Area 14
Buckingham....Dist 3/Area 19	Patrick..........Dist 6/Area 42
Campbell......Dist 3/Area 20	Pittsylvania.....Dist 6/Area 43
Caroline......Dist 1/Area 44	Powhatan.........Dist 1/Area 06
Carroll.......Dist 4/Area 25	Prince Edward....Dist 3/Area 21
Charles City..Dist 1/Area 03	Prince George....Dist 5/Area 36
Charlotte.....Dist 3/Area 21	Prince William...Dist 7/Area 11
Chesterfield..Dist 1/Area 06	Pulaski..........Dist 4/Area 24
Clarke........Dist 2/Area 13	Rappahannock.....Dist 2/Area 12
Craig.........Dist 6/Area 40	Richmond.........Dist 1/Area 02
Culpeper......Dist 2/Area 15	Roanoke..........Dist 6/Area 40
Cumberland....Dist 3/Area 19	Rockbridge.......Dist 6/Area 39
Dickenson.....Dist 4/Area 29	Rockingham.......Dist 3/Area 16
Dinwiddie.....Dist 1/Area 07	Russell..........Dist 4/Area 28
Essex.........Dist 1/Area 02	Scott............Dist 4/Area 27
Fairfax.......Dist 7/Area 09	Shenandoah.......Dist 2/Area 14
Fauquier......Dist 2/Area 12	Smyth............Dist 4/Area 26
Floyd.........Dist 6/Area 42	Southampton......Dist 5/Area 34
Fluvanna......Dist 3/Area 19	Spotsylvania.....Dist 2/Area 05
Franklin......Dist 6/Area 41	Stafford.........Dist 2/Area 05
Frederick.....Dist 2/Area 13	Surry............Dist 5/Area 36
Giles.........Dist 4/Area 24	Sussex...........Dist 5/Area 36
Gloucester....Dist 5/Area 33	Tazewell.........Dist 4/Area 28
Goochland.....Dist 1/Area 04	Warren...........Dist 2/Area 13
Grayson.......Dist 4/Area 25	Washington.......Dist 4/Area 27
Greene........Dist 3/Area 18	Westmoreland.....Dist 1/Area 02
Greensville...Dist 5/Area 35	Wise.............Dist 4/Area 30
Halifax.......Dist 3/Area 23	Wythe............Dist 4/Area 26
Hanover.......Dist 1/Area 01	York.............Dist 5/Area 37
Henrico.......Dist 1/Area 01	
Henry.........Dist 6/Area 42	
Highland......Dist 6/Area 38	
Isle of Wight.Dist 5/Area 34	## Incorporated Cities
James City....Dist 5/Area 37	
King George...Dist 1/Area 44	Chesapeake.......Dist 5/Area 32
King & Queen..Dist 1/Area 03	Hampton..........Dist 5/Area 32,37
King William..Dist 1/Area 03	Newport News.....Dist 5/Area 32,37
Lancaster.....Dist 1/Area 02	Norfolk..........Dist 5/Area 32
Lee...........Dist 4/Area 30	Portsmouth.......Dist 5/Area 32
Loudon........Dist 7/Area 10	Virginia Beach...Dist 5/Area 32

<u>VIRGINIA: COMMONWEALTH AGENCIES</u> (Continued)

<u>Department of Corrections</u>
```
 39.120      Primary Operations: State Facilities
 39.900      Secondary Operations: State Facilities
453.050R     Richmond State Prison (KSL346)
453.275      Richmond State Prison (KSL346)
```

<u>State Capitol</u>
```
155.130      State Police: Office Building Security (KJE262)
155.250      Maintenance: Office Buildings
155.490      State Police: Capitol Square (KJE262)
453.725      Capitol Buildings: Operations
```

<u>Department of Transportation</u>
<u>Highway Department</u>
```
 33.060      Hampton(KAN873/KLJ259/KZT483) / Virginia Beach(KJL634)
 45.680      Chesapeake Bay Bridge Tunnel
 45.760      Statewide (unknown use)
 72.820      Richmond(KIM25) / Salem(KIA43)
 75.700      Richmond(KIM25)
151.025      Jonesville(KXZ65) / Wyse(KRY94)
154.025      Statewide Bridges & Tunnels (Hillsville-KKV211)
156.225      Bland County(WAN349)
159.180      Salem(KIA44/KIX98)
453.850      Statewide Bridges & Tunnels
```
<u>State Highway Administration</u>
```
 47.220      F1: Briston, Lynchburg, Staunton, Fredericksburg
 47.340      F2: Culpepper, Interstate Motorist Assistance Patrol
 47.280      F3: Northern Virginia, Suffolk
 47.300      F4: Salem
```

STATE HIGHWAY ADMINISTRATION DISTRICT MAP

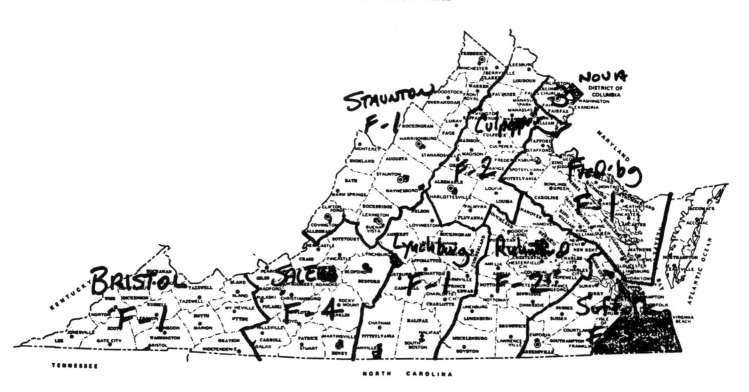

VIRGINIA: COMMONWEALTH AGENCIES (Continued)

Department of Transportation
State Highway Administration

STATION CALL SIGNS (with indication of Authorized channel useage)

Station	Call Sign	Channels	Station	Call Sign	Channels
Abington	KID537	Fl	Long Mountain	KIE817	Fl/F4
Accomack	KID544	Fl/Fl/F4	Louisa	KIC256	Fl/F4
Albemarle	KIC255	Fl/F4	Luray	KIC640	Fl
Amherst	KID563	Fl	Marion	KRF324	Fl
Appomattox	KID562	Fl	Marshall	KUY449	F4
Arlington	KFG598	Fl/F2/F4	Massanutten	KEW980	Fl/F4
Ashland	KID553	Fl/F4	Massaponox	KRF321	Fl
Bedford	KIC929	Fl/F3/F4	McKenney	KUB902	F4
Bland County	KTE716	Fl	Moccasin Gap	KRF322	Fl
Brookvale	WRE241	Fl/F2/F4	Montgomery County	KUY326	Fl/F3
Chesapeake	KID540	Fl/F2	New Kent County	KUB904	F4
Christianburg	KIC933	Fl/F3/F4	Newport News	KIP711	Fl/F2/F4
Church Road	KNAT711	F4	Norfolk	KFY442	Fl/F2/F4
Colonial Hgts	KIG861	F2/F3/F4	Norfolk	KKR435	Fl/F2/F4
Covington	KLR267	Fl	Norfolk	KRZ309	F2
Croaker	KUB901	F2	Norfolk	KNBN811	F2
Culpepper	KIC641	Fl/F4	Norton	KIF670	Fl/F3/F4
Danville	KKV741	Fl	Orange	WSB902	F4
Dillwyn	KID560	Fl	Patrick County	KRR914	F3
Dublin	KLE692	Fl/F3/F4	Petersburg	KID555	Fl/F4
Eastville	KKV746	F2	Petersburg	KNCX507	F4
Edinburg	KIC251	Fl/F4	Portsmouth	KGJ696	Fl/F3/F4
Falmouth	KID552	Fl/F4	Post Oak	WYF985	Fl
Fancy Gap	KEF516	F3	Prince George's Co.	WRE240	F4
Farmers	KID549	Fl	Prince George's Co.	KRP726	F4
Farmville	WRE239	Fl/F4	Richmond	KBP891	Fl/F2/F4
Fishersville	KUG785	Fl/F4	Richmond	KIH361	Fl/F4
Floyd	KIK322	Fl/F3/F4	Richmond	KIL265	Fl/F4
Franklin	KID545	Fl/F2	Rocky Mount	KIX930	Fl/F3/F4
Fredericksburg	KID552	Fl/F4	St. Stephen	KSL264	Fl
Free Union	WSB852	F4	Salem	KIA415	Fl/F3/F4
Freemont	KRD323	Fl	Saluda	KID551	Fl
Gainsville	KNCX508	F4	Sandy Hook	KYJ775	Fl/F4
Gloucester	KNBL335	Fl	Seaford	KLL708	F2
Green County	KLX772	F4	Smithfield	KQN713	F2
Hague	WRE242	Fl/F2/F4	South Hill	KID558	Fl/F4
Halifax	KID559	Fl	Stafford	KIL710	Fl
Hampton	KII401	Fl/F2/F4	Surry	KFF391	F2
Hanover County	WBJ947	F4	Tappahannock	KAR314	Fl
Harrisonburg	KIC254	Fl	Tazewell	KID539	Fl
Henrico County	KVM211	F4	Troutville	KSL986	F3
Hillsboro	WSB854	F4	Verona	KGY326	Fl/F4
Hillsville	KIC932	Fl/F3/F4	Victoria	KRO349	F4
Independence	KRZ307	Fl/F3	Warsaw	KID552	Fl/F4
King George	KID550	Fl	Warsaw	KID548	Fl
King William	KSL263	Fl	White Oak	KID561	Fl
Leesburg	KIC257	Fl/F4	Williamsburg	KII258	Fl/F2
Lexington	KIC248	Fl/F4	Winchester	KIC253	Fl
			Yorktown	KIP713	Fl/F2/F4

VIRGINIA: COMMONWEALTH AGENCIES   (Continued)

Department of Natural Resources: Forestry Conservation
Forest Fire Detection and Prevention
170.475   Statewide Base & Mobil
171.425   Statewide Base & Mobil
172.275   Statewide Base & Mobil / Statewide Mobil Relay System
Forestry Operations
159.360M   F1: Statewide Car to Car & Tactical
151.415R   F2: Statewide Operations (Mobil relay) (Input on 159.225)
159.330R   Statewide Operations (Mobil relay) (Input on 151.265)
159.300R   Western State Operations
159.465R   Richmond Operations (Input on 151.900?)
151.370R   Eastern Shore Ops / Statewide Tac (Input on 151.190)
151.475   Statewide Tactical
151.285   unknown use

Division of Parks and Recreation
151.235   Statewide Primary Operations
151.400   Statewide Secondary Operations
               WZM761 Appomattox   WZM766 Dublin   WZM771 Mouth of Wil.
               WZM762 Cumberland   WZM767 Green Bay   WZM772 Scottsburg
               WZM763 Chesterfield   WZM768 Marion   WZM773 Stuart
               WZM764 Clarksville   WZM769 Millboro   WZM774 Surry
               WZM765 Clinchport   WZM770 Montross   WZM775 Virginia Beach
                                                          WZM776 Williamsburg
 39.060M   Statewide low power mobils (KA2696)
171.235   Statewide general use (also 171.400)

Fish and Game Department
159.435R   Statewide Wardens (Input on 151.340)
               KFG620 Bland-Co/KUN576-Clarke Co/KEV421-Kings Hwy/KVJ804-Pittsylvania
151.280R   Statewide Operations (Input on 159.420)
151.460   Statewide Wardens
151.430M   Richmond Operations (KJX28)
 44.800M   Eastern Shore Operations - Wachapreague (also on 44.960M)

Miscellaneous State Government
 37.040   N.Va. Comm. College (Allexandria/Manassas/Sterling/Woodbridge)
154.100   William & Mary College (Williamsburg-KRM663)
155.040R   State Building & Construction Inspectors (Input on 156.015)
155.160   Statewide EMS Net (WXY535) (also 155.205 / 155.280 / 155.340)
155.820R   Agriculture Dept / Emergency Svc Office (Input on 153.995)
155.895R   Virginia Office of Emergency Services (Input on 158.820)
169.425   Energy & Emergency Services(also 170.250 / 171.125 / 171.825)
453.425R   State Division of Mines & Quaries (KNHU770)
453.450   Department of Telecommunications (WRA405) (also 453.725)
453.875   Port Authority (Norfolk-KQS519)(also 453.925/453.950/453.975)
488.3375R   State Government - unknown use (Fairfax area - KNR683-7)

United States Government: National Park Service
163.125   Manassas National Battlefield Park
166.900   Skyline Drive / Shenandoah National Park
167.175R   Blue Ridge National Parkway (Input on 166.375)
168.425   Harper's Ferry National Park
168.475   Prince William National Forest Park
417.975   Wolf Trap Farm Park

VIRGINIA: ALEXANDRIA CITY

Alexandria City Police (KLU321)

460.375R	F1:	Citywide Dispatch
460.075R	F2:	Tactical
460.050R	F3:	Service / Data
460.375M	F4:	Car to Car
460.075M	F5:	Car to Car
460.050M	F6:	Car to Car
155.070B		Tactical & Detectives (KIC737) (Mobils on 158.970)
453.550R		P-MARS: Washington Metro Intersystem (KLY674/KIC737)

TEN CODES (standard except the following:)
10-65B Net Message: Check banks on your beat
10-100 Open compound gate

Alexandria Fire Department

154.430R	F1:	"MAIN" Dispatch & Pager (KIE943) (Input on 154.070)
153.845M	F2:	"FIREGROUND" (KL7188)
154.430	F3:	"STANDBY" Backup Simplex Dispatch (KIE943)
154.265	F4:	"NOVA" Northern Virginia Mutual Aid Net (KAN472)
154.280	F5:	"MUTUAL AID" D.C. Metro Area Net (KIE943)
460.525R		"EMS" Hospital Communications (KLO294)
		Med Channels 1-10 (KIU623)

FIRE STATIONS
51	315 Prince Street (Old Town)
52**	213 East Windsor Avenue (North End)
53*	2801 Cameron Mills Road (Dez Rav)
54	900 Second Street (Headquarters)
55***	1210 Cameron Street
56**	4609 Seminary Road
57	3301 Duke Street
58*	175 North Paxton Street (West End)

*   Wagon & Truck
**   Wagon & Medic
*** Wagon/Truck/Medic

EMS CODES
1 Public Service
2 Non Life Threat
3 Life Threatening

City Government
39.040	County Sheriff: Dispatch & Operations (KZE600)
39.500	County Sheriff: Statewide SIRS-1 Network (KZE600)
39.540	County Sheriff: Statewide SIRS-2 Network (KZE600)
453.625R	Department of Public Works (KUX305)
453.650	City Buses (KLL534)
464.525	Public School System (WSH712)
494.8125R	Sanitation Authority (KNT344)

State and Federal Governments
159.135B	SPD: District 7 (Alexandria-KNAA586) (Mobils on 155.460)
47.280	DOT-3: Northern Virginia Division
37.040	Northern Virginia Community College (Alexandria-KZQ579)
40.930	Cameron Station (U.S. Army)
140.250	U.S. Navy
142.950	Cameron Station (U.S. Army)
167.975	Cameron Station (FEMA)
409.825	U.S. Coast Guard

VIRGINIA: ARLINGTON COUNTY

County Police (KLO266)

453.825R	F1:	Primary Dispatch
453.500R	F2:	Emergency / Administrative / Car to Car
453.275R	F3:	Secondary Dispatch / Tactical
453.325R	F4:	Administrative / Data / Sheriff's Office
453.100R	F5:	Mobil Data Terminal (non-voice)
453.300M	F6:	Vice Squad (simplex)
154.740P		Pager (KIB346)
453.550R		P-MARS: D.C. Metro Intersystem (WAF586)

TEN CODES (Standard except following:)

10-05 Confidential Information	10-66 Call Home (no emergency)
10-13 Officer needs Assistance	10-67 Non-Emerg Mess. at Station
10-18 Meet officer	10-71 Check Officer's Status
10-26 On Portable Radio Unit	10-75 10-7 with papers at...
10-27 Request to go direct to...	10-85 Time and Number
10-30 Check for Parking Tickets	10-87 Advise Impound Number
10-31 Check for Suspicious Person	10-91 Bank Check at...
10-39 Going to Admin. Channel	10-93 On Security Check
10-40 Back on Primary Channel	10-97 Silent Alarm
10-65 Out of Service to Eat	10-98 Audio Alarm

UNIT IDENTIFICATION: Patrol Division (D = District)
District 1: North Patrol
District 2: South Patrol
    Scout 01 Shift Lieutenant
    Scout 02 Shift Sergeant
    Scout 03 Shift Sergeant
    Scout 04 Shift Sergeant
    Scout D0 District Corporal
    Scout D1 District Corporal
    Scout D2-D9 District Patrol

UNIT IDENTIFICATION: Countywide Units
    Unit 1   Police Chief
    Car 2xx   Services Division
    Car 3xx   Operations Division

County Fire Department

154.130R	F1:	Dispatch (KIC338) (Input on 153.890)
155.865	F2:	Fireground (KSX323)
154.280	F3:	D.C. Metro Area Mutual Aid (KIC338)
154.265	F4:	NOVA - Northern Virginia Mutual Aid (KAN472)
453.050		MODAT Communications (KNAB406)
155.340		HEAR Network (KNHT333)
		Med Channels 1-10 (WXP320-1/KXZ733)

UNIT IDENTIFICATION (X = Fire Station)
7x Fire/Rescue units
8x Staff & Administration

VIRGINIA: ARLINGTON COUNTY (Continued)

Fire Department (continued)

FIRE STATIONS (NOTE: addresses are approximate)
```
01  1000  Edgewood at Columbia Pike
02   700  George Mason Drive at Wilson Boulevard
03  2000  Akland at Lee Highway
04  1000  Irving at 10th Street
05   900  18th Street at Hayes Street
06        Washington Street North at Route 66 (Falls Church)
07        31st Stret at 31st Road
08  4800  Lee Highway at Culpepper Street
09  3600  18th Street at Oakland Street
10  1500  Wilson Boulevard
31        Fort Meyers
```

County Government
```
159.120R    Public Works (KIY328-9/KJF65-6/KEG635/KQN893)
453.600R    County Sheriff: Dispatch & Operations (KVM281)
 39.500     County Sheriff: Statewide SIRS-1 Network (KVB950)
 39.540     County Sheriff: Statewide SIRS-2 Network (KVB950)
155.055     Public Works (KLU644)
155.895R    County Schools (KRC671) (Input on 158.805)
816.9875M   Allocated for future use (KB33534)
817.9875M   Allocated for future use (KB33534)
818.9875M   Allocated for future use (KB33534)
819.9875M   Allocated for future use (KB33534)
820.9875M   Allocated for future use (KB33534)
```

State and Federal Governments
```
159.135B    VSP: District 7 (Alexandria-KNAA586) (Mobils on 155.460)
 47.280     DOT-3: Northern Virginia Division (KFG598)
```
Arlington Station
```
164.445     Military Police
164.475     Military Police
```
Army Comm Center
```
148.410     RTT
```
Pentagon
```
 32.870B    VIP Taxi Network (Mobils on 32.530)
 36.710     Armed Forces Police (Metro D.C. Network)
 36.990     Fire Network
 36.510     Armed Forces Base Link (Metro D.C. Network)
142.000     Motor Pool F1
142.100     Motor Pool F2
143.175     Taxi Control
142.000     Taxi Control
```
Fort Meyers
```
 36.550     Fire Department F1
 36.990     Fire Department F2
 36.710     Military Police (Metro D.C. Armed Forces Police Net)
165.060     Base Security
148.665     Ceremonial Network
```

VIRGINIA: FAIRFAX COUNTY

County Police

460.175R	F1:	Districts 3,5 (KLR247)
460.125R	F2:	Districts 2,6 (KLR248)
460.300R	F3:	Districts 4,7 (KXX365)
460.225R	F4:	District 8, SOD/CID/Admin. (KLR249)
131.000		County Police Helicopter
462.575		County Police Training Center
453.550R		P-MARS: Washington Metro Intersystem (WAC339)

POLICE DISTRICTS   (patrol units)
```
        HQ - Fairfax
         2 - Mt. Vernon    (Scout Cars 20-26)
         3 - McLean        (Scout Cars 30-39)
         4 - Mason         (Scout Cars 40-49)
         5 - Reston        (Scout Cars 50-53)
         6 - Franconia     (Scout Cars 60-67)
         7 - W.Springfield (Scout Cars 70-77)
         8 - Chantilly     (Scout Cars 80-83)
```

NEW FAIRFAX
COUNTY POLICE
RADIO SYSTEM

Ch.#1 854.1375
Districts 4, 7

Ch.#3 853.3375
Districts 3, 5

Ch.#8 853.6375
District 8

Additional
frequencies
which will
be used in
switch from
460MHz:

853.1875
853.4875
853.7875
853.9625
854.2875

System may
become trunked

DISTRICT MAP

VIRGINIA: FAIRFAX COUNTY (Continued)

County Police

UNIT IDENTIFICATION
  Scout = Patrol units
  Unit = Individual ID
  CIB   = Headquarters Criminal Investigation Bureau
  CIS   = District Criminal Investigation Section
  ID   = Criminalistics
  CP   = Crime Prevention units
  CA   = Crime Analysis units
  Car Dx= Watch Commander (D=District)
  Car D = Captain-Station Commander (D=District)
          Fairfax 1 / Fairfax 2 = Bell Helicopters

TEN CODES (Standard except following:)
  10-17 Warrant
  10-99 No paper work necessary

RESPONSE CODES
  Code 1   Non-Emergency Response
  Code 2   Semi-Emergency (no lights or siren)
  Code 3   Emergency (Use lights and siren)

RADIO SIGNALS

01 Contact...by phone	16 Leaving area to...	38 Lost/Found Property
A Advise your phone #	17 Bank Check at...	39 Prowler
I Contact...immed.	18 House Check at...	40 Robbery
02 Contact...by teletype	19 Radar set up at...	I In Progress
03 Report to...	20 Traffic Complaint	41 Service
I Immediately	21 Trespassing	42 Sex Offenses
04 Meet complainant	22 Abandoned Auto	R Rape
06 Intoxicated Person	23 Alarm Sounding	43 Stake-out
D In automobile	24 Animal Bite	44 Stolen Automobile
P Pedestrian	D Dog Bite	R Recovered
X Drunk	25 Assault	45 Suicide
07 Larceny	26 Bad Check	A Attempt
S Shoplifter	27 Breaking & Entering	46 Suspicious Situation
09 Accident: Prop Damage	I In Progress	A Automobile
I Personal Injury	S Safe Job	P Person
F Fatal	28 Escort	W Person with weapon
10 Ambulance Run	29 Family Trouble	47 Vandalism
F Fatal (DOA)	30 Fire Alarm	48 Warrant
11 Hit&Run: Prop Damage	A Automobile	49 Bomb Threat
I Personal Injury	31 Firearms Violation	50 Loud Party
F Fatal	32 Juvenile Case	51 Phone Threat
12 Jail Break	34 Mental Case	52 No Units Available
13 Officer In Trouble	35 Missing / Runaway	53 Miscellaneous Call
I Station trouble	36 Murder	54 Disorderlies
15 Unlawful assembly	37 Open Door / Window	
F Fight in Progress		
R Riot		

VIRGINIA: FAIRFAX COUNTY (Continued)

Fire Department

460.575R	F1:	Dispatch (KXX528)
460.600R	F2:	Fire Marshalls & Hospital Communications (KJI905)
460.625R	F3:	Hospital Communications & NOVA Patch (KXX528)
460.575M		Fireground Operations (KXX528)
154.265		NOVA - Northern Virginia Mutual Aid Net (KIF337)
154.280		Washington Metro Area Mutual Aid Network (KIF337)
46.080		Volunteer Alert (KIF337)
46.180		Volunteer Alert (KIF337)
460.525		Hospital Communications (KUX359)
460.550		Hospital Communications (KUX359)
		Med Channels 1-8 (WRG823/KXU359) / Call 1-2 (WLZ890)

TEN CODES
```
10-61  D.O.A.
10-65  Request Police
```

FIRE STATIONS

01	McLEAN	1440	Old Chain Bridge Road
02	VIENNA	400	Center Street
04	HERNDON	680	Spring Street
08	ANNANDALE	7128	Columbia Pike
09	MT. VERNON	2601	Sherwood Hall Lane
10	BAILEY'S CROSS ROADS	3601	Madison Lane
11	PEN DAW	6624	Hulvey Terrace
12	GREAT FALLS	9916	Georgetown Pike
13	DUNN LORING	2148	Gallows Road
14	BURKE	9501	Burke Lake Road
15	CHANTILLY	400	Walney Road
16	CLIFTON	12645	Chapel Road
17	CENTREVILLE	5856	Centreville Road
18	JEFFERSON	3131	Hodge Place
19	LORTON	7701	Armistead
20	GUNSTON	10417	Gunston Road
21	NAVY-VALE	12504	Bennet Road
22	SPRINGFIELD	7011	Backlick Road
23	GUINEA ROAD	8914	Little River Turnpike
24	WOODLAWN	8701	Lukens Lane
25	RESTON	1820	Wichle Avenue
26	EDSALL ROAD	5316	Caroline Place
27	WEST SPRINGFIELD	6140	Rolling Road
28	SEVEN CORNERS	2949	Sleepy Hollow Road
29	TYSON'S CORNER	1560	Spring Hill Road
30	MERRIFIELD	8739	Lee Highway
31	FOX MILL	2610	Reston Avenue
32	FAIRVIEW	5600	Burke Center Parkway
33	FAIRFAX	10101	Lee Highway
34	OAKTON	10511	Rose Haven Street
	TRAINING CENTER	4600	West Ox Road

VIRGINIA: FAIRFAX COUNTY (Continued)

County Government

33.020	Board of Inspectors (KLJ619)
37.900	Civil Defense Network (KDE218-9)
39.160	Animal Control and County Sheriff (KIB950)
39.540	County Sheriff: Statewide SIRS-2 (KIB950)
39.660	County Sheriff: Dispatch (KIB950)
45.280	County Libraries (KSI860)
48.180	Water Dept/Public Works/Construction/Admin (KER936/KBK655)
151.805	Public Schools (WRQ325)
154.995R	Board of Education: Maintenance & Admin. (Input on 154.100)
158.880	Board of Education: Buses (KFL84/WGL91)
159.105R	Highway Department & Snowplows (KLE763) (Input on 151.100)
159.225R	Parks Division (KJF955) (Input on 151.220)
453.250R	County Government Common & Public Works (KXZ947)
453.675R	MODAT Communications (KSZ947)
464.625	Public School Security (WSC660)
855.9625R	Allocated for Future use (KNFU763)
855.9875R	Allocated for Future use (KNFU763)

Municipalities

453.975R	Fairfax City Police (KLL569/KXJ226)
460.600R	Fairfax City Fire Fl: County Dispatch (KJI905)
154.235	Fairfax City Fire F2: City Dispatch & Fireground (WXT676)
46.400	Fairfax City Fire Department Volunteer Alert (KYB756)
	NOTE: Fairfax City uses Med Channels 1-8 (WXT706)
	Fairfax City Fire Station 1 - 10200 Lee Highway
	Fairfax City Fire Station 2 - 10000 Lee Highway
	Fairfax City Fire Station 3 - 4000 University Drive
45.160	Fairfax City Government (KAT232)
494.3875	Fairfax City Government (KWT817)
453.925R	Falls Church City Police: Dispatch (KVA433)
154.800M	Falls Church City Police: Tactical/Admin
45.080	Falls Church City Government (KIB229/KIB232/KIQ737)
453.850R	Herndon Police Department (KRS401)
45.200	Herndon City Government (KVX908)
151.400	Reston Home Owner's Association (KOE312)
151.755	Reston Home Owner's Association (KSR249)
155.700R	Vienna City Police: Dispatch (KIK552) (Input on 154.800)
156.090M	Vienna City Police: Car to Car
45.240	Vienna City Government (KCP589)

State and Federal Governments

159.135B	VSP District 7 (Alexandria-KNAA586) (Mobils on 155.460)
47.280	DOT-3: Northern Virginia Division
488.3375R	State Government - unknown use (Fairfax Area - KNR683-7)
462.575	Northern Virginia Police Training Center (KAB5264/KAC8221)
41.370	Federal Highway Administration Research Center (McLean)
41.410	Federal Highway Administration Research Center (McLean)
417.975	National Park Service: Wolf Trap Farm

VIRGINIA: LOUDON COUNTY

County Sheriff   (KIG504/KQN900)
```
39.780B     Fl: Primary Dispatch (Mobils on 39.720)
39.540      F2: Back up Dispatch (SIRS-2: Statewide Sheriff Utility Ch)
39.500      F3: Emergencies (SIRS-1: Statewide Sheriff Emergency Channel)
155.970M        Portable units
156.030M        Portable units
453.550         P-MARS: Metro Washington Intersystem (WAC343)
```

> NOTE: Use standard 10 codes listed at back of book.
> UNIT ID: 3 digit number - 1st indicates shift:
>
> 1xx   Midnight shift
> 2xx   Day shift
> 3xx   Evening shift

Fire Department (KIU862)
```
46.380      Fl: Dispatch
46.160      F2: Fireground
46.320      F3: Truck to Truck / Training
46.400      F4: Rescue phone patch
154.280         Mutual Aid Network
154.010M        Unknown use
46.040          Rescue squad (WXK553)
155.175M        Rescue squad (KNEG680)
                Med Channels 1-10 (KKD216)
```

FIRE STATIONS
01 Leesburg Fire	10 Luckets Fire
02 Purcellville Fire	11 Sterling Fire
03 Middleburg Fire/Rescue	12 Lovettsville Fire/Rescue
04 Round Hill Fire/Rescue	13 Loudon Rescue
05 Hamilton Fire	14 Purcelville Rescue
06 Ashburn Fire	15 Sterling Rescue
07 Aldie Fire	16 Neersville Fire/Rescue
08 Philomont Fire	17 Hamilton Rescue
09 Arcola Fire/Rescue	

TEN CODES (Standard x/)
```
10-10 Subject to call at...
10-13 Emergency--Send Police
10-19 Return to Station
10-21 Call Station by Phone
10-33 Emergency Traffic
10-61 Dead on Arrival
10-65 Police Needed
    I  Immediately
10-97 Arrived at Scene
10-98 Returning in Scene
10-99 Return out of Service
```

County Government
```
45.480      Sanitation Department (KTI539)
37.260      School Board (KSO626)
155.220M    School Board
158.775R    County Operations (KSO626) (Input on 154.965)
158.745M    County Operations (KSO626)
```

Municipalities
```
453.725R    Leesburg City Police: Dispatch (KSZ881)
158.910M    Leesburg City Police: Tactical
```

State and Federal Governments
```
159.135B    VSP District 7 (Alexandria-KNAA586) (Mobils on 155.460)
47.340      DOT-2: Culpeper Division
37.040      Northern Virginia Community College (Sterling-KXQ996)
168.425     Harper's Ferry National Park (National Park Service)
```

VIRGINIA: PRINCE WILLIAM COUNTY

County Police (KLX941)

453.475R	F1:	West Dispatch
453.375R	F2:	East Dispatch
453.150R	F3:	Special Operations Division / Car to Car
453.700R		Allocated for Future Expansion
453.550		P-MARS: Washington Metro Intersystem (WAC346)
154.650		unknown use (WAC346)

TEN CODES (Different from Standard)   UNIT ID

10-11 Warrant Svc	10-67 Death Rpt	10-84 Missing Person	
10-35 Bad Check	10-68 Firearms	10-85 Trespasser	0xx Officials
10-39 Phone call	10-69 Disorderly	10-86 Radar	1xx CID
10-40 Narcotics	10-71 Park. Viol	10-87 Loitering	2xx Patrol Div
10-43 Port. Radio	10-72 Animal Compl	10-89 Larceny	3xx Patrol Div
10-47 Vandalism	10-73 Jail Break	10-91 Aband Auto	4xx SOD
10-48 Shoplifter	10-75 Susp Person	10-92 Rape	5xx Support/Admin
10-60 Adult Court	10-78 Barricade	10-93 Loud Party	6xx Muni. PD
10-61 Juv. Court	10-79 Hostage	10-95 Bomb threat	7xx Support/Admin
10-62 Burglary	10-80 Auto Theft	10-98 Veh Repair	8xx Misc/Muni PD
10-65 No tags	10-82 Armed Rob.	10-100 Tac Resp	
10-66 Med Exam.	10-83 Visitor		

Fire Department (KIW334/KIV960)

154.370	F1:	Fireground
154.325	F2:	Dispatch
154.445	F3:	Fireground
154.280	F4:	Mutual Aid
154.265		NOVA Mutual Aid (Northern Virginia Network)
154.295		Allocated for Future use
154.145		unknown use
		Med Channels 1-10 (KML321)

FIRE STATIONS (NOTE: OWL = Occoquan/Woodbridge/Lorton)

01 Manassas	05 Nokesville	09 Manassas Park	13 Dale City
02 OWL (Occoquan)	06 Coles District	10 Dale City	14 OWL (Lorton)
03 Dumfries-Triangle	07 Lake Jackson	11 Stonewall Jackson	15 Evergreen
04 Gainesville	08 Yorkshire	12 OWL (Woodbridge)	20 Vint Hill

County Government

39.680	County Sheriff (KJS688) (also 39.50 SIRS-1 / 39.54 SIRS-2)
45.120	Department of Public Works (KIQ820)
45.320	School Board (KZW857)
153.725	County Utilities
154.115	unknown use (KNGK755)
155.940	County Sheriff & Jail Operations (KNFR881)

Municipalities

453.200R	Manassas City Police F1: Dispatch (KAG257)
453.425R	Manassas City Police F2: Secondary & DPW (KIG367)
154.400	Manassas City Fire Department (KIC482)
453.775R	Manassas Park Town Police (KWM842)

State and Federal Governments

159.135B	VSP: District 7 (Alexandria-KNAA586) (Mobils on 155.460)
47.340	DOT-2: Culpeper Division (Gainesville-KNCX508)
37.040	Northern Va. Comm. College
163.125	Manassas National Battlefield Park (National Park Service)
168.475	Prince William Forest Park (National Park Service)

AMATEUR RADIO NETWORKS

DISTRICT OF COLUMBIA
```
147.240R   WB4FQR  (Input-147.840)
224.500R   W3NKF   (Input-222.900)
449.975R   WA3KOK  (Input-444.975)
```

DELAWARE
Bethany Beach
```
147.180R   W3HTB   (Input-147.780)
147.075R   K3JL    (Input-147.675)
```
Dover
```
146.970R   W3HZW   (Input-146.370)
147.195R   W3HZW   (Input-147.795)
```
Newark
```
145.170R   K3RBP   (Input-144.570)
224.960R   WB3JVX  (Input-222.360)
443.050R   WB3JVX  (Input-448.050)
```

New Castle
```
146.700R   WR3ACV  (Input-146.100)
146.955R   WB3JTK  (Input-146.355)
```
Wilmington
```
146.730R   WR3ABA  (Input-146.130)
147.225R   WA3QLS  (Input-147.825)
224.400R   WB3DPJ  (Input-222.400)
224.540R   AD3M    (Input-222.940)
```

NORTHERN VIRGINIA
Alexandria
```
146.655R   WD4PDP  (Input-146.055)
146.685R   W4HFH   (Input-146.085)
147.315R   W4HFH   (Input-147.915)
444.600R   W4HFH   (Input-449.600)
```
Annandale
```
449.850R   WR4AQB  (Input-444.850)
```
Arlington
```
147.045R   WA4YVM  (Input-146.445)
444.000R   K8ZOA   (Input-449.000)
```
Fairfax
```
146.790R   W4LBL   (Input-146.190)
146.910R   K4VYN   (Input-146.310)
```
Falls Church
```
145.350R   W4AQD   (Input-144.750)
444.450R   WB8CRK  (Input-449.450)
```
McLean
```
147.210R   WD4lWG  (Input-147.810)
```

Manassas
```
146.970R   WICRO   (Input-146.370)
444.225R   WD4JCE  (Input-449.225)
```
Sterling
```
145.390R   WN9HGB  (Input-144.790)
145.270R   WD4JCE  (Input-144.670)
449.675R   WN9HGB  (Input-444.675)
```
Tyson's Corner
```
146.910R   K4VYN   (Input-146.310)
223.940R   K4GCM   (Input-222.340)
449.750R   K4JYF   (Input-444.750)
443.500R   WB6GUS  (Input-448.500)
```
Woodbridge
```
147.240R   WB4FQR  (Input-147.840)
444.900R   WB4FQR  (Input-449.900)
```
Alexandria
```
223.940R   K4GCM   (Input-222.340)
```

MARYLAND (Listed by Counties)

ALLEGANY COUNTY
Cumberland
```
145.450R   WA3III  (Input-144.850)
146.880R   WR3AGI  (Input-146.280)
444.000R   AJ3S    (Input-449.000)
```
Frostburg
```
147.390R   K3CCC   (Input-147.990)
```

ANNE ARUNDEL COUNTY
Annapolis
```
145.330R   W3VRD   (Input-144.730)
449.475R   W3EAO   (Input-444.475)
```
Crownsville
```
146.700R   WA3PJQ  (Input-146.100)
```
Davidsonville
```
147.105R   W3VPR   (Input-147.705)
223.880R   N3AKP   (Input-222.280)
```
Glen Burnie
```
146.805R   WA3PJQ  (Input-146.205)
443.700R   WA3MEJ  (Input-448.700)
```
Harmans
```
448.925R   W3YVV   (Input-443.925)
```
Odenton
```
444.700R   WA3PGC  (Input-449.700)
```

AMATEUR RADIO NETWORKS (MARYLAND continued)

BALTIMORE CITY		
Citywide		
146.670R	K3SP	(Input-146.070)
147.030R	W3DID	(Input-147.630)
147.285R	W3BPX	(Input-147.885)
449.325R	K3SP	(Input-444.325)
443.400R	W3DID	(Input-448.400)
East Baltimore		
147.240R	WR3AFI	(Input-147.840)
223.840R	WR3AFI	(Input-222.240)
449.550R	WR3AFI	(Input-444.550)
West Baltimore		
147.345R	WR3AGS	(Input-147.945)
224.380R	W3HMO	(Input-222.780)
224.940R	WR3AKN	(Input-223.340)
443.550R	WA3WLO	(Input-448.550)
North Baltimore		
146.940R	WA3KOK	(Input-146.340)
224.240R	N3IC	(Input-222.640)
449.650R	WA3KOK	(Input-444.650)
Northwest Baltimore		
145.130R	WA3DZZ	(Input-144.530)
224.800R	WA3DZZ	(Input-223.200)
443.350R	WA3DZZ	(Input-448.350)
BALTIMORE COUNTY		
Freeland		
29.620R	K3SP	(Input- 29.520)
Lutherville		
145.210R	K3VC	(Input-144.610)
CALVERT COUNTY		
Chesapeake Beach		
145.450R	W3PY	(Input-144.850)
CARROLL COUNTY		
Westminster		
145.410R	K3PZN	(Input-144.810)
449.875R	K3PZN	(Input-444.875)
FREDERICK COUNTY		
Frederick		
146.730R	WR3ABL	(Input-146.130)
147.060R	WA3OHI	(Input-147.660)
448.750R	WA3OHI	(Input-443.750)
444.800R	WR3ABL	(Input-449.800)
HARFORD COUNTY		
Bel Air		
146.775R	K3GUX	(Input-146.175)
Harve de Grace		
146.850R	K3UAV	(Input-146.250)
443.100R	K3UAV	(Input-448.100)
HOWARD COUNTY		
Columbia		
147.135R	K3CUJ	(Input-147.735)
147.390R	WR3AGP	(Input-147.990)
Jessup		
146.760R	WA3DZD	(Input-146.160)
224.760R	WA3DZD	(Input-223.160)
444.100R	WA3DZD	(Input-449.100)

MONTGOMERY COUNTY		
Bethesda		
145.290R	K3YGG	(Input-144.690)
Burtonsville		
443.650R	WA3TKW	(Input-448.650)
Damascus		
224.580R	WR3AHS	(Input-222.980)
Gaithersburg		
146.955R	WR3AKP	(Input-146.355)
448.600R	WR3AKP	(Input-443.600)
Potomac		
147.270R	WR3ACF	(Input-147.870)
Rockville		
145.250R	W3RCN	(Input144.650)
146.640R	WR3ABM	(Input-146.040)
146.460M		
Silver Spring		
147.000R	K3WX	(Input-146.400)
147.180R	WA3WAD	(Input-147.780)
443.450R	WB3ARZ	(Input-448.450)
Wheaton		
53.250R	WB3DBU	(Input- 52.250)
PRINCE GEORGE'S COUNTY		
Adelphi		
145.370R	WB3FRW	(Input-144.770)
Ashton		
147.000R	K3WX	(Input-146.400)
Cheltenham		
147.150R	WA3OPC	(Input-147.750)
Cheverly		
146.610R	WR3ABC	(Input-146.010)
College Park		
145.490R	W3AEX	(Input-144.890)
Greenbelt		
146.835R	W3ZM	(Input-146.235)
146.880R	W3MZG	(Input-146.280)
Upper Marlboro		
443.300R	WB3IUT	(Input-448.300)
ST. MARY'S COUNTY		
Lexington Park		
146.640R	WR3ACP	(Input-146.040)
146.865R	W3NET	(Input-146.265)
TALBOT COUNTY		
Easton		
147.045R	WA3GVI	(Input-146.445)
WASHINGTON COUNTY		
Hagerstown		
146.940R	W3CWC	(Input-146.340)
147.090R	K3UMV	(Input-147.690)
WICOMICO COUNTY		
Salisbury		
146.820R	WB3FOW	(Input-146.220)
146.985R	WA3YII	(Input-146.385)
WORCESTER COUNTY		
Ocean City		
147.180R	W3HTB	(Input-147.780)
443.450R	WD4OXQ	(Input-448.450)

INTERNATIONAL AIRPORTS

WASHINGTON AIR TRAFFIC CONTROL CENTER
    Note: A=Aircraft / B=Ground Control
    --listings are for high altitude ATC

120.350B	Patuxent, Maryland	133.025A	Buena Vista, Virginia
125.450A	Green Bay, Virginia	133.275A	Buck's Elbow, Virginia
127.750A	Buck's Elbow, Virginia	133.725A	Aircraft
128.150A	Norfork, Virginia	134.225A	Charlestown, West Virginia
132.025B	Clinton, Maryland	134.625A	Buck's Elbow, Virginia
132.225A	Norfolk, Virginia	135.200A	Aircraft
132.275B	Somerville, Virginia	135.400A	Buena Vista & Green Bay, VA
132.950A	Flint Hill, Virginia	135.500A	Aircraft
		135.525B	Clinton, Maryland

WASHINGTON AIR TRAFFIC CONTROL CENTER
    Note: A=Aircraft / B=Ground Control
    --miscellaneous listings

120.300B	National Airport App/Dep	127.100B	National Airport App/Dep
122.400A	Richmond, Virginia FSS	133.800B	National & Dulles Airports
122.600B	Arlington, Virginia FSS	134.200B	National & Dulles Airports

BALTIMORE-WASHINGTON INTERNATIONAL AIRPORT (Anne Arundel County, Maryland)

43.840	Airport Limos/Buses	KAS454	127.800	ATIS
75.000	FAA		128.050	Clearance Delivery
109.700	FAA		132.125	Air Traffic Control
111.700	FAA		151.715	Page Airlines	KWS345
115.100T	ATIS/VORTAC/FSS		151.955	Friendship Flying Svc	WRJ488
118.050	Clearance Delivery		154.980	Airport Utilities
119.000	Approach Control: North		162.300	Windshear
119.400	Tower Control		169.250	Windshear Remote Xmtr
119.700	Approach Control: South		172.175	Malsr Lite Cntl(Runway 28/33L)
120.650	Departure Control: South		226.900	Approach / Departure Control
121.100	Radar Service		228.400	Approach:North (simul 119.000)
121.500	Nationwide Emergency Channel		231.600	Approach:South (simul 119.700)
121.900	Ground Control		243.000	Nationwide Emergency Channel
122.000	FSS Weather Advisory		255.400	Radio Aids
122.100R	FSS		257.800	Tower Control
122.200	FSS		287.100	Approach Control
122.700	Eastern Flying	KXX8	307.900	Departure Control
122.800	UNICOM		325.800	Departure Control
122.900	CAP Search & Rescue		333.200	FAA
122.950	UNICOM to National Airport		333.500	FAA
123.000	UNICOM		334.700	American/Eastern/TWA Airlines
123.050	UNICOM		453.800R	Fire Department	KBQ735
123.175	Command Post		453.900R	Police Department	KBQ735
123.200	Command Post		460.650	Pan American Airlines	KXI372
123.300	Eastern Flying	KQJ7	460.750	Eastern Airlines	KLB856
123.400	Command Post		460.750	People's Express	KNCN634
123.500	Command Post		460.775	American Airlines	KVN410
123.850	Command Post		460.800	Texas International	WQM303
123.950	Command Post		460.825	World Airways	KNBL479
124.000	Radar Service		460.850	Ozark Airlines	WSC911
124.550	Approach Control		464.375	Macke Company
125.300	Departure Control: North		464.575	Hertz Rent-a-Car	WYU248
125.900	Radar Service		464.925	Marriott in Flight	KNAZ703
126.750	Clearance Delivery			

DULLES INTERNATIONAL (_____ inia)

[handwritten: 124.7 National / 119.1 / TOWER / VHF]

Freq	Description		
113.500	Radio Aids: V(		Fire Department F1
119.200	App/Dep-North(		Fire Department F2
120.100	Tower Control		FAA Police F1: Emergency
120.450	App/Dep-South		FAA Police - SWAT/Tactical
121.500	Nationwide Em(		FAA Police F2: Dispatch
121.900	Ground Contro'		Facility Maintenance
122.950	UNICOM (Pager)		FAA Police F3: Alternate
122.950	Page/Luftwaff(		FAA Windshear (p/w 162.350)
123.000	UNICOM		NASA
125.050	App/Dep-Northv		Dulles Airport-unknown use
125.500	Radar Service		Lite Cntl(Runway 1L/12/19L/30)
126.100	App/Dep-Northeast (7 -57)	243.000	Nationwide Emergency Channel
126.650	App/Dep-Northwest (226 -7)	311.000	U.S. Air Force
127.350	Clearance Delivery	321.000	U.S. Air Force
127.900	Radar Service	334.100	United Airlines
129.025	Pegasus Air / Capitol Helicop.	334.700	American & United Airlines
129.150	British Airways	348.600	Ground Control
129.200	American Airlines	351.100	App/Dep-South (simul 120.450)
129.225	American Airlines	384.900	App/Dep-NE (simul 126.100)
129.300	United Airlines	388.000	Tower Control
129.650	Colgan Air	390.900	App/Dep-NW (simul 126.650)
129.700	Pan American Airlines	409.200	U.S. Air Force
129.800	Americair	409.300	Gate Operations/Mobil Lounges
130.100	US Air	415.125	Tower/Gnd Cntl/Mobil Lounges
130.225	Brannif & TWA Airlines	452.650	Airtrans Buses to National Apt
130.525	People's Express	460.650	Pan American Airlines KKG421
130.550	Western Airlines	460.675	Brannif
130.675	Northwest Orient	460.675	Trans World Airlines KLC377
130.750	Eastern Airlines	460.700	Eastern Airlines
130.900	Eastern Airlines	460.700	Comm Air KVC417
131.150	Fairfax County Police Copter	460.725	United Airlines KCU388
131.700	Northwest Orient	460.750	Eastern Airlines KLN586
131.750	Republic Airlines	460.775	American Airlines KRP541
131.950	Air Virginia	460.825	Page Aviation
131.975	Continental	460.875	Air France KVV361
134.850	ATIS	464.325	Airinc WQU522
135.850	FAA Flight Check	464.675	Avis Rent-a-car KSU715
162.350	FAA Windshear	978.000	American Airlines
164.495	Dulles Airport-unknown use	979.000	United Airlines

WASHINGTON AIR TRAFFIC CONTROL CENTER
    Note: A=Aircraft / B=Ground Control
    --listings are for low altitude ATC

Freq	Location	Freq	Location
118.750A	Westminster, Maryland	132.550B	Dunn Loring, Virginia
123.850A	Whaleyville, Virginia	133.550A	Patuxent, Maryland
123.900B	Dunn Loring, Virginia	133.650B	Falls Church, Virginia
124.050A	Green Bay, Virginia	133.900B	Dunn Loring & Whaleyville, VA
124.250A	Buck's Elbow, Virginia	134.150B	Cumberland,MD / Dans Rock,VA
125.850A	South Boston, Virginia	134.300B	Somerville, Virginia
128.600B	Falls Church, Virginia	135.000B	Clinton, Maryland
132.550A	Aircraft		

[handwritten: National tower 124.7 > VHF / 119.1 -]

35.140	DC Rent-A-Car	KJN443
75.000	FAA	
108.200	Radio Aids: VOT	
108.500	FAA	
109.900	FAA	
111.000	Radio Aids:VOR/DME / Tower(B)	
118.100	Departure Control: West	
118.300	Approach Control: East	
119.100	Tower Control: Primary	
119.850	Approach Control: West	
120.750	Tower (Copters) (simul 119.1)	
121.050	FAA	
121.500	Nationwide Emergency Channel	
121.700	Ground Control	
122.000	FSS Flight Watch	
122.100R	FSS Aircraft Transmit	
122.200	FSS Common En Route	
122.600	FSS Airport Advisory	
122.750	UNICOM: Air to Air	
122.950	UNICOM to BWI / Butler Aviat.	
123.025	UNICOM: Helicopters	
123.050	UNICOM: Med Star Helipad	
123.075	UNICOM: Helicopters	
124.000	Approach Control	
124.200	Approach Control: East	
124.700	Approach Control: West	
126.550	Departure Control: East	
128.250	Clearance Delivery/Pre-Taxi	
129.000	Hinson & Suburban Aviation	
129.150	British Airways	
129.200	American Airlines	
129.225	Capitol Helicopters	
129.300	United Airlines	
129.450	United Airlines	
129.500	Delta Airlines	
129.650	Air Virginia / Colgan Air	
129.700	Eastern / Empire / Pan Am	
129.800	Piedmont Airlines	
130.100	US Air	
130.350	Northwest Orient	
130.400	Eastern Airlines	
130.450	Eastern Airlines: Airborne	
130.500	US Air	
130.620	Trans World Airlines	
130.820	Eastern Airlines: Shuttle	
131.000	Eastern Airlines	
131.225	New York Air (Apple)	
131.325	Midway Airways	
131.700	Northwest Orient	
131.850	Delta Airlines	
131.950	Pan American Airlines	
132.650	ATIS	
151.655	Americar Rental	KMAQ370
151.805	Allied Aviation	KJU477
151.955	Marriott-In-Flight	KNFR992
151.955	Sky Chef	KNAR623
154.515	D & H Parking Service	KNAQ427
154.540	National Airport Shuttle Bus	
158.460	Airport Terminal Service	
162.2125	Airport Paging	
164.825	Fire Department	
165.4125	Maintenance Network	
165.500	FAA Police F1: Emergency	
165.6375	FAA Police - SWAT/Tactical	
165.6625	FAA Police F2: Dispatch	
165.7625	FAA Windshear Tones	
167.125	U.S. Postal Service	
169.275	Noise Abatement	
169.300	FAA Windshear Tones	
169.375	FAA Windshear (p/w 169.300)	
170.175	NASA	
171.3375	U.S. Coast Guard	
172.175	Lite Cntl (Runway 18)	
173.050	FAA	
243.000	Nationwide Emergency Channel	
255.400	Radio Aids/Approach/Departure	
257.600	Tower / Ground Control	
269.000	Approach: East (simul 124.200)	
306.300	Approach Control	
322.300	Approach: West (simul 119.850)	
329.900	National Airport-unknown use	
333.800	National Airport-unknown use	
338.200	Approach Control	
343.000	Misc Private Airlines	
343.700	Departure Control	
396.100	Departure Control	
408.175	Maint: Aircraft Flight Insp.	
409.325	U.S. Coast Guard	
416.875R	PD/CAP (408.825I/410.900I)	
452.650	Airtrans Buses to Dulles Apt	
460.650	United Airlines Ch.A	KGG805
460.675	Trans World Airlines	KQR912
460.700	US Air	KFU435
460.725	United Airlines Ch.B	KRJ333
460.750	Eastern Airlines	KLN589
460.775	American Airlines	KXA937
460.775	US Air	
460.800	Piedmont Airlines	KRD777
460.825	Delta Airlines	KXM522
460.850	Empire & Pan Am Airlines	
460.850	National Airlines	KFM782
460.875	NY Air	WQU675/WQY735
462.125	Hertz	WZL507/KLI409/WXR809
463.500	Int'l Total Svc (Security)	
464.250	Airline Baggage, Inc.	KQK431
464.375	Budget Rent-A-Car	WYS525
464.400	Dollar Rental	
464.450	Dollar Rental	WZY675
464.875	Air I	
464.925	Eastern Airlines	KQW634
464.975	Hertz Rental	KNAQ526/WYV670
495.6875	Ransome Airlines	KWW765
499.2375	Transport Luggage	WIC618
978.000	Misc Private Airlines	
979.000	Misc Private Airlines	

MILITARY AND GOVERNMENT AIRPORTS

ANDREWS AIR FORCE BASE (Prince George's County, Maryland)

113.100	ATIS (simulcasts 269.900)	165.010	Base Operations
118.400	Tower	167.975	FEMA
119.300	Washington Ctr Approach	169.595	Base Motor Pool
121.500	Nationwide Emerg Channel	172.950	Medivac Operations
121.800	Ground Control	173.485	Fire & Crash Crews
122.850	PTD/Single Free Approach	173.560	Medical Network
124.000	National Airport Approach	173.5875	Fire & Crash Crews
125.350	Approach / Departure	173.685	Medical Network
125.650	Washington Ctr Approach	236.600	Tower
127.550	Clearance Delivery	269.500	Washington Ctr Departure
128.350	Radar Service (PAR)	269.900	ATIS (simulcasts 113.100)
130.650	Military Airlift Command	275.800	Ground Control
138.720	Naval Air Field	289.600	Tower
140.400	Tactical Operations	294.500	Washington Ctr Approach
140.445	U.S. Marine Corps HQ	344.600	PMSV: Metro (Weather)
143.450	Radio Wire Integration	351.200	U.S. Air Force Reserves
143.800	U.S. Air Force Reserves	371.800	Command Post
143.950	MARS	372.200	PTD: Pilot to Dispatcher
148.065	Disaster Preparedness	393.100	Clearance Delivery
148.275P	U.S. Air Force	407.425	Command Post Switchboard
149.205	Military Police	413.000	Security Police F1
149.175	Ground Operations	413.200	Maintenance Network
162.925	Airevac Ambulance	413.275	Security Police F2
163.4625	Security	413.375	Security Police

DAVIDSON AIR FORCE BASE - FORT BELVOIR (Fairfax County, Virginia)

52.750FM	Navagational Operations	150.555	Military Police
118.100	Washington Departure Cntl	163.425	Base Transportation
118.850	Radar Service	166.750	Fire Department
119.850	Washington Approach Cntl	229.400	Tower
119.950	Radar Service	241.000	Tower
121.900	Ground Control	245.200	Ground Control/Clnc Deliv
126.300	Tower	322.300	Washington Approach Cntl
		343.700	Washington Departure Cntl

DOVER AIR FORCE BASE (Kent County, Delawaware)

121.900	Ground Control	173.560	Medical Network
125.550	Clearance Delivery	173.590	Fire & Crash Crews
125.900	Stage II Radar Service	225.400	Ground Control
126.500	Tower	273.500	ATIS
128.000	Approach Control	289.400	Clearance Delivery
130.650	Command Post	324.500	Departure Control
135.1xx	Approach Control	327.500	Tower
139.9xx	Approach Control	339.100	Approach Control
148.545	Military Police	342.500	PMSV: Metro
173.200	Base Security	349.400	Command Post
173.440	Base Security	359.300	Stage II Radar Service
		372.200	PTD: Pilot to Dispatcher

MILITARY AND GOVERNMENT AIRPORTS

FEDERAL AVIATION ADMINISTRATION (Prince George's County, Maryland)

109.600	Federal Aviation Admin.	257.200	Federal Aviation Admin.
110.500	Federal Aviation Admin.	269.500	Washington Ctr. Departure
111.500	Federal Aviation Admin.	269.900	Andrews AFB: ATIS
113.100	Andrews AFB: ATIS	275.000	Federal Aviation Admin.
118.400	Andrews AFB: Tower	289.600	Andrews AFB: Tower
118.950	Federal Aviation Admin.	294.500	Washington Ctr. Approach
119.300	Washington Ctr. Approach	301.500	Federal Aviation Admin.
119.900	Approach / Departure	316.700	Federal Aviation Admin.
121.800	Andrews AFB: Ground Cntl.	329.600	Federal Aviation Admin.
122.850	UNICOM / PTD	332.900	Federal Aviation Admin.
124.000	National Apt.: Approach	335.500	Federal Aviation Admin.
125.350	Federal Aviation Admin.	360.800	Federal Aviation Admin.
128.350	Andrews AFB: Radar	363.800	Radar Approach
165.6125	Maintenance Network	379.200	Federal Aviation Admin.
236.600	Andrews AFB: Tower	389.000	Federal Aviation Admin.
		393.100	Andrews AFB: Clnc Deliv

GLEN L. MARTIN STATE AIR FORCE BASE (Baltimore County, Maryland)

115.100	Radio Aids: VORTAC	126.200	Tower
116.600	Radio Aids: VOR	143.800	Army Reserves
119.000	BWI Apt: North Approach	149.525	Fire/Crash/Ambulance
121.300	Tower	163.485	Security
121.700	Ground Control	243.000	Nationwide Emerg Channel
122.800	UNICOM	253.400	Ground Control
122.950	UNICOM	287.100	BWI Apt: Approach Cntl.
123.200	Command Post	297.200	Tower
125.300	BWI Apt: North Departure	307.900	BWI Apt: Departure Cntl.
		347.200	Colt Control: Command Post

PATUXENT NAVAL AIR STATION - TRAPNELL FIELD (St. Mary's County, Maryland)

117.600T	Radio Aids: VORTAC/FSS	140.700	Fire Department
120.050	Approach / Departure	148.375	U.S. Navy MARS
120.350	Federal Aviation Admin.	276.200	ATIS
122.100R	FSS	277.400	Federal Aviation Admin.
123.300	U.S. Navy	281.800	Approach / Departure
123.350	U.S. Navy	321.000	U.S. Air Force
123.650	Tower	336.400	Ground Control
126.200	Ground Control/Clnc Deliv	340.200	Tower
134.100	Radar Service	344.400	Tower
135.150	Radar Service	354.800	Advisory Service
140.580	Security	356.200	PMSV: Metro (Weather)
		413.450	U.S. Air Force

MILITARY AND GOVERNMENT AIRPORTS

PHILLIPS AIR FORCE BASE - ABERDEEN PROVING GROUND (Harford County, Md)

34.100	Tower		165.185	Military Police
36.690	Emergency Operations		165.590	Military Police
36.890	Emergency Operations		170.025	Army Engineers
108.400T	ATIS / Radio Aids		173.410	Fire & Crash Crews
121.500	Nationwide Emerg. Channel		229.600	Tower
121.900	Ground Control		241.000	Tower / Air Nat. Guard
124.550	BWI Apt: Approach Cntl.		243.000	Nationwide Emerg Channel
126.150	Tower / Air to Air		287.100	BWI Apt: Approach Cntl.
126.750	BWI Apt: Clnc. Delivery		307.900	BWI Apt: Departure Cntl.
165.035	Ambulance Network		373.800	Ground Control
165.060	Base Security		407.325	Gire & Crash Crews
			407.475	Fire & Crash Crews

QUANTICO MARINE CORPS TRAINING CENTER (Prince William County, Virginia)

41.950	Tower		149.130	Military Police-Secondary
125.800	Tower		149.350	Fire Department
126.200	Approach / Departure		149.450	Ambulance Network
134.100	Radar Service		150.125P	Post Engineer Pager
140.100	MCAS Crash & Rescue Teams		312.200	Approach / Departure
149.100	Military Police: Primary		340.200	Ground Control / Tower
			360.200	Tower

TIPTON AIR FORCE BASE - FORT MEADE (Anne Arundel County, Maryland)

32.500	U.S. Army		163.175	Base Security
46.790	U.S. Army		163.475	Base Security
49.700	U.S. Army		163.535	Military Police F2
49.800	U.S. Army		163.560	Military Police F1
119.700	BWI Apt: South Approach		167.975	FEMA
121.500	Nationwide Emerg Channel		173.460	U.S. Army
121.750	Ground Control		226.900	BWI Apt: App/Dep
127.000	Tower / VFR Advisory Svc.		227.100	Ground Control
128.750	U.S. Air Force		241.000	Air National Guard
132.600	Air Traffic Control		243.000	Nationwide Emerg Channel
132.950	Air Traffic Control		248.200	Tower / VFR Advisory Svc.
133.150	Air Traffic Control		287.100	BWI Apt: Approach Cntl.
133.200	Pilots & Radar Station		296.200	U.S. Air Force
139.250	U.S. Army		301.600	U.S. Air Force
140.000	U.S. Army		407.300	Fire Department
141.025	U.S. Army		407.475	U.S. Army
141.325	U.S. Army		407.575	U.S. Army
142.350	U.S. Army		411.075	N.R.C.
143.995	MARS		412.975	U.S. Army
150.425	U.S. Army		413.525	U.S. Army
150.450	U.S. Army			
150.475	U.S. Army			
150.525	U.S. Army			
150.575	U.S. Army			

WASHINGTON, DC MUNICIPAL AIRPORTS

WASHINGTON HOSPITAL CENTER
123.050   Hospital Heliport   WHR8

DELAWARE MUNICIPAL AIRPORTS

DUPONT MUNICIPAL AIRPORT
114.000   Radio Aids: VORTAC

GEORGETOWN MUNI (Sussex Co.)
112.600   Radio Aids
122.800   UNICOM
125.900   Approach / Departure
128.000   Approach / Departure

KENTON MUNICIPAL AIRPORT
111.400   Radio Aids: VORTEC/ENO
122.100R Radio (Transmit:111.400)

LAUREL AIRPORT (Sussex Co.)
122.800   UNICOM

MIDDLETOWN APT (New Castle Co.)
122.700   UNICOM
123.500   Flight School
125.000   Approach / Departure

MILFORD AIRPARK (Sussex Co.)
122.800   UNICOM   KCR3
128.000   Approach / Departure

NEW CASTLE APT (New Castle Co.)
122.700   UNICOM
122.800   UNICOM
123.300   Flight School
453.325R Airport Security   KXD290

REHOBOTH BEACH (Sussex Co.)
112.600   Radio Aids
122.800   UNICOM
128.000   Dover Approach/Departure
339.100   Dover Approach/Departure

SMYRNA AIRPORT (Kent County)
122.800   UNICOM   WFH5

SUMMIT AIRPARK (New Castle Co.)
114.000   Radio Aids
122.700   UNICOM
125.000   Phili. Approach/Departure
323.100   Phili. Approach/Departure

SUSSEX CO. AIRPARK (Sussex Co.)
112.600   Radio Aids
122.800   UNICOM
128.000   Dover Approach/Departure
339.100   Dover Approach/Departure

WATERLOO MUNICIPAL AIRPORT
112.100R Radio (Transmit:117.900)

WILMINGTON APT. (New Castle Co.)
 34.150   Air Nat Guard: Fire/Crash
 38.600FM Navagational Operations
114.000   Radio Aids: VOTREC
121.700   Ground Control
122.950   UNICOM
123.300   Flight School
123.500   Flight School
123.950   ATIS
125.000   Phili. Approach/Departure
126.000   Wilmington Tower
148.200   Air Nat Guard: Security
275.800   Ground Control
305.400   Wilmington Tower
323.100   Phili. Approach/Departure
343.000   Command Post ("Seabee")

WYOMING AIRPARK (Kent County)
122.800   UNICOM

VIRGINIA MUNICIPAL AIRPORTS

DAVIS FIELD (Prince William Co.)
123.000   UNICOM
123.300   Page Beachcraft   KQL9

LEESBURG-GODFREY (Loudon Co.)
122.800   UNICOM
123.300   Century Aviation   WFS3
          Janelle Aviation   WJW3
390.900   Approach / Departure

WOODBRIDGE MUNI (Prince Wm. Co.)
122.800   UNICOM

DAVIS FIELD-MANASSAS (Fairfax Co)
113.500R Radio Aids: VOTRAC/AML
120.450   Dulles Apt: App/Dep
121.650   Clearance Delivery
122.700   UNICOM
123.000   UNICOM
123.200   NASA
123.300   Page Beachcraft   KQL9
126.100   Approach / Departure
351.100   Dulles Apt: App/Dep

MARYLAND MUNICIPAL AIRPORTS

ABERDEEN REGIONAL (Harford Co.)
255.400	FAA Flite Service (BWI)
371.900	Approach / Departure

ANNE ARUNDEL COUNTY AIRPARK
123.200	Flight School
123.300	Flight School

AQUA-LAND-CLIFTON (Charles Co.)
111.800	Radio Aids: VORTAC
122.700	UNICOM
122.800	UNICOM

BALTIMORE AIRPARK (Balt. Co.)
115.100	Radio Aids: VORTAC
123.000	UNICOM
	Baltimore Aviation KTJ3

BAY BRIDGE APK (Queen Anne Co.)
123.000	UNICOM

BENNETT FIELD (Wicomico Co.)
122.800	UNICOM
123.200	NASA

CAMBRIDGE MUNI (Dorchester Co.)
114.500	Radio Aids: VORTAC
123.000	UNICOM
127.950	Patuxent NAS App/Dep
134.100	Patuxent NAS App/Dep
257.000	Dorchester County

CARROLL COUNTY MUNICIPAL
117.900T	Washington FSS/VORTAC
122.100R	Washington FSS
122.700	UNICOM
	Chesapeake Aviation KCM2
	Spanair KIN8
125.300	BWI Apt: North Approach
126.750	BWI Apt: Clearance Deliv.
287.100	BWI Apt: Approach Control
307.900	BWI Apt: Departure Cntl.

CLEARVIEW AIRPARK (Carroll Co.)
117.900T	Washington FSS/VORTAC
122.100R	Washington FSS
122.800	UNICOM
	Clearview Management WLQ2
125.300	BWI Apt: North Departure
126.750	BWI Apt: Clearance Deliv.

COLLEGE PARK APK (Pr. George Co)
122.800 / 123.000	UNICOM

CRISFIELD MUNI (Somerset Co.)
122.800	UNICOM

CUMBERLAND MUNI (Allegany Co.)
110.500	Military Aircraft/FAA
112.300	Radio Aids: VOTRAC
118.550	Air National Guard
122.300	Martinsburg,W.Va. FSS
122.350	Martinsburg,W.Va. FSS
122.800	UNICOM
124.400	Cleveland,Oh. App/Dep
127.255	Military Aircraft/FAA
255.400	FAA Flite Service
257.700	Military Aircraft/FAA
287.900	Military Aircraft/FAA
327.100	Cleveland,Oh. App/Dep

DAVIS FIELD (Montgomery Co.)
122.800	UNICOM
	Laytonsville Flying KHR9

DEEP CREEK APK (Anne Arundel Co)
122.800	UNICOM / Airpark KMW6

EASTON MUNICIPAL (Talbot Co.)
113.700	Radio Aids: VORTAC
122.800	UNICOM / Airport KEP3
123.500	Calypso Airways KBX3
135.000	Approach / Departure

ESSEX SKYPARK (Baltimore Co.)
122.700	UNICOM
154.515	Coleman Aviation WXM888

FREDERICK MUNI (Frederick Co.)
109.000T	Martinsburg,W.Va. FSS/VOR
117.900	Radio Aids: VORTAC
119.000	BWI Apt: North Approach
122.100R	Martinsburg,W.Va. FSS
123.000	UNICOM
123.300	Mid Atlantic Soaring WQJ2
125.300	BWI Apt: North Departure
142.155	U.S. Air Force
287.100	BWI Apt: Approach Control
307.900	BWI Apt: Departure Cntl.

FREEWAY AIRPORT (Pr. George Co.)
122.700	UNICOM

GARRETT COUNTY MUNICIPAL
112.300T	Morgantown,W.Va. FSS/VORTAC
122.100R	Morgantown,W.Va. FSS
122.800	UNICOM
124.400	Cleveland,Oh. Ctr App/Dep

GRANTSVILLE APT (Garrett Co.)
112.300T	Morgantown FSS/VORTAC
121.100R	Mortantown,W.Va. FSS

MARYLAND MUNICIPAL AIRPORTS

HARFORD COUNTY INDUSTRIAL APK
122.800 UNICOM

HYDE FIELD (Pr. George's Co.)
122.800 UNICOM
        Beacon Flying Svc. WIT5

JOHNS HOPKINS HOSPITAL
123.050 Balt. City Helipad WHJ8

LEWISTOWN MUNI (Frederick Co)
148.185/150.195/165.035 U.S.A.F.
268.000/287.500/293.500 U.S.A.F.

MARYLAND AIRPARK (Charles Co.)
111.000 Radio Aids: VOR/DME
122.700 UNICOM

MEXICO FARMS (Carroll Co.)
122.800 UNICOM

MIDDLE RIVER (Balt. Co.)
116.600 Radio Aids: VOR

MONTGOMERY CO AIRPARK
109.000 Radio Aids: VOR
113.500 Radio Aids: VORTAC
119.000 BWI Apt: North Approach
122.700 UNICOM (Primary)
122.800 UNICOM
123.200 NASA
123.500 Gibson Aviation WGM4
125.300 BWI Apt: North Departure
126.750 BWI Apt: Clearance Deliv.

NOTTINGHAM APK (Pr. George Co)
113.700T Washington FSS/VORTAC
122.100R Washington FSS

OCEAN CITY (Worcester Co.)
112.100R Salisbury FSS
112.400T Salisbury FSS
114.500 Radio Aids: VORTAC
122.800 UNICOM

PARK HALL (St. Mary's Co.)
117.600 Radio Aids: VORTAC

PRINCE GEORGE'S CO APK
122.800 UNICOM

ST. MARY'S COUNTY AIRPARK
117.600T Salisbury FSS/VORTAC
122.100R Salisbury FSS
122.800 UNICOM
134.100 Patuxent NAS App/Dep

SALISBURY-WICOMICO CO APT
 75.000 / 108.700 FAA
114.500T Salisbury FSS/VORTAC
121.500 Nationwide Emerg Channel
122.030 Weather Advisory
122.100R Salisbury FSS
122.200 Salisbury FSS/Tower
122.300 Salisbury FSS/Tower
122.800 / 122.950 UNICOM
123.100 Search & Rescue
123.200 Flight School
123.600 Salisbury FSS/Tower
135.150 Air Traffic Control
172.175 Federal Aviation Admin.
243.000 Nationwide Emerg Channel
255.400 FSS
330.500 Federal Aviation Admin.

SNOW HILL (Worchester Co.)
112.400T Salisbury FSS/VOTRAC
122.100R Salisbury FSS/VORTAC

SUBURBAN APK (Pr. George's Co.)
121.600 FCC
122.700 UNICOM
        Suburban Airservice KUJ5
123.300 Suburban Airservice KVU4
123.400 / 123.450 Flight School
243.200 FCC

WASHINGTON COUNTY REGIONAL
 34.200 / 34.550 U.S. Air Force
 75.000 / 111.900 FAA
109.800T Martinsburg FSS/Radio Aid
115.000 Radio Aids: VORTAC
120.300 Tower
121.900 Ground Control
122.100R Martinsburg,W.Va. FSS
122.950 UNICOM
123.200 Fairchild Industries WWM0
123.500 Flight School
134.500 Washington Center App/Dep
138.350 U.S. Air Force / FAA
153.095 Fairchild Industries
169.325 Federal Aviation Admin.
233.400 U.S. Air Force
265.200 U.S. Navy / U.S. Air Force
265.700 Tower
309.600 / 398.800 U.S. Air Force
334.700 Henson Aviation
464.675 Henson Aviation

WESTMINSTER APK (Carroll Co.)
117.900T Washington FSS/VORTAC
121.100R Washington FSS

WASHINGTON METRO AREA TRANSIT AUTHORITY

161.385	Transit Police (KSL840-1)
160.260	Rail Ops F1: Red Line
160.380	Rail Ops F2: Blue/Orange
160.605	Rail - New Carlton Yard
160.620	Rail - Start Up Freq
161.025	Rail - Systemwide Maint.
161.235	Rail - Brentwood Yard
44.560	Bus - Supers/Repair Truck
496.4625	Bus F1: Systemwide Calling
496.5875	Bus F2: Prince George's Co
496.5125	Bus F3: Washington, D.C.
496.5375	Bus F4: DC-Montgomery Co.
496.5625	Bus F5: DC-Montgomery Co.
496.4875	Bus F6: Virginia
496.6125	Bus F7: Supervisors
496.3375 / 496.4375	Bus-Future use
462.625	Snow Desk (winter only)

AMTRAK - Northeast Corridor

160.800	F1: Road Channel #1
161.070	F2: Road Channel #2
161.515R	F3: Maintenance of Way
161.295R	F4: Police Dispatch
161.205M	F5: Police Car to Car
161.635	F6: Maintenance
160.920R	F7: Future Road Channel
452.900	Station Administration
416.125	Metroliner Phones:MD/NJ
416.175	Metroliner Phones:DEL/PA/NJ
416.225	Metroliner Phones:DEL/NJ
416.875	Metroliner Phones:DEL/PA/NJ/NY
416.925	Metroliner Phones:MD/NJ
416.975	Metroliner Phones:MD/PA/NJ

161.280/160.935/161.160/160.830/161.190

Police Codes (Different from Standard)

10-00	Emergency
10-05	Repeat Message
10-10	Car/Person Check
10-11	Additional Units
10-12	Req. Supervisor
10-13	Req. Other PD
10-14	Req. Ambulance
10-15	Req. Fire Dept.
10-16	Prisoner in Custody
10-17	Wants/Warrants Check
10-18	Return to your HQ
10-19	Cal your HQ
10-24	Alarm Sounding
10-26	Prepare to Copy
10-45	Accident
10-46	Train in Emergency
10-47	Train Protection
10-48	Stoning/Shooting
10-49	Passenger Assist
10-50	Disorderly Person
10-82	Hostage Situation
10-88	Bomb Threat
10-99	Assist Officer

BALTIMORE MASS TRANSIT ADMINISTRATION

160.395	Subway - Road Channel
161.085	Subway - Police Department
161.475	Subway - Yard Channel
161.565	Subway - Maintenance
494.3375R	Buses F1
494.4375R	Buses F2
494.6125R	Buses F3
494.6375R	Buses F4
494.7625R	Security F1: Primary
494.8125R	Security F2: Secondary
494.9625R	Supervisors F1
495.0375R	Supervisors F2

UNION STATION (Washington, D.C.)

160.290	F1: Switching
160.350	F2: Baggage/Food/AMTRAK
160.440	F3: Police Department
161.445	Police Dept - Alt.
161.265/161.370	New Allocations

CONRAIL

160.800	F1: Road Channel
161.070	F2: Road & Yard
160.710	F3: Maintenance
161.130	F4: Maintenance
160.860	F3: Hump Yard
160.980	F4: Kenilworth Yard
160.560	Police Dispatch
161.520	Car Department

CHESSIE SYSTEM

160.230	F1: Road Channel
160.320	F2: Road Secondary/Yard
160.530	F3: Yard - Brunswick,MD
161.160	F4: Yard - Fred/Balt, MD
160.785	Maintenance of Way
160.875	Police Department

161.400/160.890/160.470/161.070

RICHMOND, FREDERICKSBURG & POTOMAC

161.550	F1: Road
161.550B	F2: Disp (Train-161.490)
161.355	F3: Police & Supervisors
160.275	Potomac Yard F1: Switching
160.335	Potomac Yard F2
160.485	Potomac Yard F3: Welding
160.770	Potomac Yard F4: Car Dpt.
161.100	Potomac Yard-So'bound Hump
161.280	Potomac Yard-No'bound Hump

SOUTHERN RAILWAY

160.950	F1: Road Channel
160.245B	F2: Disp (Train-160.830)
160.500	F3: Mobil Freight & Agents
161.205	F4: Police Department

MISCELLANEOUS RAILROADS

160.590/160.845	Patapsco&Buck Rivers
161.250/161.190	Norfolk & Western

METRO D.C.: NETWORK NEWS MEDIA

ABC Television Network (Arlington, VA)

455.0875	F1:	Disp/Assign Desk	KQB201
455.5875	F2:	Engineering	KQA998
450.5875	F3:	Production	KQB200
450.4125	F4:	IFB Feed	KQA999
455.6125	F5:	unknown use	
450.1125	F6:	unknown use	
495.6625		ABC-TV Network	

ABC Radio Network

455.3500	F1:	unknown use	KQB324
455.7000	F2:	unknown use	KQB324
450.6500	F3:	unknown use	
450.8500	F4:	IFB Feed	KQB324/KXZ929
450.7250		(p/w 455.7250)	

Cable News Network

452.9750	F1:	Engineering	WXV785
453.0000	F2:	Dispatch	WXV785
453.0000R	F3:	IFB Feed	WXV785
450.0875		Cable News Network	
152.9900		Cable News Network	

CBS Television Network

450.1500	F1:	Desk/Cues	KQA986
450.4875	F2:	Production	KQA986
450.0500	F3:	Tech/Engineering	
450.2875	F4:	News Desk	KQA986
450.8000R	F5:	IFB Feed	KQA986
455.8000I	F5:	input to above	
450.5125R	F6:	Tech/Engineering	KQA986
455.5125I	F6:	input to above	
450.6125R	F7:	IFB Feed	KQA986
450.2875R	F8:	Camp David Remote	KQA986
154.6250		CBS-TV Net KWB585/KWB401	
153.3500		CBS-TV Network	

CBS Radio Network

455.2500	F1:	unknown use	KES329
455.4500	F2:	unknown use	KES329
455.6500	F3:	unknown use	KES329

Metromedia, Inc.

816.3375	Metromedia, Inc.
820.3375	Metromedia, Inc.
816.5875	Metromedia, Inc.
820.5875	Metromedia, Inc.

NBC Television Network (comb w/WRC-TV)

450.4500	F1:	Local Engineering	KAH290
450.5500	F2:	Net Engineering	KFR952
455.1500	F3:	Local Production	KAH290
455.8500	F4:	Net Production	KFR952
161.670		Net/Loc Dispatch	KFT442
450.6750		(p/w 455.6750)	
450.8750		(p/w 455.8750)	
450.0750		Cues	
455.9000		NBC-TV Network	

METRO D.C.: NETWORK NEWS MEDIA

NBC Radio Network

450.3125	F1:	Newsdesk	WQB268
455.4125	F2:	Engineering	KQB268
455.7500	F3:	Dispatch	KAH290
455.0500	F4:	Newsroom	KAH290
450.9250		IFB Feed (p/w 455.925)	KA4274
455.3125		NBC Radio Network	
153.2900		NBC Radio Network	
153.1100		NBC Radio Network	

METRO D.C.: LOCAL NEWS MEDIA

WJLA-TV (ABC-Ch 7)

455.5500	F1:	Dispatch	KFB376
455.1125	F2:	Cueing	KGB261

WDVM-TV (CBS-Ch 9)

450.2125	601:	Assign. Desk	KFT601
450.7500	344:	News Desk	KVM344
153.2300		WDVM-TV	

WTTG-TV (Metromedia-Ch 5)

161.7300	F1:	Disp/Metro Trf.	KGI343
161.7600	F2:	Alt/Metro Trf.	KGI343
152.8700		WTTG-TV	KV9166

WRC-TV (NBC-Ch 4) (see also NBC list)

153.0500	Local Disp & Feed	WHE854
153.1700	Local Use	

WETA-TV (PBS-Ch 26) (Arlington, VA)

455.1875	WETA-TV	KKN789
455.2875	WETA-TV	KKN789
455.3875	WETA-TV	KKN789

WMAL-AM Radio (ABC)

161.7000	Traffic Helicopter	
455.2125R	Disp/Pager (450.650I)	KKN764

WTOP-AM Radio (CBS)

450.3500	Traffic Helicopter	KQS282
455.6500	Alt Operations	KA8851
161.7600	Emerg Bdcstg Service	KJB595

Miscellaneous Radio

450.2500	WASH-FM Trf. Copter	KCG901
450.7000	WPGC-AM Trf. Copter	
161.6400	WPGC-AM Cues	KFT442
166.2500	WAVA-FM (Arl,VA)	KIY549
455.6500	WDON (Wheaton, MD)	KTB790
455.7500	WDON (Wheaton, MD)	KTB790
151.6550	WEAM (Falls Church,VA)	KSP759
161.6400	WWDC-AM	KGZ973
170.1500	Emergency Broadcasting Svc.	

METRO D.C.: Washington Post

154.5150	unknown use	KNAX310
154.5400	Security	
173.2250	P.G. Co. MD Delivery	KDG633
173.2750	Wash., D.C. Delivery	KNFH942
173.3250	Arl., VA Delivery	KDG633
173.3750	Mont Co. MD Delivery	KJE545
464.5000	Dispatch	
464.7750	unknown use	WYF547
496.0125	unknown use	KXS842

METRO D.C.: TRAFFIC MEDIA

496.1625	Metro Trf Cntl: Dtwn	KNQ228
450.925B	Metro Trf Cntl (455.925M)	
862.4875	Metro Traffic Control	
863.4875	Metro Traffic Control	
864.4875	Metro Traffic Control	
865.4875	Metro Traffic Control	
462.6750	REACT: Primary Metro, DC	
462.6000	REACT: Secondary Metro, DC	
462.6250	REACT: Prince George's Co.	
462.7000	REACT	
122.7500	Traffic Helicopters Common	

METRO D.C.: MISCELLANEOUS MEDIA

461.4000	Ace Federal Reporter	KCF361
453.0000	Action Movie News	WXU784
450.8000	Associated Press	WZB774
455.4500	Associated Press	WZB774
455.5000	Associated Press	WZB774
173.3250	Broadcast News Svc.	KNCD665
173.3750	Broadcast News Svc.	KNCD665
453.0000	Broadcast News Svc.	KNAS221
161.6400	Capitol Broadcasters	KGZ973
450.5125	Channel 50, Inc.	WHE703-4
461.4250	Channel 50, Inc.	KNCA469
450.1500	Columbia Bdcstg.	KQR742
450.9500	Columbia Bdcstg.	KQR752
464.5000	Columbia General Media	
455.6125	CONUS	
452.9750	Dow Jones, Inc.	KBC912
463.9500	Eastern Video System	KNCW438
450.1875	Gannett Radio	
450.2875	Howard University	KA3670
455.2875	Howard University	KA3670
450.5875	Howard University	KA3670
455.5875	Howard University	KA3670
452.9750	Mobile Video Service	WSH608
852.1625	Mobile Video Service	KNAN847
161.6400	Mutual Broadcasting	WHE980
455.4125	Mutual Broadcasting	KA7474
455.4875	Mutual Broadcasting	KA7474
152.9300	Mutual Broadcasting	KA7474
152.9900	Mutual Broadcasting	KA7474
151.6550	National Geographic	KFT684
461.4000	Newsletter Services	KNCS975
452.9750	Time, Inc.	KNAX816
153.2750	UPI Film Pick-up	
452.9750	United Press Int'l.	KVS951
450.2500	Viacom	KR4782
452.9750	Wall Street Journal	
854.8375	Washington Times	
854.0875	Washington Times	
455.7500	Westinghouse Bdcstg.	KSQ963

BALTIMORE AREA LOCAL NEWS MEDIA

WBAL-TV (CBS-Ch 11) (Hearst Corp.)

450.0875	F1: unknown use	KZH878
450.1125	F2: unknown use	KZH878
450.1875	F3: unknown use	KZH878
450.2125	F4: unknown use	KZH878

WJZ-TV (ABC-Ch 13) (Westinghouse Bdc.)

450.3875	F1: unknown use	KGI294
455.3875	F2: unknown use	KGI294
450.5500	News Desk	KAN346

WMAR-TV (NBC-Ch 2)

450.3125	unknown use	KVX339
455.3125	unknown use	KVX339
464.3500	unknown use	KYL268

BALTIMORE MISCELLANEOUS MEDIA

450.3500	A.S. Abell Publ. Co.	KDV346
455.3500	A.S. Abell Publ. Co.	KDV346
173.2250	A.S. Abell Publ. Co.	KJA459
173.3750	A.S. Abell Publ. Co.	KJA459
450.6500	Baltimore County	KA4424
166.2500	Baltimore Radio Show	KLS700
450.0500	Hearst Corporation	
450.1500	Hearst Corporation	
450.2500	Hearst Corporation	
455.6500	Hearst Corporation	KZH878
455.7500	Hearst Corporation	KFY358
455.9500	Hearst Corporation	KZH895
464.3250	Hearst Corporation	KSP936
170.1500	Hearst Corporation	
173.2750	Hearst Corporation	KGG946
450.0500	Key Broadcasters	KJR580
450.2500	Key Broadcasters	KJR580
455.0500	Key Broadcasters	KJR580
463.8500	Metro Traffic Control	
464.5500	Metro Traffic Control	
450.0500	Metromedia, Inc.	KJU393
450.1500	Metromedia, Inc.	KJU393
450.2500	Metromedia(Trf Copter)	KJU393
455.2500	Metromedia, Inc.	KJU393
455.4500	Metromedia, Inc.	KJU393
153.1700	Nationwide Communic.	KK7657
455.0500	Nationwide Communic.	WYR245
455.8500	Nationwide Communic.	WYR245
450.5125	Plough Broadcasting	KEH598
455.7500	Plough Bdcstg.	KFY364/KGK952
450.6500	WBAL - News Desk	
450.6125	WBAL Radio	
450.5125	WCAO	
161.7300	WCBM (Metromedia)	KRN705
161.7600	WCBM (Metromedia)	KRN705
161.7300	WFBR-AM	
166.2500	WFBR-AM Trf Copter	
161.6400	WITH Radio	KEK706
455.0500	WPOC Radio Trf Copter	
455.6125	WRAI Radio	
450.9500	Westinghouse Broadcasters	

MARYLAND MISCELLANEOUS MEDIA

154.6250	Anne Arundel County	(Arnold)	KAL925
463.9250	Associated Photographers	(Towson)	KDR201
947.5000	Atlantic Broadcasting	(Ocean City)	KQA984
161.6400	Bel Air Broadcasting	(Bel Air)	KVL841
173.3250	Caroline County Newspapers		
161.6400	Carroll County Broadcasting	(Westminster)	KFG618
161.7000	Carroll County Broadcasting	(Westminster)	KFG618
161.7300	Carroll County Broadcasting	(Westminster)	KFG618
161.7600	Carroll County Broadcasting	(Westminster)	KFG618
161.7000	Chesapeake Broadcasting	(Harve De Grace)	KUH574
153.3500	Continental Radio	(Leonardtown)	KP8219
161.6700	Continental Radio	(Leonardtown)	KRN295-6
463.7250	Council Press	(Bethesda)	WRR472
946.8750	Crystal Broadcasting	(La Plata)	WCX647
947.1250	Crystal Broadcasting	(La Plata)	
161.6700	Cumberland Broadcasting	(Cumberland)	
161.7300	Cumberland Broadcasting	(Cumberland)	
166.2500	Hagerstown Broadcasting	(Hagerstown)	KOP331
170.1500	Hagerstown Broadcasting	(Hagerstown)	KGN467
948.0000	Hagerstown Broadcasting	(Hagerstown)	WAC225
151.6550	Homes & Land Magazine	(Millersville)	WRU470
173.3250	Independent Newspapers	(Denton)	KSD694
161.7600	Inter Urban Broadcasting	(Laurel)	KW8636
166.2500	Jim Gibbons Radio	(Frederick)	KGZ551
170.1500	Jim Gibbons Radio	(Frederick)	KGZ550
151.6550	Key Broadcasting	(Lexington Park)	KOL216
450.0500	Key Broadcasting	(Lexington Park)	KJX807
450.2500	Key Broadcasting	(Lexington Park)	KJX807
455.0500	Key Broadcasting	(Lexington Park)	KJX807
152.8700	Mackk Broadcasting	(Aberdeen)	
161.7000	Mackk Broadcasting	(Aberdeen)	KBQ419
161.7600	Mardel Communications	(Salisbury)	KQA919
155.0850	Maryland Public Broadcasting	(Owings Mills)	
154.5400	National Geographic	(Gaithersburg)	KNAT230
467.7500	National Geographic	(Gaithersburg)	
453.0000	News American	(Towson)	WZZ800
161.6700	Prettyman Broadcasting	(Salisbury)	KGI452
455.2500	RAU Radio	(Annapolis)	KRI505
455.2500	RAU Radio	(Crownsville)	KRI506
455.4500	RAU Radio	(Hagerstown)	KA3513
455.5500	RAU Radio	(Hagerstown)	KA3513
947.3750	RAU Radio	(Hagerstown)	WBJ969
947.6250	RAU Radio	(Hagerstown)	WBJ969
161.6700	RKO General	(Bethesda)	KHZ807
161.7000	RKO General	(Bethesda)	KHZ807
161.7300	RKO General	(Bethesda)	KHZ807
161.7600	RKO General	(Bethesda)	KHZ807
464.8500	Record Publishing	(Rockville)	KNAR236
153.2900	Regional Broadcasting	(Halfway)	KGI346
463.9750	Random House	(Westminster)	
161.6400	WBOC-TV (CBS-Ch 16)	(Salisbury)	KGU251
161.6700	WBOC-TV (CBS-Ch 16)	(Salisbury)	KGU251
161.7000	WBOC-TV (CBS-Ch 16)	(Salisbury)	KGU250
161.7300	WBOC-TV (CBS-Ch 16)	(Salisbury)	KGU250
161.7600	WBOC-TV (CBS-Ch 16)	(Salisbury)	KGU250
161.7000	WTBO/WKGO	(Cumberland)	WQB244-5
161.7300	WTBO/WKGO	(Cumberland)	WQB244-5
161.7600	WTBO/WKGO	(Cumberland)	KFK812
161.6700	WTOW	(Towson)	KFK939
161.6400	Western Maryland Broadcasting	(Frostburg)	KGI458
161.7000	Western Maryland Broadcasting	(Frostburg)	KGI458

VIRGINIA MISCELLANEOUS MEDIA

461.6500	Alderson Reporting	(Arlington)	WYQ369
173.2750	Columbia Newspapers	(Alexandria)	KDZ977
461.2500	Interstate Photography	(McLean)	WXL278
464.9500	Journal Newspapers	(Arlington)	KUD613
851.7875	Kelly Press	(Falls Church)	WQP533
951.9000	Metcom, Virginia	(Alexandria)	WAK808
161.6400	Metcom, Virginia	(Falls Church)	WQB269
161.7000	Metcom, Virginia	(Falls Church)	WQB269
161.7300	Metcom, Virginia	(Falls Church)	WQB269
947.0000	Metroplex Communications	(Alexandria)	WGW942
161.7600	National Broadcasting	(Fairfax)	KGH975
161.6400	Newcomb Broadcasting	(Falls Church)	KG3420
161.6700	Newcomb Broadcasting	(Falls Church)	KG3420
161.6400	Radio Wage	(Leesburg)	KIY629
161.7000	Radio Wage	(Leesburg)	KIY629
161.7600	Radio Wage	(Leesburg)	KIY629
151.9250	Reynolds Photo	(Manassas)	
461.5500	Trader Publications	(Arlington)	KJW720
173.2250	USA Today	(Arlington)	

DELAWARE MISCELLANEOUS MEDIA

161.7300	Dover Broadcasting	(Dover)	
161.7600	Dover Broadcasting	(Dover)	
173.3250	Independent Newspapers	(Dover)	KKL430
173.3250	Independent Newspapers	(Millsboro)	KSD697
173.2250	News Journal Company	(Wilmington)	KZX571
173.3250	News Journal Company	(Wilmington)	KZX571
161.7300	RAU Radio	(Dover)	KJT982
161.7600	RAU Radio	(Dover)	KJT982
161.6700	Scott Broadcasting	(Georgetown)	KLQ217-8
152.4800	WBOC	(Hazlettville)	WYD641

MARINE BAND ALLOCATION TABLE

NOTE: All are Ship/Ship and Ship/Shore unless otherwise noted

156.300	F6:	Intership Safety (Ship/Ship only)
156.350	F7:	Commercial
156.400	F8:	Commercial (Ship/Ship only)
156.450	F9:	Commercial
156.500	F10:	Commercial
156.550	F11:	Commercial
156.600	F12:	Port Operations / U.S. Coast Guard
156.650	F13:	Navagational
156.700	F14:	Port Operations / U.S. Coast Guard
156.750	F15:	Environmental/Hydrographic (Ships Receive Only)
156.800	F16:	Distress / Calling
156.850	F17:	State Control (Ship/Shore only)
156.900	F18:	Commercial
156.950	F19:	Commercial
157.000	F20:	Port Operations (Coast Rx on 161.600)
157.050	F21:	U.S. Coast Guard
157.100	F22:	U.S. Coast Guard
157.150	F23:	U.S. Coast Guard
157.200	F24:	Marine Phone (Ship/Shore only—Coast Rx on 161.800)
157.250	F25:	Marine Phone (Ship/Shore only—Coast Rx on 161.850)
157.300	F26:	Marine Phone (Ship/Shore only—Coast Rx on 161.900)
157.350	F27:	Marine Phone (Ship/Shore only—Coast Rx on 161.950)
157.400	F28:	Marine Phone (Ship/Shore only—Coast Rx on 162.000)
156.275	F65:	Port Operations
156.325	F66:	Port Operations
156.375	F67:	Commercial (Ship/Ship only)
156.425	F68:	Non-Commercial
156.475	F69:	Non-Commercial (Ship/Shore only)
156.525	F70:	Non-Commercial (Ship/Ship only)
156.575	F71:	Non-Commercial (Ship/Shore only)
156.625	F72:	Non-Commercial (Ship/Ship only)
156.675	F73:	Port Operations
156.725	F74:	Port Operations
156.875	F77:	Commercial / Oil Tankers (Ship/Ship only)
156.925	F78:	Non-Commercial (Ship/Shore only)
156.975	F79:	Commercial
157.025	F80:	Commercial
157.075	F81:	U.S. Coast Guard
157.125	F82:	U.S. Coast Guard
157.175	F83:	U.S. Coast Guard Auxiliary
157.225	F84:	Marine Phone (Ship/Shore only—Coast Rx on 161.825)
157.275	F85:	Marine Phone (Ship/Shore only—Coast Rx on 161.875)
157.325	F86:	Marine Phone (Ship/Shore only—Coast Rx on 161.925)
157.375	F87:	Marine Phone (Ship/Shore only—Coast Rx on 161.975)
157.425	F88:	Commercial (Ship/Ship only)

IMPORTANT TAXICAB FREQUENCY NOTES

The frequencies listed in the taxi section are for the base only if the cab companies operate between 152.270 and 152.465. The mobile channels for each company cab are listed below. To determine the mobile channel for 452MHZ cabs, simply add 5MHz.

152.270B/157.530M // 152.285B/157.545M // 152.300B/157.560M
152.315B/157.575M // 152.330B/157.590M // 152.345B/157.605M
152.360B 157.620M // 152.375B/157.635M // 152.390B/157.650M
152.450B/157.665M // 152.420B/157.680M // 152.435B/157.695M
152.450B 157.710M // 152.465B/157.725M // (B=Base / M=Mobile)

IMPORTANT BUSINESS SECTION NOTES

"Trunked" radio systems in the 800MHz band are now being utilized and only some of these frequencies are included in the business section due to the difficulty in their listening and their listing (multiple channels are shared between many businesses and they are constantly alternating frequencies)...College frequencies listed included Campus Police as well as buildings and grounds, escort services, etc....The major ambulance frequencies are included in the County Listings - Private and hospital ambulance as well as security, paging and administration freqs are found in the business section - Hospital paging frequencies: 35.640/35.680/43.680/ 152.0075/157.450/157.470/163.250 as well as the following (which are also business paging frequencies): 157.740/154.625/158.460/ 152.480/465.000/462.750-.900...Listings "0.0000" in the Communications Section are radio companies with ability to operate on all frequencies....Mobile only frequencies include 154.570/154.600, and frequencies listed with a 4 number - 2 letter call sign.

Special Agencies

463.3250 AFSCME	(Washington DC)	KNBT886
151.6250 Ameri. Psychiatric	(Washington DC)	
464.5000 Ameri. Public Transit	(Washington DC)	
461.8500 Ameri. Traffic Control	(Falls Church VA)	WSC348
154.5400 Anne Arundel Alarmers	(Glen Burnie MD)	
151.8950 Arlex Association	(Arlington VA)	WSG581
464.4500 Arlington Soccor Asc.	(McLean VA)	KNBY680
151.7550 Army Distaff Hall	(Washington DC)	KAK411
462.7500 Asbury Methodist Home	(Gaithersburg MD)	WYT757
464.0500 Baltimore Auto Recover	(Towson MD)	WQM816
154.5150 Baltimore Goodwill	(Arbutus MD)	KUC452
464.6375 Baltimore Orioles	(Baltimore MD)	
154.5150 Bible Speaks	(Baltimore MD)	WYS348
154.5150 B'nai Israel Congrega.	(Rockville MD)	KDH225
154.5400 Boy Scouts of America	(Rockville MD)	KBU298
151.6250 Brotherhood Rail/Air	(Rockville MD)	
462.1250 Burke Center Conserva.	(Arlington VA)	WQL435
466.7000 C R Amusements	(Seaford DE)	WBZ681
461.7000 C R Amusements	(Smithvile MD)	KBN386
464.3500 CBS Snow Removal	(McLean VA)	WYH605
461.6750 Capitol Center	(Washington DC)	
151.6850 Capitol Ctr.-Food Ops.	(Landover MD)	
151.8950 Capitol Ctr.-Sec/Maint	(Landover MD)	
467.8000 Capitol's Hockey Team	(Landover MD)	
151.8350 Carroll Collection	(Westminster MD)	KGP999
464.6500 Carroll Co. Seniors	(Westminster MD)	WXU430
461.9750 Catholic Cemeteries	(Bethesda MD)	KX0260
462.5500 Church of Jesus Christ	(Kensington MD)	KAA9903
462.5500 City of Baltimore	(Baltimore MD)	KAB0381
463.3500 Columbia Amusement	(Towson MD)	KIS452
154.5400 Columbia Country Club	(Chevy Chase MD)	WSM319
464.6750 Commons at Courthouse	(Rockville MD)	WXX842
464.5000 Comm. Workers America	(Washington DC)	
154.5400 Community Action	(Alexandria VA)	KKU769
462.0250 Conditioned Air	(Washington DC)	
465.8000 D.C. Special Olympics	(Washington DC)	
462.1000 Del Mar Va Amusement	(Willards MD)	WXV327
151.8950 Delaware Theatrical	(Camden DE)	WRT726
154.5700 Downtown Jaycees	(Washington DC)	
151.7750 Dundalk Community Co.	(Dundalk MD)	KNCU835
463.3750 Easter Seal Society	(Silver Spring MD)	
152.4800 Eastern Central Dist.	(Hazlettville DE)	WXM503
154.6000 Exhibit Aids	(Arlington VA)	KRB926
464.1500 Exhibit Aids	(Arlington VA)	KRB926
151.7450 Explorers of America	(Hyattsville MD)	KIK257
464.1000 Fair Winds Gun Club	(Chestertown MD)	
151.8050 First State Amusement	(Millsboro DE)	KZG787
461.0625 Folger Library	(Washington DC)	
151.8650 Greater Baltimore	(Baltimore MD)	KG0248
151.9250 Ho Co Retarded Asc.	(West Friends MD)	WXQ428
152.4800 Holy Cross Church	(Hazlettville DE)	WQP4686
154.5150 Holy Sisters	(Silver Spring MD)	WXV560
464.2500 Institute Modern Art	(Arlington VA)	WZR716
464.2500 Institute Modern Art	(Baltimore MD)	WZR716
463.4750 Inter-American Agency	(Baltimore MD)	WQL847
463.6000 International Union	(Baltimore MD)	WRX411
462.6000 Ivy Hill Cemetery	(Alexandria VA)	KAC3885
462.7000 James William Sheriff	(Oxon Hill MD)	KAC5115
157.7400 Jefferson Memorial	(Alexandria VA)	KG0891
463.7750 Jewish Council	(Rockville MD)	
154.5400 Jockey Club	(Washington DC)	
463.5500 K & P Eviction	(Arlington VA)	
851.7125 Kendall Demonstration	(Wheaton MD)	WQP379
35.9200 Laborers Int'l Union	(Midland MD)	KZG552
463.6250 Laborers Int'l Union	(Washington DC)	
151.6850 Laurel Center	(Laurel MD)	WSC420
151.6550 Laurel Race Track	(Laurel MD)	
495.9375 Lloyd Publicity	(Catonsville MD)	KZK589
461.1250 Mackee, Inc.	(Rockville MD)	
461.2500 Mackee, Inc.	(Rockville MD)	
151.7450 Maryland Bail Bonds	(Ocean City MD)	WZF899
463.3250 Maryland Bail Bonds	(Silver Spring MD)	KUE580
463.5500 Maryland Bail Bonds	(Silver Spring MD)	KNFT398
154.6000 Maryland Environ Svc.	(Annapolis MD)	
464.9750 Maryland Hist. Soc.	(Baltimore MD)	
464.2750 Franklin Park Watch	(McLean VA)	
151.6850 Merriweather Post Pav	(Columbia MD)	
461.5875 Merriweather Post Pav	(Columbia MD)	
154.5700 Mid Atlantic Golf	(Glyndon MD)	
154.6000 Mid Atlantic Golf	(Glyndon MD)	
47.5000 Montgomery Retireds	(Silver Spring MD)	
151.6250 Muscular Dystrophy	(Washington DC)	
464.5000 Nat'l Manufacturers	(Washington DC)	
154.6250 National 4-H Council	(Chevy Chase MD)	KSD487
154.5150 National Presbytarian	(Washington DC)	KUS918
464.425B Old Post Office Pav.	(Washington DC)	
464.525M Old Post Office Pav.	(Washington DC)	
151.7450 Pan American Sanitary	(Washington DC)	
151.8950 Park Fairfax Improve	(Alexandria VA)	WXB474
463.9500 Parking Management	(Washington DC)	KRD909
852.2625 Parking Management	(Washington DC)	KNBP732
464.8250 Philips Harborplace	(Baltimore MD)	
852.2625 Philson's Trash	(Washington DC)	KBBV427
464.9750 Pimlico Racetrack	(Baltimore MD)	
154.5400 Potomac Gardens	(Gaithersburg MD)	WS0731
464.4750 Protestant Episcopal	(Alexandria VA)	KSP881
463.2750 Protestant Episcopal	(Washington DC)	WQK715
462.6750 REACT: Metro DC	(Washington DC)	
462.6750 REACT: Herndon Ops.	(Vienna VA)	
462.6750 REACT: E. Baltimore	(Baltimore MD)	
462.6750 REACT: Cascade Team 2	(Pen Mar MD)	KAB6305
462.6000 REACT: Metro DC sec.	(Falls Church VA)	
462.6250 REACT: P.G. County	(Oxon Hill MD)	KAD0393
462.7000 REACT: Metro DC Alt.	(Washington DC)	KAB5269
151.6250 Rouse Co.	(Columbia MD)	
462.6500 SWR Ratcheteers	(Rockville MD)	KAC7389
461.3500 Salon Services	(Washington DC)	
464.1250 Security Auto Rcvry.	(Towson MD)	KMG919
35.0800 Shore Litter, Inc.	(Salisbury MD)	KGG296
496.0625 T.A.A.A.C.	(Annapolis MD)	KZG390
464.0000 The Salvation Army	(Baltimore MD)	KVX359
466.6000 Tidewater Amusement	(Delmar DE)	WDA795
151.6250 Tournament Players	(Bethesda MD)	
499.6375 Town Center Building	(Queenstown MD)	WIE733
461.3500 Traffic Control Maint	(Midland MD)	WYP598
42.9600 Tri State Amusement	(Hagerstown MD)	WYS495
461.4250 United Planning Org.	(Silver Spring MD)	WXR866
151.7150 Village of Cross Key	(Baltimore MD)	KAM7413
151.6250 Washington Cathedral	(Washington DC)	
151.8950 Washington National	(Largo MD)	KNBB901
154.5150 W Baltimore Community	(Baltimore MD)	KXY577
31.6000 Westminster Rotary	(Westminster MD)	KXN819
461.7750 Wicomico Humanitarian	(Eden MD)	KWK231
464.8750 Wild World	(Mitchellville MD)	KNFS220
464.9750 Wild World	(Mitchellville MD)	KNGS220
154.6000 Woodmont Country Club	(Rockville MD)	

BUSINESS UPDATES & CORRECTIONS

SPECIAL AGENCIES

181.000	National Football League	Washington, D.C.	
180.600	National Football League	Baltimore, MD	

HOSPITALS & AMBULANCES

155.160	Alexandria Hospital	Alexandria, VA	
151.655	Allegany Ambulance	Frostburg, MD	
33.080	American Ambulance Service	Georgetown, DEL	
47.580	American Amb & Oxygen Service	Baltimore, MD	
33.080	American Legion Ambulance Service 8	Georgetown, DEL	KOE419
155.280	Broadcreek Medical Services	Bethel, DEL	KNGN384
155.205	Cochran Equipment Company	Middletown, DEL	KAX278
154.540	Columbia Hospital	Washington, D.C.	
155.205	Delaware Ambulance Service	Wilmington, DEL	KNAI395
155.175	George's Creek Ambulance Service	Lanaconing, MD	KNIB800
462.175	Huntemann Ambulance	Washington, D.C.	
155.220	Medical Transport Service	Newark, DEL	
155.220	New Castle Medical Society	Wilmington, DEL	
453.0125M	American Red Cross	Washington, D.C.	KB21192
155.400	St Francis Hospital	Wilmington, DEL	
453.125	Washington County Hospital	Hagerstown, MD	KNIY604
155.280	Wilmington Medical Center	Wilmington, DEL	

SECURITY & DETECTIVE

464.125	Eagle Security	Gaithersburg, MD	
460.975	Wells Fargo	Washington, D.C.	

MALLS & STORES

464.475	Commons at Courthouse	Rockville, MD	
462.000	Montgomery Ward	Silver Spring, MD	
151.805	Salisbury Mall Associates	Salisbury, MD	
151.925	Beltway Mall	Greenbelt, MD	
151.895	Capital Plaza	Landover, MD	
151.625	Prince George's Plaza	Hyattsville, MD	
464.675	Hunt Valley Mall	Cockeysville, MD	KNBE658
151.995	Montgomery Mall Security F1	Rockville, MD	
151.775	Montgomery Mall Security F2	Rockville, MD	
464.325	Tysons Corner Mall	McLean, VA	

HOTELS & INNS

154.540	Columbia Country Club	Chevy Chase, MD	WSM319
35.060	Marriott Corporation	Arlington, VA	KXI509
151.625	Marriot Corporation	Washington, D.C.	

SCHOOLS

47.500	Alexander School	Silver Spring, MD	
155.235	Indian Creek School	Crownsville, MD	

PROPERTY MANAGEMENT

31.160	Watergate West	Washington, D.C.	KO9121
151.775	Watergate Improvement	Washington, D.C.	KRF857
154.540	Promenade	Bethesda, MD	

COLLEGES

462.650	George Mason University	Fairfax, VA	

UTILITIES

451.325	Chesapeake & Potomac: Maintenance	Baltimore, MD	
153.080	Western Electric	Baltimore, MD	
153.905	Washington Suburban Sanitary Comm.	Washington, D.C.	KV2262

Washington Suburban Sanitary Commission: Radio Codes

01	On Duty	06	Talk Slowly	11	No Messages
02	Off Duty	07	Acknowledge	12	Time Check
03	Radio Test	08	Repeat	13	Request Materials
04	Receive Poorly	09	Weather		
05	Receive Well	10	Any Messages?	99	EMERGENCY

TRANSPORTATION

462.700	Air Lines Pilots Association	Washington, D.C.	KAD3772
464.675	Avis Rent-A-Car	Washington, D.C.	WYN514
464.450	B.P. Auto Rental	McLean, VA	KNBQ920
464.325	National Car Rental	Washington, D.C.	KNAY511
461.950	Thrifty Rent-A-Car	Washington, D.C.	KNQY418

TAXIS

853.4375	Barwood Cab F1: Bethesda Dispatch	Bethesda, MD
854.4375	Barwood Cab F2: Wheaton Dispatch	Bethesda, MD
855.4375	Barwood Cab F3: Delivery Service	Bethesda, MD
157.620M	Dial Cab (mobiles)	Washington, D.C.
157.530M	Silver Spring Taxi (mobiles)	Silver Spring, MD
157.590M	Takoma-Langley Taxi (mobiles)	Silver Spring, MD
157.680M	Weaver Cab (mobiles)	Silver Spring, MD

TOWING

462.025	Columbia Road Exxon	Silver Spring, MD
468.250	Montgomery Mall Texaco	Rockville, MD
461.100	Professional Towing	Silver Spring, MD
463.975	Schwartz & Bowie Towing	Rockville, MD

AMERICAN AUTOMOBILE ASSOCIATION

150.905	Washington, D.C.	UNITS 01-09
150.965	Montg. Co., MD - lower	UNITS 10-20
452.600	Montg. Co., MD - upper	UNITS 21-30
452.525	P.G. Co., MD	UNITS 40-49
452.575	Northern Virginia	UNITS 50-69
452.550	Northern Virginia	UNITS 50-69
150.950	Common to all except Montg. Co., MD	

TRUCKING

496.2125	Area Wide Delivery	Washington, D.C.
159.990	Call-A-Messenger	Washington, D.C.

MOBIL PHONES: RCC & PAGING

451.325	AT&T	Washington, D.C.

COMMUNICATIONS

151.625	Motorola, Inc.	Washington, D.C.
851.4875	RCA Corporation	Baileys Crossroads, VA
461.125	RCA Corporation	College Park, MD
461.250	RCA Corporation	Richmond, VA
461.975	RCA Corporation	College Park, VA
462.125	RCA Corporation	Alexandria, VA

Hospitals & Ambulances

Freq	Name	Location	Call
151.7150	Alexandria Hospital	(Alexandria VA)	
155.3400	Alexandria Hospital	(Alexandria VA)	KQM661
462.7500	Alexandria Hospital	(Alexandria VA)	WXB460
461.5500	Alexandria Medical	(Arlington VA)	KKN901
155.2800	Allegany County	(Cumberland MD)	KVI526-8
155.3800	Allegany County	(Cumberland MD)	KAB226
155.2800	Allegany County	(Frostburg MD)	KVF504
155.3550	Allegany Memorial	(Cumberland MD)	
463.3500	American Medical Lab	(McLean VA)	KYK988
152.4800	Andreas Rauer MD	(Hazlettville DE)	WQD644
816.9875	Animal Welfare League	(Arlington VA)	
152.4800	Ann Webb MD	(Easton MD)	WRN407
155.2200	Annapolis Emergency	(Annapolis MD)	KWX598
453.1250	Anne Arundel General	(Anne Arundel MD)	WXP320
152.0075	Arlington Hospital	(Arlington VA)	KQR348
152.0075	Arlington Hospital	(Arlington VA)	WRL827
155.2200	Arlington Hospital	(Arlington VA)	KQR348
154.5400	Associated Radiological	(Hagerstown MD)	WYV757
155.4000	BEEB Hospital	(Lewes DE)	KNGA800
35.6800	Baltimore County General	(Randallstown MD)	KQF735
158.4600	Baltimore County General	(Randallstown MD)	KNBH227
155.2800	Baltimore Sinai Hospital	(Baltimore MD)	
464.9250	Baltimore Sinai Hospital	(Baltimore MD)	
157.7400	Bon Secour Hospital	(Baltimore MD)	KNBN734
47.5000	Bond Street Vet	(Westminster MD)	KGC867
46.0000	Capitol Ambulatory	(Dover DE)	WZM980
35.6800	Capitol Hill Hospital	(Washington DC)	KTK951
155.1600	Capitol Hill Hospital	(Washington DC)	KQR447
155.3400	Capitol Hill Hospital	(Washington DC)	KWF688
463.3250	Cardoza Health Clinic	(Washington DC)	KNCA204
35.6400	Carroll County General	(Westminster MD)	WRB436
155.2800	Carroll County Medical	(Westminster MD)	KXE547
163.2500	Carroll County Medical	(Westminster MD)	KGW662
33.0800	Carroll County Vet	(Westminster MD)	KVN481
155.2050	Carroll Manor	(Hyattsville MD)	
154.5400	Catoctin Veterinary	(Leesburg VA)	KSC372
47.5000	Centers for Handicapped	(Silver Spring MD)	KSJ510
151.6850	Chestertown Animal Hospital	(Chestertown MD)	KNCL911
33.0400	Chevy Chase Rescue	(Bethesda MD)	
155.2200	Children's Hospital	(Baltimore MD)	WSZ319
155.2200	Children's Hospital	(Washington DC)	KWJ303
155.2800	Children's Hospital	(Washington DC)	KNFQ334
155.2350	Chimes	(Baltimore MD)	KZJ953
157.4500	Church Hospital	(Baltimore MD)	WQL711
155.1600	Church Hospital	(Baltimore MD)	
152.2200	Columbia Hospital	(Washington DC)	KQM659
157.4500	Columbia Hospital	(Washington DC)	KQM659
464.5250	Commonwealth Hospital	(Fairfax VA)	KNBV717
155.2650	Commonwealth of Maryland	(Baltimore MD)	KUQ682
151.6550	Community Group Health	(Washington DC)	KZK732
464.7250	Companion Animal Hospital	(Cooksville MD)	KNS806
154.6000	Constant Care Health Center	(Baltimore MD)	
47.6600	Countryside Animal Hospital	(Mountain Lake MD)	KIN600
464.2750	D C M Ambulance	(Arlington VA)	KCH649
155.2950	Dickey County Memorial	(Ellendale MD)	KBP842
163.2500	Dickey County Memorial	(Ellendale MD)	KBP842
33.0600	District of Columbia	(Washington DC)	KGA842
155.1600	District of Columbia	(Washington DC)	KTH398
155.2500	District of Columbia	(Washington DC)	KLG615
461.9000	Doctor's Bag	(Wilmington DE)	
155.2200	Doctor's Hospital	(Lanham MD)	KEC410
163.2500	Doctor's Hospital	(Lanham MD)	KEC410
152.4800	Doctor's Hospital	(Washington DC)	WXU991
152.4800	Dorchester General	(Cambridge MD)	KNAZ799
154.5400	Dr. Amarillo	(Hagerstown MD)	WYU515
152.4800	Dr. Basilio Bautista	(Hazlettville DE)	WQU202
45.9600	Dr. Fowble	(Timonium MD)	KYG510
152.4800	Dr. Leslie Robinson	(Hazlettville DE)	WXV572
464.8500	Dr. RJ Wilson	(Rockville MD)	KNAZ914
464.8500	Dr. Robert Wilson	(Gaithersburg MD)	KNAZ914
35.1200	Dr. Rokus -Veterinarian	(Leesburg VA)	KMM266
152.4800	Dr. Zaragona	(Hazlettville DE)	WRK885
152.4800	Drs. Mroz & Bengzon	(Hazlettville DE)	WYQ399
462.1000	Eastern Medical Specialists	(Towson MD)	KNBG522
155.2650	Eastern Shore Hospital	(Cambridge MD)	KZO326
47.4600	Eastport VFD	(Annapolis MD)	KJB939
460.5250	Fairfax County	(Falls Church VA)	KXU359
460.5500	Fairfax County	(Falls Church VA)	KXU359
35.6400	Fairfax Hospital	(Falls Church VA)	KRZ906
154.5400	Fairfax Hospital Assn.	(Falls Church VA)	WYW268
152.0075	Fallston General	(Fallston MD)	WYC666
453.0750	Franklin Square Hospital	(Baltimore MD)	WSU296
155.4000	Franklin Square Hospital	(Baltimore MD)	
155.4000	Franklin Square Hospital	(Baltimore MD)	
462.9000	Frederick Memorial	(Frederick MD)	KNCL266
151.7750	Frederick Memorial Hospital	(Frederick MD)	KRK727
33.0400	Frederick Peterson	(Sparks MD)	KSP219
155.1600	Frostburg Area Ambulance	(Frostburg MD)	WSV456
45.9600	G. Wade Compton	(Port Tabaco MD)	
155.2800	Garrett County	(Garrett County MD)	KBP682
37.9000	Garrett County Memorial	(Oakland MD)	KGF872
155.2050	George Washington Univ. Hosp.	(Washington DC)	
163.2500	Georgetown University Hospital	(Washington DC)	KVP791
47.5400	Glade Valley Animal Hospital	(Frederick MD)	KGC370
463.2000	Go-Ambulance Systems	(Baltimore MD)	WRO715
158.4600	Good Samaritan Hospital	(Baltimore MD)	WSU208
154.5700	Good Samaritan Hospital	(Baltimore MD)	
158.4600	Good Samaritan Hospital	(Baltimore MD)	
151.8650	Greater Baltimore Med Center	(Baltimore MD)	
157.4500	Greater Baltimore Memorial	(Baltimore MD)	KNBX249
155.2200	Greater Southeast	(Washington DC)	KWV669
157.4500	Greater Southeast	(Washington DC)	KWV669
154.5400	Gynecology-Obstetrics	(Hagerstown MD)	WYX858
154.5400	Hagerstown Eye Specialists	(Hagerstown MD)	WYY688
154.5400	Hagerstown Surgical	(Hagerstown MD)	WYR355
163.2500	Harford Memorial	(Havre de Grace MD)	KVV926
155.4000	Harford Memorial	(Havre de Grace MD)	KNBT906
155.4000	Holy Cross Hospital	(Silver Spring MD)	KVF708
465.0000	Holy Cross Hospital	(Silver Spring MD)	WXG675
157.4500	Hospital Commission	(Cheverly MD)	WSY256
35.9000	Hospital for Mentally Ill	(Georgetown DE)	WYY769
47.6600	Howard Baker	(Hagerstown MD)	KCK301
155.4000	Howard County General	(Columbia MD)	WQX246
163.2500	Howard University Hospital	(Bethesda MD)	KLX858
155.2800	Howard University Hospital	(Washington DC)	KLX858
163.2500	Howard University Hospital	(Washington DC)	KLX858
463.8000	Huntmann Ambulance	(Washington DC)	KQR300
463.3250	Ironsides Medical Transport	(Silver Spring MD)	KES793
47.6600	Irvin Frock	(Reisterstown M)	KGD483
155.2800	Jensco	(Baltimore MD)	KZF976
163.2500	Johns Hopkins Hospital	(Baltimore MD)	KLL620
461.7750	Johns Hopkins Hospital	(Baltimore MD)	WXJ233
151.8950	Johns Hopkins Hospital	(Baltimore MD)	

155.4000 Johns Hopkins Hospital	(Baltimore MD)	
495.9125 Katzen Eye Group	(Baltimore MD)	
462.7750 Kent General Hospital	(Dover DE)	
33.0400 Kent Queen Annes	(Chestertown MD)	KEV440
155.2950 Keswick Home	(Baltimore MD)	KGU436
33.0200 Laurel Volunteer Rescue	(Laurel MD)	KGD400
155.1750 Leland Memorial Hospital	(Riverdale MD)	WRG852
157.4500 Leland Memorial Hospital	(Riverdale MD)	WRG852
47.5800 Leroy Manlove	(Elkton MD)	KNBT448
46.0400 Louden County Volunteer	(Leesburg VA)	
152.0075 Louden Memorial	(Leesburg VA)	WQD226
155.4000 Louden Memorial Hospital	(Leesburg VA)	KUN586
461.3750 Loudoun Memorial	(Leesburg VA)	
35.0600 Maple Springs Veterinary	(Rockville MD)	KZH211
155.2200 Maryland General	(Baltimore MD)	KXF717
152.0075 Maryland General Hospital	(Baltimore MD)	KXF717
462.0000 Maryland Medical Lab	(Silver Spring MD)	KKR757
461.2000 Maryland Medical Labs	(Towson MD)	KBT507
496.6875 Maryland S.P.C.A.	(Baltimore MD)	KNS732
47.6600 McClellan Veterinary	(Frederick MD)	
35.1000 McDonald Ambulance	(Cumberland MD)	KZJ298
155.2950 Medi-Care	(Baltimore MD)	KNAD271
464.9500 Medic-Trans	(Waldorf MD)	KNBZ259
462.7250 Medical Service Systems	(Baltimore MD)	KAC8492
31.2400 Medical Transport	(Frederick MD)	KNAY265
152.4800 Medical Transport Svc.	(Hazlettville DE)	WXG768
33.1000 Memorial Hospital	(Easton MD)	KGX406
155.4000 Memorial Hospital	(Easton MD)	KFA555
47.5400 Metropolitan Ambulance	(Glen Burnie MD)	KGC911
163.2500 Milford Memorial Hospital	(Milford DE)	
163.2500 Milford Memorial Hospital	(Milford DE)	KQS641
37.9000 Milford Memorial Hospital	(Milford DE)	KQ5641
155.2650 Montecello Hospital Center	(Baltimore MD)	
154.5150 Montgomery County General	(Olney MD)	
152.2200 Mount Vernon Hospital	(Alexandria VA)	KCE605
155.1600 Mount Vernon Hospital	(Fairfax VA)	
47.5400 Mountain Top Vet Center	(Garrett County MD)	
37.9000 Nanticoke Memorial Hospital	(Seaford DE)	KRT709
152.4800 Nanticoke Memorial Hospital	(Seaford DE)	WYE978
155.3400 National Orthopedic	(Arlington VA)	KJX247
155.1600 North Arundel Hospital	(Arlington VA)	
157.4500 North Arundel Hospital	(Glen Burnie MD)	KVN478
163.2500 North Charles General	(Baltimore MD)	WXP336
155.2950 Northern Virginia Ambulance	(Alexandria VA)	
155.2200 Ocean City Ambulance	(Ocean City MD)	KUE565
35.0600 Peachtree Veterinary	(Beallsville MD)	KNFA872
155.2950 Peninsula General Hospital	(Salisbury MD)	KWV469
163.2500 Peninsula General Hospital	(Salisbury MD)	KWV469
155.1600 Prince George's General	(Cheverly MD)	
43.6800 Prince William Hospital	(Manassas VA)	KRI640
155.1600 Prince William Hospital	(Manassas VA)	KRI640
33.1000 Professional Ambulance	(Falls Church VA)	KKD680
155.2950 Providence Center	(Annapolis MD)	KNCE721
37.9800 Providence Hospital	(Washington DC)	KLJ280
155.1600 Providence Hospital	(Washington DC)	KLR351
158.4600 Providence Hospital	(Washington DC)	KQI207
163.2500 Provident Hospital	(Baltimore MD)	WYG261
152.4800 R C Davison MD	(Hazlettville DE)	WQU636
461.3500 R.E. Olsen DVM	(Frederick MD)	WSH641
47.4200 Red Cross	(Pikesville MD)	WRX842
47.4200 Red Cross	(Rockville MD)	
47.6200 Red Cross	(Rockville MD)	
47.4200 Red Cross	(Salisbury MD)	WZU308
462.9375 Red Cross	(Washington DC)	
47.4200 Red Cross	(Washington DC)	KGC525
47.6600 Reistertown Veterinary	(Reistertown MD)	
47.4600 Robert Mouser DVM	(Clifton VA)	KBT788
47.6600 Roger Olsen	(Frederick MD)	KGE980
155.3250 Sacred Heart Hospital	(Cumberland MD)	
152.3600 Sacred Heart Hospital	(Cumberland MD)	KVI525
34.6800 Shady Grove Adventist	(Rockville MD)	WRG556
464.4750 Shady Grove Adventist	(Rockville MD)	WRD264
157.4500 Sheppard & Enoch	(Towson MD)	WYX505
155.2800 Sibley Memorial	(Washington DC)	KQR356
33.0800 Sibley Memorial	(Washington DC)	KQS640
33.1600 Silver Spring Ambulance	(Takoma Park MD)	KYS416
495.9625 Silver Spring Ambulance	(Washington DC)	
453.1750 South Baltimore General	(Baltimore MD)	WSU299
155.2800 South Baltimore General	(Baltimore MD)	
37.9800 South Garrett County Rescue	(Garrett County MD)	
35.6800 Southern Maryland Hospital	(Clinton MD)	KMK737
33.1000 Springfield Hospital	(Sykesville MD)	KSS995
47.5000 Squire Veterinary	(Upper Marlboro MD)	KVV653
461.3000 Squire Veterinary	(Waldorf MD)	WQL712
155.1600 St. Agnes Hospital	(Baltimore MD)	KVZ540
453.0250 St. Agnes Hospital	(Baltimore MD)	WSU298
155.2650 St. Elizabeth Hospital	(Washington DC)	
155.4000 St. Joseph Hospital	(Towson MD)	KNBG333
152.0075 St. Joseph Hospital	(Towson MD)	KNBG333
155.2650 St. Mary's Hospital	(Leonardtown MD)	
151.8050 St. Mary's Hospital	(Leonardtown MD)	
155.2650 State of Maryland	(Cumberland MD)	WXF737

155.2800 Suburban Hospital	(Bethesda MD)	KWO636
47.5000 Suburban Vet Med Center	(Damascus MD)	
154.5400 Surgical Associates	(Hagerstown MD)	WYV900
157.4500 Taylor Manor Hospital	(Ellicott City MD)	WSL447
47.5000 Thelma Sherbert	(North Beach MD)	KGH307
47.5800 Town & Country Animal Clinic	(Olney MD)	KGD657
152.4800 Union Hospital	(Elkton MD)	KCF914
155.2800 Union Memorial	(Baltimore MD)	
152.0075 Union Memorial Hospital	(Baltimore MD)	KGW332
154.5150 Union Memorial Hospital	(Baltimore MD)	KXT733
47.4600 Walter Hastings	(Cambridge MD)	KGB359
157.4500 Washington Adventist	(Takoma Park MD)	KQN717
155.1600 Washington County	(Hagerstown MD)	KEY840
155.2800 Washington County	(Hagerstown MD)	KWM633-5
155.4000 Washington County	(Hagerstown MD)	KWI762
123.0500 Washington Hospital	(Washington DC)	WHR8
462.7500 Washington Hospital	(Washington DC)	KWM483
151.9550 Washington Hospital	(Washington DC)	
816.9875 Washington Humne Society	(Washington DC)	
35.6400 Washington Sanitarium	(Takoma Park MD)	KUV615
157.7400 Washington Sanitarium	(Takoma Park MD)	KRD505
462.6250 Wheaton Volunteer	(Wheaton MD)	KAB1720
462.6500 Wheaton Volunteer	(Wheaton MD)	

Security & Detective

851.1125 A B C Security	(Birdville MD)	KRX751
460.9500 A D T Alarms	(Baltimore MD)	KNCV690
464.7500 A1 Lock & Safe	(Arlington VA)	WXQ818
496.9375 ABC Fire Protection	(Falls Church VA)	KB2300
151.7450 ABC Security	(Annapolis MD)	KFQ412
154.5700 ADT Alarms	(Baltimore MD)	
460.9500 ADT Alarms	(Washington DC)	KGG395
463.3500 ADT Alarms	(Washington DC)	
461.9000 Accurate Security	(Wilmington DE)	
495.9625 Action Investigation	(Falls Church VA)	KNO227
151.6250 Action Investigative	(Alexandria VA)	
498.9625 Action Investigative	(Alexandria VA)	WIB287
464.4500 Action Investigative	(McLean VA)	KNFA805
464.8500 Action Lock & Door	(Rockville MD)	WSX787
463.5500 Action Security	(Arlington VA)	KNBD313
461.4000 Admiral Security	(Washington DC)	KRF285
461.6750 Admiral Security	(Washington DC)	WZE245
460.9250 Alarm Specialists	(Silver Spring MD)	
461.3750 Alarm Systems	(Oxon Hill MD)	
463.2250 Alarmsmith	(Waldorf MD)	KNCM431
154.5150 Albert Detective	(Glen Burnie MD)	KWK692
463.8250 Alexandria Alarm	(Falls Church vA)	KNAT760
851.7875 Allied Safe & Lock	(Falls Church VA)	WQA432
151.6250 Allied Security	(Frederick MD)	
463.4250 Allied Security	(Silver Spring MD)	KSU358
151.7150 Allstate Alarm	(Glen Burnie MD)	KNBR630
464.6250 American Security	(Silver Spring MD)	KNCL555
463.9000 Annapolis Lock & Key	(Birdville MD)	KNBL728
154.5400 Anne Arundel Alarm	(Glen Burnie MD)	KXF298
463.3250 Apollo Detective	(Washington DC)	
462.0750 Apollo Detective	(Wheaton MD)	KNFC730
851.7875 Approved Fire Protection	(Falls Church VA)	WQP424
154.5150 Area Safe & Lock	(Alexandria VA)	KKD602
463.4000 Armstrong Prof. Security	(Washington DC)	WXX849
461.5500 Atlantic Security	(Alexandria VA)	WXE210
461.5500 Atlantic Security	(Alexandria VA)	WXV539
461.5500 Atlantic Security	(Arlington VA)	WXE211
463.8750 Atlas Guard	(Washington DC)	WQL612
460.9750 Baker Protective	(Arlington VA)	KAR525
460.9750 Baker Protective	(Cantonsville MD)	KYT696
460.9750 Baker Protective	(Washington DC)	WCH26
464.4250 Baker Protective	(Woodlawn MD)	
464.7500 Baldinos Lock & Key	(Arlington VA)	KQT269
461.1500 Beltway Alarm	(Bethesda MD)	WRT849
461.0250 Betco Security	(Wheaton MD)	WRV736
463.5250 Bob's Locksmith	(Midland MD)	WST436
35.9400 Bomarc Investigative	(Salisbury MD)	KNA0915
154.5400 Boone Investigative	(Frederick MD)	WXK448
44.4000 Brinks	(Bethesda MD)	KJK651
159.4950 Brinks	(Bethesda MD)	
463.3750 Burns Security	(Rockville MD)	
464.1250 Burns Security	(Towson MD)	
461.6750 Burns Security	(Washington DC)	KLW691
468.9750 Burns, Inc.	(Georgetown DE)	WCA618
463.9750 Burns, Inc.	(Hillsboro DE)	KCG956
151.6250 CES Security	(Baltimore MD)	
461.6750 Capitol Center	(Washington DC)	
462.1500 Carl Mark Security	(Falls Church VA)	KNCD819
151.7150 Carolina Security	(Arlington VA)	WXG996
461.1250 Central Investigation	(Falls Church VA)	KUW424
461.1250 Central Investigative	(McLean VA)	KUW423
461.1250 Century Investigation	(Baltimore MD)	WZE964
495.9125 Century Investigation	(Baltimore MD)	KNO617

Freq	Name	Location	Call
461.6750	Colorado Security	(Washington DC)	KNAY395
151.8650	Confidential Service	(Lewes DE)	WXX877
461.5750	Construction Security	(Arlington VA)	KNCT968
464.9000	Crest Lock Co.	(Towson MD)	KNBX367
463.3750	Crime Control	(Rockville MD)	KZM309
464.1250	Crime Control	(Towson MD)	KZM310
468.3750	Crime Control, Inc.	(Pikesville MD)	WBN644
461.2000	Custom Security	(Hagerstown MD)	WSB403
461.1000	Del Mar Va Safe & Lock	(Ocean City MD)	WRO522
151.8950	Dennis Detective	(Severna Park MD)	KTR361
159.8250	Dunbar Armored	(Washington DC)	
464.0750	Eagle Security	(Silver Spring MD)	WQV677
35.7000	East Coast Investigative	(Baltimore MD)	KEJ650
463.3000	Easters Lock & Key	(Baltimore MD)	KNCF568
461.7750	Eccles Security	(Silver Spring MD)	WRE705
463.9500	Econ Alarm	(Towson MD)	WRK353
461.9500	Efec Security	(Washington DC)	KNAY544
154.5700	Electrical Security	(Washington DC)	KT3459
461.0000	Electro Protective	(Rockville MD)	KIQ242
461.0000	Electro Protective	(Towson MD)	KNAO656
464.2000	Empior Security	(Washington DC)	
464.8500	Equitable Investigative	(Rockville MD)	KNBC457
159.8250	Federal Armored	(Baltimore MD)	KAS451
159.8250	Federal Armored	(Fairfax VA)	KXZ295
159.8250	Federal Armored	(Washington DC)	KGQ227
461.0500	General Alarm	(Baltimore MD)	
463.9500	Gilbert Security	(Falls Church VA)	
463.9500	Glessner Protective	(Hagerstown MD)	KQJ417
851.1625	Globe Security	(Baltimore MD)	WXV874
151.7750	Green Investigation	(Hampstead MD)	KTP216
151.7750	Green Investigation	(Towson MD)	KTP216
462.1000	Guardian Security	(Washington DC)	KZQ205
154.6000	Guardian Security	(Washington DC)	
461.0250	H & H Security	(Wheaton MD)	WYK540
461.4000	H&H Investigators	(Washington DC)	
154.6000	Halifax Security	(Washington DC)	KNY456
495.6625	Hank's Lock & Key	(Laurel MD)	KNS518
464.0500	Harris Fire Protection	(Towson MD)	WRS500
462.0250	Hill's Capitol Security	(Washington DC)	KNM456
463.6000	Hill's Capitol Security	(Washington DC)	
496.6875	Home Security Svc.	(Falls Church VA)	KNQ437
460.9250	Honeywell Alarms	(Arlington VA)	KZE913
154.6000	Honor Guard Security	(Rockville MD)	
151.8050	Howard Security	(Baltimore MD)	KWU849
461.9750	Howard Security	(Bethesda MD)	KCG422
461.8750	Howard Security	(Cantonsville MD)	KCG422
466.1750	Industrial Security	(Cambridge MD)	WCX557
461.1750	Industrial Security	(Smithville MD)	KKS650
463.8500	Intelligence Research	(Silver Spring MD)	WQE294
469.3750	International Security	(Arlington VA)	
464.1750	Intersec	(Washington DC)	KVL441
464.8750	Interstate Intelligence	(Washington DC)	KLB399
464.8500	Intntnl. Investigative	(Rockville MD)	KNBD616
464.2500	Investigations, Inc.	(Arlington VA)	KAD581
463.4500	K-9 Sentries	(Washington DC)	KNB836
461.8000	Kastle Security	(Washington DC)	KKX429
461.6500	King Investigative	(Arlington VA)	KNAW397
151.6550	Laurel Race Track	(Laurel MD)	
463.4250	Leonard Security	(Silver Spring MD)	WYU334
151.6550	Lermens Lock & Safe	(Gambrills MD)	WRP318
461.4250	Liberty Detective	(Baltimore MD)	KCN378
464.3000	Liberty Security	(Baltimore MD)	WYD493
464.3000	Liberty Security	(Baltimore MD)	WZM785
464.3000	Liberty Security	(Chevy Chase MD)	WZM784
35.8000	Lloyd Detective	(Baltimore MD)	WYK859
151.8350	Lock & Key Service	(Camp Springs MD)	WSK231
151.8650	Lock Out Alarm Systems	(Glen Burnie MD)	
498.7125	Locks Unlimited	(Falls Church VA)	WXJ926
43.0000	M S Investigative	(Randallstown MD)	KOI839
460.9250	Marriott Security Systems	(Arlington VA)	
35.1800	Marva Pen Alarm	(Hagerstown MD)	WXM925
463.6000	Marybipp Security	(Baltimore MD)	
495.5625	Maryland Capitol Security	(Silver Spring MD)	KB5652
460.9250	Master Alarm	(Baltimore MD)	KTB631
461.1000	McCracken Security	(Silver Spring MD)	
463.5000	Metro Detective	(Washington DC)	
463.6500	Metro Intl. Investigating	(Cantonsville MD)	KNBR6478
463.9500	Metro Protective	(Washington DC)	WYF770
463.6250	Metropolis Detective	(Bethesda MD)	KST293
463.5000	Metropolitan Detective	(Washington DC)	KAY772
495.7125	Miller Protective Svcs.	(Arlington VA)	KGE530
464.7500	Montgomery Cnty. Investigative	(Silver Spring MD)	
464.5750	Montgomery County	(Germantown MD)	KNBC719
464.6250	Naitonal Security	(Washington DC)	
35.1200	National Detective	(Baltimore MD)	KGG306
464.6250	National Detective	(Washington DC)	KAR374
151.6850	National Protective	(Alexandria VA)	WRJ980
461.6750	National Safe & Lock	(Washington DC)	KST291
151.9550	National Security	(Washington DC)	
461.0750	Northern Security	(Falls Church VA)	WRK747
495.7625	Pinkertons	(Falls Church VA)	KNT220
31.2000	Pinkertons	(Washington DC)	KTD740
461.9000	Pinkertons	(Washington DC)	KNBF733
154.5700	Pinkertons	(Washington DC)	
31.2400	Pinkertons	(Washington DC)	
461.1000	Pittman Detective	(Silver Spring MD)	KKN515
151.7750	Professional Lockmaster	(Derwood MD)	WXA396
462.5500	Protection Service	(Arlington VA)	KAB0984
463.6500	Protection Services	(Midland MD)	WZL406
461.2000	Protection Services	(Williamsburg MD)	WYV791
151.6250	Protective Security	(Washington DC)	KA39109
151.7750	Public Security	(Towson MD)	WRI413
160.1400	Purolator Armored	(Baltimore MD)	KGG245
160.1400	Purolator Armored	(Oxon Hill MD)	KIU589
151.7450	RM Security	(Ocean City MD)	WZQ303
496.1125	Rampart Security	(Rockville MD)	KW7932
496.1125	Rampart Security	(Silver Spring MD)	KZG391
461.9000	Rankin Security	(Washington DC)	WSN711
466.5250	Resorts Investigation	(Oak Orchard DE)	KNAZ383
462.1235	Revels Security	(Arlington VA)	WSX337
463.8250	Rollins Lock & Key	(Falls Church VA)	WQV295
496.7125	Rose Lock & Safe	(Annapolis MD)	
461.0750	Rosedale Lock & Key	(Baltimore MD)	WRL225
463.4000	S & C Security	(Oxon Hill MD)	KNFP976
462.1000	Securiguard	(Silver Spring MD)	KNFN750
461.9750	Security Administration	(Baltimore MD)	KXS784
463.5250	Security Alarm	(Frederick MD)	WRJ237
151.6850	Security Concepts	(Reston VA)	KMH445
461.4500	Security Investigative	(Falls Church VA)	KNCS942
460.9000	Security, Inc.	(Bethesda MD)	KNFP733
462.2500	Security, Inc.	(Bethesda MD)	
460.9000	Security, Inc.	(Washington DC)	KNFP773
464.6250	Setry Detective	(Silver Spring MD)	WSF944
461.4235	Silver Fox Investigating	(Baltimore MD)	WQN673
464.7500	Simmons Investigative	(Arlington VA)	KIW256
151.6550	Simmons Security	(Washington DC)	
154.6000	Sonitrol Security	(Baltimore MD)	WQS620
461.6500	Sonitrol Security	(Baltimore MD)	WQS620
42.9600	Sound & Alarm Svc.	(Hagerstown MD)	WYS492
461.0750	State Side Detective	(Falls Church VA)	WXB696
463.2500	State Wide Security	(Bethesda MD)	WYZ854
495.7125	Stateside Detective	(Falls Church VA)	KNR342
461.0750	Stateside Detective	(Falls Church VA)	
31.2400	Statewide Security	(Washington DC)	KLZ445
463.5750	Sting Security	(Rockville MD)	WRI665
461.2500	Suburban Investigation	(Wheaton MD)	KKD623
151.8650	Suburban Investigative	(Cheverly MD)	
151.8650	Suburban Investigative	(Cheverly MD)	KYE571
463.9250	The Wackenhut Corp.	(Bethesda MD)	WQS639
461.5000	Trans American Security	(Silver Spring MD)	WSW211
461.7250	Tri State Security	(Hagerstown MD)	WRT808
463.3500	Tri-State Canine	(Fairfax VA)	
463.3500	Virginia Safe & Lock	(McLean VA)	KNCE319
464.3250	Wackenhut	(Washington DC)	KYL337
464.6500	Wells Fargo	(Arlington VA)	KXQ523
464.4250	Wells Fargo	(Baltimore MD)	
461.9250	Wells Fargo	(Washington DC)	KNCQ617

Banks

Freq	Name	Location	Call
154.6000	Baltimore Federal	(Baltimore MD)	
151.7550	Carendon Bank & Trust	(McLean VA)	KBN625
464.8500	Diversified Equity	(Waldorf MD)	WYS319
151.7450	Equitable Trust	(Baltimore MD)	KWD471
151.8650	Equitable Trust	(Baltimore MD)	KWD471
851.2875	Equitable Trust	(Silver Spring MD)	KNBT303
851.4375	Equitable Trust	(Towson MD)	KNBT303
464.3000	Farmer's Bank	(Hazlettville DE)	KYJ770
151.8650	Fidelity & Deposit	(Baltimore MD)	KSS596
464.8500	Fidelity Bond	(Waldorf MD)	WXA313
42.9600	First Federal Saving	(Hagerstown MD)	WRS836
463.4250	First National Bank	(Baltimore MD)	KNAT338
464.3750	First Virginia Banks	(Falls Church VA)	
151.9550	Int'l Bank for Reconstruction	(Washington DC)	KNY544
151.8950	Maryland Casualty	(Baltimore MD)	KTQ882
464.5250	Maryland Casualty	(Baltimore MD)	KNCL496
495.7625	Riggs National Bank	(Falls Church VA)	KNS895
464.4000	United Virginia Bank	(Alexandria VA)	

Malls & Stores

Freq	Name	Location	Call
35.0800	Bell's Trading Post	(Annapolis MD)	KNAG885
151.7450	Blue Hen Mall	(Dover DE)	KNAQ437
464.5750	Cumberland Mall	(Lavale MD)	KNAH266
151.8050	Eastpoint Mall	(Baltimore MD)	WSP644
464.4750	Fairoaks Mall	(Fairfax VA)	WSQ891
464.4250	Frederick Mall Associates	(Frederick MD)	KNBI311
464.1750	Giant Foods	(Annapolis MD)	WSB378
461.6500	Giant Foods	(Arlington VA)	WYY471

464.2500 Giant Foods	(Arlington VA)	KIR961
851.9875 Giant Foods	(Bethesda MD)	WQ0949
151.7150 Giant Foods	(Jessup MD)	KNFA825
151.7750 Giant Foods	(Jessup MD)	KMH852
151.7750 Giant Foods	(Landover MD)	KIR958
151.7750 Giant Foods	(Lanham MD)	KMH849
464.2750 Giant Foods	(Towson MD)	KIR960
851.9875 Giant Foods	(Towson MD)	WQ0944
463.9500 Giant Foods	(Towson MD)	WYY472
154.5150 Harundale Mall	(Glen Burnie MD)	KTV984
496.0375 Hecht Company	(Baltimore MD)	KZN974
154.5400 Hecht Company	(Silver Spring MD)	
495.0375 Hecht Company	(Silver Spring MD)	
464.7000 Lake Forest Mall	(Gaithersburg MD)	
464.8250 Landover Mall	(Landover MD)	
151.9250 Leisure World	(Silver Spring MD)	KUJ494
496.0375 Leisure World	(Silver Spring MD)	KNR804
154.6000 Linpro Lakeside Plaza	(Germantown MD)	
461.1500 Lohmans	(Bethesda MD)	
158.4600 Longfellow Restaurant	(St. Michaels MD)	WQC529
154.6250 Lord & Taylor	(Fairfax VA)	KNAC809
151.8050 Mall Management	(Baltimore MD)	WRO740
151.8350 Marlow Heights Shopping	(Marlow Hgts. MD)	WYZ848
151.7750 Maryland Way Restaurant	(Annapolis MD)	WQJ540
151.7750 Maryland Way Restaurant	(Waldorf MD)	WQJ540
151.9550 May Stores	(McLean VA)	KNFH644
151.9550 May Stores	(Silver Spring MD)	KNFH646
151.9550 May Stores	(Washington DC)	KNFH645
151.9550 May Stores -Montgomery Mall	(Bethesda MD)	KON982
151.9550 Maza Gallarie	(Washington DC)	
464.6250 Maza Gallerie	(Washington DC)	
154.5400 Montgomery Ward	(Baltimore MD)	KEZ363
464.4750 Montgomery Ward	(Baltimore MD)	KAP208
464.4250 Neiman Marcus	(Washington DC)	KIN454
464.5750 Neiman Marcus	(Washington DC)	KIN454
460.6625 Renaissance Plaza	(Baltimore MD)	
30.9200 Sales Center	(Lexington Park MD)	KJL214
154.5700 Security Square Center	(Baltimore MD)	
495.8875 Sloane, Inc.	(Silver Spring MD)	
461.9250 St. Mary's Realty	(Leonardtown MD)	KNBR206
495.8875 Tony's Superbowl	(Hyattsville MD)	KB2304
464.5750 Valley Mall	(Hagerstown MD)	KNBI312
464.8250 Wheaton Plaza	(Wheaton MD)	WSA788
463.9000 Wheaton Plaza	(Wheaton MD)	
464.8250 White Flint Mall	(Rockville MD)	
463.9000 White Flint Mall	(Rockville MD)	
151.6550 Woodward & Lothrop	(Rockville MD)	
151.6550 Woodwardxc & Lothrop	(Washington DC)	

Hotels & Inns

462.5750 Annapolis Hilton Inn	(Annapolis MD)	KAC9044
462.9000 Anthony House	(Washington DC)	
152.4800 Atlantic Sands Motel	(Rehoboth DE)	WYU592
151.8950 Baltimore Country Club	(Baltimore MD)	WYS289
462.5750 Baltimore Hilton	(Baltimore MD)	
151.9250 Bethesda Marriott	(Bethesda MD)	WSG346
151.8950 Boardwalk Inn	(Ocean City MD)	WYW788
154.6000 Bonnie View Country Club	(Washington DC)	
30.8800 Capital Hilton	(Washington DC)	KUN246
151.7750 Capitol Hilton	(Washington DC)	KXY474
154.6000 Colonial Manor Motel	(Rockville MD)	
462.8750 Columbia Inn	(Columbia MD)	KNBB943
154.5150 Congressional Country Club	(Bethesda MD)	
461.4250 District Hotel Supply	(Bethesda MD)	KLO784
152.4800 Dover Country Club	(Hazlettville DE)	WXW321
464.3750 Dupont Plaza	(Washington DC)	KNBW925
462.8000 Embassy Row Hotel	(Washington DC)	KNFQ810
465.0000 Embassy Square	(Washington DC)	WRF208
154.6250 Fairfax	(Washington DC)	WXC381
35.0800 Four Seasons	(Washington DC)	WRN605
151.8950 Four Seasons	(Washington DC)	WRE709
465.0000 Gaithersburg Marriott	(Gaithersburg MD)	KNBE854
463.7500 Gateway Motel	(Ocean City MD)	WZQ603
157.6200 Golden Sands Club	(Ocean City MD)	WRU419
151.6550 Guest Quarters	(Alexandria VA)	KNCA599
464.4250 Guest Quarters	(Washington DC)	KNCV707
461.4000 Guest Services	(Washington DC)	KAI663
151.6550 Hampshire Motor Inn	(Langley Park MD)	WQJ528
464.5250 Harambee House	(Washington DC)	WXX326
27.4500 Hay Adams	(Washington DC)	WQT310
151.7450 Hay Adams	(Washington DC)	KEF658
151.7150 Hilton	(Washington DC)	KFP831
154.5700 Hobbits Glen Golf Course	(Columbia MD)	
154.6250 Holiday Inn	(Aberdeen MD)	
151.6850 Holiday Inn	(Alexandria VA)	WSU232
151.8050 Holiday Inn	(Baltimore MD)	KWH883
35.0800 Holiday Inn	(Bethesda MD)	KTB535
151.6850 Holiday Inn	(Bethesda MD)	KJU320

154.6250 Holiday Inn	(Gaithersburg MD)	WYD839
461.9250 Holiday Inn	(Washington DC)	KNAW367
464.3750 Holiday Inn	(Washington DC)	KNBQ579
464.5750 Holiday Inn	(Washington DC)	KNAM670
151.8950 Holiday Inn -Thomas Circle	(Washington DC)	WSG554
496.1625 Howard Johnson's	(Alexandria VA)	KNR621
464.5250 Howard Johnson's	(Washington DC)	KYO746
31.2400 Howard Johnson's	(Washington DC)	KYO746
464.7750 Hyatt Regency	(Arlington VA)	KNBQ558
464.3750 Hyatt Regency	(Washington DC)	KZO479
154.5400 International Hotel	(Linthicum MD)	KUS807
151.8050 International Inn	(Washington DC)	KMH641
464.5250 L'Enfant Plaza	(Washington DC)	KXT587
464.8250 L'Enfant Plaza	(Washington DC)	KXW614
461.5250 Linden Hill Hotel	(Bethesda MD)	WQN551
35.0600 Loews	(Washington DC)	KUJ401
151.7750 Madison	(Washington DC)	KDJ502
462.8750 Madison	(Washington DC)	WSY553
151.7750 Madison	(Washington DC)	
151.9550 Marriott	(Arlington VA)	KNFR992
151.9550 Marriott	(Arlington VA)	WRO317
464.5250 Marriott	(Bethesda MD)	WRC526
151.9250 Marriott	(Bethesda MD)	
465.0000 Marriott	(Washington DC)	WQE879
464.6750 Marriott	(Washington DC)	WQQ603
151.9250 Marriott	(Washington DC)	
151.8350 Marriott -Crystal City	(Arlington VA)	WRO317
35.0800 Marriott Dulles	(Chantilly VA)	KKN858
154.5400 Marriott Dulles	(Chantilly VA)	KVJ336
460.9250 Marriott Security Systems	(Arlington VA)	
467.8250 Metropolitan Hotel	(Washington DC)	KE2601
154.5400 Mount Vernon Motor Lodge	(Alexandria VA)	KLI716
464.6250 Preston Country Club	(Silver Spring MD)	WYJ887
35.0800 Quality Inn	(Arlington VA)	KDO651
464.8250 Ramada Inn	(Alexandria VA)	KXE960
465.0000 Ramada Inn	(Beltsville MD)	WYW256
157.7400 Ramada Inn	(Dover DE)	KKM776
154.5400 Ramada Inn	(Falls Church VA)	WYZ972
154.5400 Ramada Inn -Seminary	(Alexandria VA)	WSY586
461.1000 Ramada Renaissance	(Washington DC)	
151.7550 Sheraton	(Washington DC)	KSB417
464.9750 Sheraton	(Washington DC)	WSX236
464.5750 Sheraton Carlton	(Washington DC)	KQE398
465.0000 Sheraton Motor Inn	(New Carrolton MD)	
151.9550 Sheraton Motor Inn	(Washington DC)	KA20474
154.6000 Sheraton Park Hotel	(Washington DC)	KSB417
464.5750 Sheraton Park Hotel	(Washington DC)	KSB417
464.9750 Sheraton Potomac	(Rockville MD)	
154.5150 Sheraton Washington	(Washington DC)	KXL909
151.9550 Shoreham Americana	(Washington DC)	KXA887
464.9750 Springfield Hilton	(Springfield VA)	WZK606
151.6550 State Line Motel	(Delmar MD)	KNCH304
151.8650 Stouffer's Inn	(Arlington VA)	
151.8650 Toby Tank Inn	(Salisbury MD)	KGO580
464.4750 Tysons Westpark	(McLean VA)	KNAM418
462.8000 Vista International	(Washington DC)	
35.0800 Washington Hotel	(Washington DC)	KUD478
464.4750 Washington Hotel	(Washington DC)	WZS734
151.7450 Watergate Improvement	(Washington DC)	KRF857
151.7750 Watergate Improvement	(Washington DC)	KRF857
151.7450 Watergate South	(Washington DC)	KJU721
31.1600 Watergate West	(Washington DC)	KO9121
151.7450 Watergate at Landmar	(Alexandria VA)	KZC716
152.4800 William Hill Manor	(Easton MD)	KNCF956
464.9250 Woodmont Country Club	(Rockville MD)	KNBX654

Colleges

462.8000 American College	(Bethesda MD)	KKZ464
151.7450 American University	(Washington DC)	KJO549
151.8950 American University	(Washington DC)	WZY851
464.4250 Campus Escort Service	(College Park MD)	KKM498
464.5750 Catholic University	(Washington DC)	KDH222
154.5400 Chesapeake College	(Wye Mills MD)	KWK816
151.8050 College of Notre Dame	(Baltimore MD)	KCV343
154.5400 Columbia Union College	(Takoma Park MD)	KRX904
154.5150 Columbia Union College	(Takoma Park MD)	
151.7450 Gallaudet College	(Washington DC)	KNCY740
154.5400 Gallaudet College	(Washington DC)	KRD874
464.4500 George Washington	(McLean VA)	KNFR623
151.7150 George Washington	(Washington DC)	KJQ813
151.8650 George Washington	(Washington DC)	WYP441
154.6000 George Washington	(Washington DC)	KJQ813
464.9250 George Washington	(Washington DC)	WRJ869
464.8750 George Washington	(Washington DC)	
151.6850 Georgetown University	(Washington DC)	KJI224
151.6850 Georgetown University	(Washington DC)	KRE804
151.9550 Georgetown University	(Washington DC)	KKO963
463.5750 Georgetown University	(Washington DC)	KNCZ276

464.4750	Georgetown University	(Washington DC)	WST474
151.9250	Goucher College	(Towson MD)	WZF209
151.7750	Harford Community College	(Bel Air MD)	KBB593
464.9750	Hood College	(Frederick MD)	WRQ340
151.7750	Howard Community College	(Columbia MD)	KVS559
30.9200	Howard University	(Washington DC)	KUV446
462.5750	Howard University	(Washington DC)	KAA8411
464.6750	Howard University	(Washington DC)	WYN529
151.8350	Howard University	(Washington DC)	
152.4800	Johns Hopkins	(Baltimore MD)	WRG321
157.5600	Johns Hopkins	(Laurel MD)	WRO531
151.8950	Johns Hopkins	(Washington DC)	KWW805
151.7150	Loyola College	(Baltimore MD)	KSS623
154.6250	Loyola College	(Baltimore MD)	KYD257
464.3750	Macke Co. -Towson State	(Towson MD)	
154.6250	Maryland Academy	(Baltimore MD)	KAW250
155.0250	Maryland State	(Princess Anne MD)	
464.1250	Montgomery College	(Rockville MD)	WQE355
154.5400	Montgomery College	(Rockville MD)	
39.5800	Montgomery College	(Takoma Park MD)	
464.3250	Morgan State University	(Baltimore MD)	KZA781
151.9250	Peabody Institute	(Baltimore MD)	
154.5150	Salisbury State	(Salisbury MD)	KWK655
464.9250	St. John's College	(Annapolis MD)	KNFA657
151.9550	Towson State	(Towson MD)	KYP312
464.8250	University of D.C.	(Washington DC)	KKS386
464.8750	University of D.C.	(Washington DC)	KKS386
464.9750	University of D.C.	(Washington DC)	KNBW586
151.8650	University of MD -also 151.895	(College Park MD)	WYJ450
154.5400	University of Maryland	(Baltimore MD)	KUI876
462.9250	University of Maryland	(Baltimore MD)	KNCB299
495.2375	University of Maryland	(Baltimore MD)	KBS891
462.9250	University of Maryland	(Burtonsville MD)	KNCB298
31.2400	University of Maryland	(College Park MD)	KVH580
151.7750	University of Maryland	(College Park MD)	WXM827
154.5400	University of Maryland	(College Park MD)	KAU839
464.4750	University of Maryland	(College Park MD)	KUL520
155.0250	University of Maryland	(College Park MD)	
453.5750	University of Maryland	(College Park MD)	KXV427
462.9250	University of Maryland	(Greenbelt MD)	KNCB300
461.0500	Virginia Polytechnic	(Bethesda MD)	WQT774
151.7450	Washington College	(Chestertown MD)	KEF344
151.9250	Wesley College	(Dover DE)	KRZ444
151.9550	Western Maryland College	(Westminster MD)	KLC901
151.9550	Western Maryland College	(Westminster MD)	

Schools

464.5250	Alexandria City School	(Alexandria VA)	WSH712
462.0500	Arundel Driving School	(Birdville MD)	KUR493
151.7150	Ballou Sr. High	(Washington DC)	WZK955
463.9625	Board of Education	(Bel Air MD)	KUH548
464.4750	Board of Education	(Cambridge MD)	WRY412
151.7150	Browne Jr. High	(Washington DC)	WQT387
47.5000	Center for the Handicapped	(Wheaton MD)	
151.7150	Coolidge Sr. High	(Washington DC)	WQL624
151.7150	Douglass Jr. High	(Washington DC)	KNCM603
151.7150	Dunbar Sr. High	(Washington DC)	WYW501
151.7150	Eliot Jr. High	(Washington DC)	KNCN550
151.7150	Kelly Miller Jr. High	(Washington DC)	WRJ847
462.1250	Kendall Elementary	(Arlington VA)	KZQ212
462.1250	Kendall Elementary	(Arlington VA)	KDO245
151.7150	Kramer Jr. High	(Washington DC)	WSC837
460.6625	MD School for the Blind	(Baltimore MD)	
154.5150	Maryland School	(Frederick MD)	KVY364
151.7150	McKinley Senior High	(Washington DC)	KNCL820
151.8050	Mt. Vernon High	(Alexandria VA)	
31.2400	No. Arundel Vocational	(Severn MD)	WRS666
151.7150	Roosevelt Sr. High	(Washington DC)	WQZ798
151.7150	Shaw Jr. High	(Washington DC)	WRF764
499.8125	Sidwell Friend's School	(Washington DC)	WIE480
151.7150	Spingarn High	(Washington DC)	WZP267
158.4600	The Milford School	(Milford DE)	WSK467
151.8950	The Park School	(Brooklandville MD)	KNBW790
151.8050	W. Springfield High	(Springfield VA)	
151.9550	W. Springfield High	(Springfield VA)	
151.7150	Woodrow Wilson High	(Washington DC)	KWB201
151.7150	Woodson Jr. High	(Washington DC)	WRE821

Cable Television

462.1500	Alexandria Cablevision	(Alexandria VA)	WQI438
496.9875	Annapolis CATV	(Birdville MD)	KNS945
461.2250	CATV General	(Harrington DE)	WQD754
461.3250	CATV General	(Harrington DE)	WQD754
461.3250	CATV General	(Oak Orchard DE)	WQD754

464.2250	CATV General	(Washington DC)	KNFK3128
463.9000	CATV General Corp.	(Birdville MD)	KNFK318
464.2250	CATV General Corp.	(Birdville MD)	KNFK318
464.5250	Colonial Cablevision	(Gambrills MD)	KNBF768
151.7450	Eastern Shore CATV	(Ocean City MD)	WZF688
154.5400	Eastern Shore CATV	(Ocean City MD)	KGX918
151.7150	Frederick Cablevision	(Frederick MD)	KUP756
151.6850	Frostburg Cable TV	(Frostburg MD)	WXT377
851.9625	Howard Cable TV	(Columbia MD)	WQP245
461.7000	Lex Par Cablevideo	(Lexington Park MD)	
157.5600	Madison Cablevision	(Elkton MD)	KZG914
496.8125	Montgomery County CATV	(Silver Spring MD)	KNR628
463.2250	Multi View Cable	(Aberdeen MD)	KVG542
468.2250	Multi View Cable TV	(Bel Air MD)	WBZ892
151.6250	Prime Cable	(Annapolis MD)	
31.3600	South Maryland Cable	(Tracey's Landing MD)	
464.5750	St. Charles CATV	(St. Charles MD)	KNAU265
464.8500	St. Charles CATV	(Waldorf MD)	KKT223
851.7125	Storer Cable	(Wheaton MD)	WQA633
151.9550	Sullivan Cable	(Cambridge MD)	KUW476
151.6250	Trans Con CATV	(Columbia MD)	
816.2375	Westinghouse	(Baltimore MD)	

Video Services

464.7500	Associated Sound Svcs.	(Falls Church VA)	
462.1500	Atlantis Sound	(Falls Church VA)	KNFH477
463.3250	Capron Company	(Washington DC)	KNCG999
461.4250	Chesapeake Sound	(Easton MD)	KYE905
463.2000	Cinema Sound	(Arlington VA)	WQD326
151.6250	Hedgepath Audio	(Takoma Park MD)	
151.6550	International Sound	(Baltimore MD)	KZA501
464.9750	International Sound	(Baltimore MD)	
151.9250	Joe Clark Productions	(Washington DC)	KNFM342
151.8950	TM Sound Associates	(Upperco MD)	
461.5000	Total Audio Visual	(Silver Spring MD)	WSK404
152.8700	Towson State University	(Towson MD)	KYP312
464.8500	Video Labs Corp.	(Rockville MD)	WQG648

Property Management

154.5150	1325 G. St. NW Building	(Washington DC)	
464.3500	A & B Development	(McLean VA)	WYF395
463.9750	Accent Mobile Homes	(Waldorf MD)	KNQ834
154.5400	Arlington Towers Assoc.	(Arlington VA)	KLW754
151.8950	B T R Realty	(Bel Air MD)	KGO321
30.9200	Baldus Real Estate	(La Plata MD)	KTH881
461.1000	Bayshore Development	(Ocean City MD)	
495.9625	Beatty Management	(Falls Church VA)	KNR494
151.7450	Bethesda Land Company	(Bethesda MD)	WSP211
464.4750	Bethesda Land Company	(Bethesda MD)	WQW732
151.7550	Brentwood Village	(Washington DC)	KQD408
463.4250	Brown Realty	(Silver Spring MD)	KUV448
154.6000	Buchanan Apartment Assoc.	(Arlington VA)	
43.0000	Camelot Mobile Home	(Lewes MD)	KVO773
151.6550	Capital Park Condominiums	(Washington DC)	KNFK481
154.5150	Capitol Park Towers	(Washington DC)	KNCA512
816.9625	Cardio Management Consultants	(Columbia MD)	
151.8650	Carri Condominium	(Ocean City MD)	WZG855
464.3750	Carriage Hill Village	(Randallstown MD)	KFJ216
151.8350	Century 21	(Baltimore MD)	KZJ929
461.8000	Charles Smith Management	(Alexandria VA)	KSF780
151.8650	Chesapeake Manor Development	(Arnold MD)	KBQ825
461.1250	City Wide Management	(Baltimore MD)	KML582
151.8650	Clarkston Apartments	(Baltimore MD)	WQH799
151.9250	Collonaide Condominium	(Washington DC)	KNFC244
461.5250	Colonies Condominium	(McLean VA)	WRX540
154.6000	Compass Realty	(Fairfax VA)	
463.8250	Connolley Homes	(Annapolis MD)	KTF409
152.4800	Country Village Apts.	(Hazlettville DE)	WZF725
464.6500	Crestwood Village	(Frederick MD)	WZA438
461.5500	Curtis Properties	(Arlington VA)	KXW478
463.8250	DFI Development	(Annapolis MD)	WQV679
496.2875	Danac Real Estate	(Bethesda MD)	KY8530
496.2875	Danac Real Estate	(Rockville MD)	KBO256
463.9750	Davitt Land	(Elkton MD)	WYS312
461.5250	Development Management	(McLean VA)	WXP813
463.2750	Dougherty Realty	(Frederick MD)	WZP869
462.1250	Eastern Shore Community	(Ocean City MD)	KNAR228
151.9250	Edgewood Management	(Baltimore MD)	WXJ470
151.9250	Elizabeth Condominium	(Chevy Chase MD)	KIV275
461.1000	Emmet Realty	(Silver Spring MD)	WYA745
154.5150	First Office Management	(Arlington VA)	KWZ809
464.4250	Foxfire Apartments	(Laurel MD)	WYL381
495.6875	Frall Developers	(Woodbine MD)	
151.6850	G H I Development	(Greenbelt MD)	WQN543

Freq	Name	Location	Call
62.1750	Georgian Towers	(Silver Spring MD)	WRJ709
33.1600	Glen Falls Realty	(Westminster MD)	KVF290
463.7500	Green Valley Development	(Hazlettville DE)	KUE250
151.6550	Grempler Realty	(Ellicott City MD)	KRU548
151.8050	Harbour Square	(Washington DC)	KQR786
35.0800	Harrison Realty	(Arlington VA)	KAI976
151.8350	Henlopen Condominium	(Rehoboth DE)	KZG931
464.3250	Huntint Towers	(Alexandria VA)	WSJ808
151.8650	Hutzells Realty	(Frederick MD)	WYV508
461.4250	Inner City Management	(Baltimore MD)	
464.5250	Inter American Development	(Washington DC)	KCT591
461.6750	John Akridge	(Washington DC)	WQO395
464.4750	Klingbell Management	(Arlington VA)	WSH887
461.2250	L & R Properties	(Baltimore MD)	
464.8250	L'Enfant Plaza Corp.	(Washington DC)	KXW614
464.5250	L'Enfant Plaza Properties	(Washington DC)	KXT587
461.1000	LWM Management	(Ocean City MD)	
464.9250	Landmark Center	(Alexandria VA)	KNBJ430
461.1000	Leland Realty	(Ocean City MD)	
461.0375	Lewinsville Retirement Home	(McLean VA)	
464.4250	M S Management	(Forestville MD)	WSD902
464.4250	M S Management Assoc.	(Baltimore MD)	KYF520
151.8050	MBG Realty	(Baltimore MD)	WXQ334
461.9000	MDC Land	(Washington DC)	WSV520
151.8050	Madison Management	(Washington DC)	KGE360
464.7750	Madison Park North Apartments	(Baltimore MD)	
496.5625	Major Development Co.	(Silver Spring MD)	KNS920
151.6850	Management Partnership	(Washington DC)	KCB885
151.8350	Mann-Reedy Realty	(Hampstead MD)	KLR646
464.9500	Margate Management	(Fairfax VA)	KZD544
464.9500	Margate Management	(Falls Church VA)	KTI381
151.6550	Mark Winkler Management	(Alexandria VA)	KWU939
30.8000	Marty's Mobile Homes	(Dover DE)	KDV284
461.1000	Maryland Condominium	(Ocean City MD)	KFJ523
462.0000	Maryland Properties	(Silver Spring MD)	KIJ467
152.4800	Mayfaur Apts.	(Hazlettville DE)	WQP616
42.9600	Mayne Realty	(Olney MD)	KQQ454
464.8500	McCormack Properties	(Towson MD)	KNBE249
35.7600	Mellott Estate	(Hagerstown MD)	KFV571
42.9600	Meyer Realty	(Westminster MD)	KZF488
42.9600	Michael Real Estate	(Hagerstown MD)	WQU618
151.8350	Miller Management	(Silver Spring MD)	
463.5000	Miller Management	(Washington DC)	KSH954
463.7500	Mills Properties	(Baltimore MD)	KNCC352
151.8050	Montebello Condominium	(Alexandria VA)	KNFT370
462.5500	Montgomery Village	(Gaithersburg MD)	KAB0432
151.8050	Monumental Properties	(Baltimore MD)	KUR571
151.7450	Morningside Heights	(Owings Mills MD)	KKU316
469.9500	Mount Vernon Realty	(Manassas VA)	WAM535
464.6000	National Capital Bldg.	(Bethesda MD)	KQM396
462.6750	National Capitol Realty	(Washington DC)	KAB3548
461.5500	Northern Virginia Development	(Arlington VA)	KLN603
463.6750	O'Conor & Flynn Realty	(Bel Air MD)	KME576
151.7450	Oakcrest Towers	(Suitland MD)	WRO728
461.8750	Ocean Pines Association	(Berlin MD)	WZG731
151.7450	Park Associates	(Mitchellville MD)	
154.5400	Parklawn Joint Venture	(Rockville MD)	KSP486
463.7750	Pavilion Apartments	(Rockville MD)	KNBQ482
154.5400	Peck Realty	(Silver Spring MD)	KLJ697
463.7000	Phoenix Development	(McLean VA)	KIW909
154.5400	Pine Acres	(Millsboro DE)	KUR747
463.7000	Powell Realty	(Williamsburg MD)	KKJ252
463.3250	Princemont Realty	(Silver Spring MD)	KCB345
151.8350	Queens Trust Realty	(Stevensville MD)	KIW847
461.3500	Quincy Development	(Baltimore MD)	KAL637
807.4125	RTM Developers	(Olney MD)	
151.7450	Real Estate Management	(Baltimore MD)	KSS486
151.6850	Realty Investment	(College Park MD)	WXG943
151.7150	Resort Realty	(Ocean City MD)	KFL339
496.0625	Reston Land Corp.	(Reston VA)	KNS290
816.9625	Rhett Realty	(Ellicott City MD)	
464.4750	Riesterstown Plaza	(Baltimore MD)	KNCF923
151.9250	River Park Homes	(Washington DC)	
496.8625	River Ridge Realty	(Damascus MD)	KNQ343
495.7625	River Ridge Realty	(Frederick MD)	KNQ343
152.4800	Rodney Village Apts.	(Hazlettville DE)	WYQ398
151.7450	Rotunda Condominium	(McLean VA)	KSD252
463.2250	Runco Realty	(Waldorf MD)	WQE220
151.7450	S & L Management	(Washington DC)	KUW351
461.1750	Seward Management	(Cantonsville MD)	KNFT296
151.7750	Siegel Management	(Owings Mills MD)	KKT672
151.6550	Southern Towers Apartments	(Alexandria VA)	KBV495
151.7750	Southview Development	(Oxon Hill MD)	KZW688
464.6750	Springhill Lakes Apts.	(Greenbelt MD)	KEU982
464.8500	Terrapin Developers	(La Plata MD)	KAH606
462.6250	Tower Villas Council	(Arlington VA)	
151.7550	Town Center Management	(Washington DC)	KVW347
463.8250	U.S. Home Corp.	(Annapolis MD)	WXE968
151.8650	Universal Housing	(Washington DC)	KKT252
461.5000	Universal Management	(Silver Spring MD)	KNBD232
151.8650	University Towers Condo	(Silver Spring MD)	
461.2750	Village in the Woods	(Landover MD)	
151.7150	Village of Cross Keys	(Baltimore MD)	
151.6850	Villani Realty	(Ocean City MD)	
461.1750	Washington Square	(Glen Burnie MD)	
464.6000	Watergate Improvement	(Washington DC)	KRF857
464.8500	Watergate Improvement	(Washington DC)	KRF857
151.7450	Watergate South	(Washington DC)	KJU721
463.9500	Western Development	(Washington DC)	KNBR938
151.8950	Westfield Realty	(Arlington VA)	WQJ914
151.9250	Williams Estates	(Baltimore MD)	KIF855
154.5400	Willoughby Properties	(Chevy Chase MD)	KSW239
462.7250	Windsor Resort	(Ocean City MD)	KAD0520
464.4250	Wire Properties	(Washington DC)	KCU572
154.5400	Woodbyne Realty	(Poolesville MD)	KIT519
151.8050	Woodner	(Washington DC)	WXP744
464.3250	Yorktowne Development	(Cockeysville MD)	WSK798
151.7450	Zalco Realty	(Ocean City MD)	WZF413
151.7750	]1055 Thomas Jefferson	(Washington DC)	KBP311

Utilities

Freq	Name	Location	Call
451.3250	American Tel & Tel	(Fairlee MD)	WYG590
451.3250	American Tel & Tel	(Faulkner MD)	KGR926
451.3250	American Tel & Tel	(Frostburg MD)	WYG591
451.3250	American Tel & Tel	(Randallstown MD)	WYG600
153.5150	Anne Arundel Utilities Ops.	(Glen Burnie MD)	
158.1750	Anne Arundel Utilities Ops.	(Glen Burnie MD)	
461.6000	Antietam Water Svc.	(Hagerstown MD)	KNAB969
153.6050	Baltimore G & E -Elec. Trouble	(Baltimore MD)	
153.6050	Baltimore G & E -Elec. Trouble	(Cockeysville MD)	KYX804
153.6050	Baltimore G & E -Elec. Trouble	(Davidsonville MD)	KGE216
153.6050	Baltimore G & E -Elec. Trouble	(Ellicott City MD)	KGA255
153.6050	Baltimore G & E -Elec. Trouble	(Essex MD)	KYX801
153.6050	Baltimore G & E -Elec. Trouble	(Glen Burnie MD)	KGC826
153.6050	Baltimore G & E -Elec. Trouble	(Jacksonville MD)	KGD387
153.6050	Baltimore G & E -Elec. Trouble	(Westminster MD)	KGA908
153.6050	Baltimore G & E -Elec.Trouble	(Woodlawn MD)	WSM928
37.7000	Baltimore G & E -Gas Constr.	(Dayton MD)	KGE223
37.7000	Baltimore G & E -Gas Constr.	(Granite MD)	KGA618
37.7000	Baltimore G & E -Gas Constr.	(Jacksonville MD)	KGD387
37.7000	Baltimore G & E -Gas Constr.	(Owings Mills MD)	KGA617
37.7000	Baltimore G & E -Gas Constr.	(Randallstown MD)	KTA315
153.5750	Baltimore G & E -Gas Service	(Granite MD)	KYX805
153.4400	Baltimore G & E -Gas Service	(Leonardtown MD)	KNAL815
153.4400	Baltimore G & E -Gas Service	(Lusby MD)	KNAL814
153.4400	Baltimore G & E -Gas Service	(Pikesville MD)	KNAL816
48.2200	Baltimore G & E -No. District	(Westminster MD)	KUU808
47.9600	Baltimore G & E -South Dist.	(Davidsonville MD)	KGE216
47.9600	Baltimore G & E -South Dist.	(Ellicott City MD)	KGA255
47.9600	Baltimore G & E -South Dist.	(Glen Burnie MD)	KGC826
48.0800	Baltimore G & E -Storm Trouble	(Jacksonville MD)	KGD387
48.0800	Baltimore G & E Storm Trouble	(Reisterstown MD)	KGG916
47.8600	Baltimore G&E -Central Distr.	(Baltimore MD)	
37.7000	Baltimore G&E -Gas Constr.	(Conowingo MD)	KLY365
451.1000	Baltimore Gas & Electric	(Baltimore MD)	
151.8950	Baltimore Gas & Electric	(Baltimore MD)	KGI947-8
42.9800	Baltimore Gas & Electric	(Baltimore MD)	
47.9200	Baltimore Gas & Electric	(Ellicott City MD)	KGB834
47.9200	Baltimore Gas & Electric	(Finksburg MD)	KGB723
47.9200	Baltimore Gas & Electric	(Glen Burnie MD)	KDN894
151.8950	Baltimore Gas & Electric	(Glen Burnie MD)	KDH713
47.9200	Baltimore Gas & Electric	(Laurel MD)	KFY656
153.6650	Baltimore Gas & Electric	(Lusby MD)	WXD211
47.9200	Baltimore Gas & Electric	(Owings Mills MD)	KDN893
47.9200	Baltimore Gas & Electric	(Pikesville MD)	KQU818
47.9200	Baltimore Gas & Electric	(Randallstown MD)	KJQ366
47.9200	Baltimore Gas & Electric	(Reisterstown MD)	KGG916
47.9200	Baltimore Gas & Electric	(Towson MD)	KDN895
47.9200	Baltimore Gas & Electric	(Westminster MD)	KGA908
47.9200	Baltimore Gas & Electric	(White Marsh MD)	KGG917
47.8200	Baltimore Gas & Electric	(Whiteford MD)	KGT724
47.9200	Baltimore Gas & Electric	(Whiteford MD)	KGG919
47.9200	Baltimore Gas & Electric	(Woodlawn MD)	WSM928
35.1600	Chesapeake & Potomac	(Baltimore MD)	KBA954
151.9850	Chesapeake & Potomac	(Baltimore MD)	KBA954
451.4000	Chesapeake & Potomac	(Baltimore MD)	KBA954
451.3000	Chesapeake & Potomac	(Baltimore MD)	
451.3500	Chesapeake & Potomac	(Baltimore MD)	
464.5750	Chesapeake & Potomac	(Baltimore MD)	
451.4500	Chesapeake & Potomac	(Charlotte MD)	KZX770
451.3500	Chesapeake & Potomac	(Oxon Hill MD)	WYX475
35.1600	Chesapeake & Potomac	(Washington DC)	WSW506
151.9850	Chesapeake & Potomac	(Washington DC)	KBQ871
451.3500	Chesapeake & Potomac	(Wheaton MD)	KSV581
816.9625	Chesapeake Lighting	(Laurel MD)	
47.8000	Chesapeake Utilities	(Georgetown DE)	KNBS623
47.8000	Chesapeake Utilities	(Salisbury MD)	KCO425
47.8000	Chesapeake Utlities	(Seaford DE)	KCO427
48.4800	Choptank Electric	(Denton MD)	KGA292

Frequency	Name	Location	Callsign
48.4800	Choptank Electric	(Pocomoke MD)	KVH849
48.4800	Choptank Electric	(Salisbury MD)	KGA294
153.6500	Columbia Gas	(Baltimore MD)	KUW769
153.6500	Columbia Gas	(Hagerstown MD)	KBJ391
153.5000	Columbia Gas	(Washington DC)	
37.6400	Conowingo Power	(Elkton MD)	KAP390
37.7800	Conowingo Power	(Elkton MD)	KAP390
451.3500	Continental Telephone	(Manassas VA)	KSS742
158.1900	Delaware Electric	(Greenwood DE)	KGA230
48.2400	Delmarva Power	(Cambridge MD)	KGA278
48.3000	Delmarva Power	(Cambridge MD)	KGA278
153.6200	Delmarva Power	(Centerville MD)	KAU458
48.2400	Delmarva Power	(Centreville MD)	KNAX536
48.3000	Delmarva Power	(Centreville MD)	KNAX536
48.2400	Delmarva Power	(Chestertown MD)	KGD634
48.3000	Delmarva Power	(Chestertown MD)	KGD634
48.3000	Delmarva Power	(Crisfield MD)	KGA273
48.3000	Delmarva Power	(Denton MD)	KGA276
48.3000	Delmarva Power	(Federalsburg MD)	KGA275
48.3000	Delmarva Power	(Georgetown DE)	KGA271
48.3000	Delmarva Power	(Grasonville MD)	KGJ3509
48.2400	Delmarva Power	(Harrington DE)	KGA281
48.3000	Delmarva Power	(Harrington DE)	KGB328
48.3000	Delmarva Power	(Laurel DE)	KGA270
48.2400	Delmarva Power	(Millington MD)	KGA280
48.3000	Delmarva Power	(Millington MD)	KGA280
48.3000	Delmarva Power	(Millsboro DE)	KGA269
48.3000	Delmarva Power	(Oxford MD)	KGA277
48.3000	Delmarva Power	(Pocomoke MD)	KGA282
48.3000	Delmarva Power	(Rehoboth DE)	KGA268
48.3000	Delmarva Power	(Rehoboth DE)	KGA268
48.2400	Delmarva Power	(Salisbury MD)	KGA573
48.3000	Delmarva Power	(Salisbury MD)	KGB329
48.2400	Delmarva Power	(Wye Mills MD)	WSP756
48.3000	Delmarva Power	(Wye Mills MD)	WSP756
35.1600	Diamond State Telegraph	(Dover DE)	KZJ692
35.1600	Diamond State Telephone	(Georgetown DE)	KZJ693
153.4550	District of Columbia Power	(Washington DC)	KVY297
158.1300	District of Columbia Power	(Washington DC)	KBZ463-4
158.1300	District of Columbia Power	(Washington DC)	KGA596
48.0200	Dover City Power	(Dover DE)	KGD466
37.5200	Eastern Shore Gas	(Ocean City MD)	KEA259
37.5200	Eastern Shore Gas	(Snow Hill MD)	KEA261
47.8000	Eastern Shores	(Dover DE)	KUA801
48.1800	Fairfax County Power	(Alexandria VA)	KER936
48.1200	Fairfax County Water	(Herndon VA)	KNFA830
153.5000	Frederick Gas	(Frederick MD)	KAV464
153.2750	General Electric	(Columbia MD)	KUW737
153.3050	General Electric	(Columbia MD)	KXQ304
451.4500	General Telephone	(Midland MD)	KNFC370
153.4850	Hagerstown Water	(Hagerstown MD)	KGF820
47.7600	Lincoln & Ellendale	(Ellendale DE)	KCJ494
152.4200	Maryland Electric	(Cumberland MD)	KJI852
153.5000	Maryland Marine Utility	(Ocean City MD)	KEZ655
153.6500	Maryland Water Works	(Bel Air MD)	KIA616
158.1600	Potomac Edison	(Clear Spring MD)	KGA613
158.2500	Potomac Edison	(Clear Spring MD)	KGA613
158.2050	Potomac Edison	(Clear Spring MD)	KGA613
158.2650	Potomac Edison	(Clear Spring MD)	KGA613
158.1600	Potomac Edison	(Clear Spring MD)	KGB550
158.2650	Potomac Edison	(Frederick MD)	KGB550
451.2750	Potomac Edison	(Hagerstown MD)	KNAX823
158.1600	Potomac Edison	(Hancock MD)	KGF949
158.2500	Potomac Edison	(Hancock MD)	KGF949
158.2050	Potomac Edison-158.265,158.160	(Frederick MD)	KGB550
37.5800	Potomac Electric	(Alexandria VA)	KIK309
37.6600	Potomac Electric	(Alexandria VA)	KIK309
37.8200	Potomac Electric	(Alexandria VA)	KIK309
451.1250	Potomac Electric	(Alexandria VA)	KIK309
451.1250	Potomac Electric	(Dickerson MD)	KGG551
451.1250	Potomac Electric	(Laurel MD)	KWC981
37.8200	Potomac Electric	(Rockville MD)	KGB383
37.5800	Potomac Electric -37.66, 37.82	(Takoma Park MD)	KGH232
37.5800	Potomac Electric -37.66,37.820	(Dickerson MD)	KGG551
451.0250	Potomac Electric -F1 Montg.Cty	(Laurel MD)	KWC981
451.0250	Potomac Electric -F1 Montg.Cty	(Rockville MD)	KWC978
451.0500	Potomac Electric -F2 D.C.	(Laurel MD)	KWC981
451.0750	Potomac Electric -F3 P.G. Cty.	(Laurel MD)	KWC981
451.1500	Potomac Electric -F4 Sprvsrs.	(Germantown MD)	WZS953
451.1500	Potomac Electric -F4 Sprvsrs.	(Takoma Park MD)	WYX474
451.1500	Potomac Electric -F4 Sprvsrs.	(Upper Marlboro MD)	WYX476
451.1750	Potomac Electric -F5 Sprvsrs.	(Rockville MD)	
451.2500	Potomac Electric -F6 Hdqrtrs.	(Alexandria VA)	KIK309
153.4700	Prince William Electric	(Manassas VA)	KIC837
153.6950	Prince William Electric	(Manassas VA)	KIC837
158.1450	Southern Maryland Electric	(Leonardtown MD)	KGA331
158.2200	Southern Maryland Electric	(Leonardtown MD)	KGA331
158.1450	Southern Maryland Electric	(White Plains MD)	KLN379
158.2200	Southern Maryland Electric	(White Plains MD)	KLN379
37.6000	Susquehanna Electric	(Conowingo MD)	WRA785
37.7800	Susquehanna Electric	(Conowingo MD)	KGB826
151.5950	Tri Gas & Oil	(Federalsburg MD)	KIX932

Frequency	Name	Location	Callsign
461.9750	Tri-County Utilities	(Bethesda MD)	WSI843
153.5300	Virginia American Water	(Alexandria VA)	KIM769
48.0400	Virginia Electric	(Alexandria VA)	KIF666
48.1400	Virginia Electric	(Alexandria VA)	KIF666
48.0400	Virginia Electric	(Alexandria VA)	KIF666
48.1400	Virginia Electric	(Alexandria VA)	KIF666
48.2800	Virginia Electric	(Alexandria VA)	KIF666
451.1750	Virginia Electric	(Alexandria VA)	
451.2250	Virginia Electric	(Alexandria VA)	
451.4750	Virginia Electric	(Alexandria VA)	
451.6750	Virginia Electric	(Alexandria VA)	
451.5250	Virginia Electric	(Arlington VA)	KLC836
37.7000	Virginia Electric	(Fairfax VA)	
451.6250	Virginia Electric	(Fairfax VA)	
451.3750	Virginia Electric	(Herndon VA)	
48.0400	Virginia Electric	(Leesburg VA)	KIE996
48.2800	Virginia Electric	(Leesburg VA)	KIE996
451.5750	Virginia Electric	(Leesburg VA)	KJE550
461.5750	Virginia Electric	(Springfield VA)	WXN863
451.4250	Virginia Electric	(Woodbridge VA)	
153.4100	Washington County	(Clear Spring MD)	WXU824
158.2200	Washington County	(Hagerstown MD)	WFB510
47.9000	Washington Gas & Light	(Chillum MD)	KGA577
47.9000	Washington Gas & Light	(Sprinfield VA)	KDN651
47.9000	Washington Gas & Light	(Springfield VA)	KGA575
451.1750	Washington Gas & Light	(Springfield VA)	KXH540
451.2000	Washington Gas & Light	(Springfield VA)	
48.5000	Washington Gas & Light	(Washington DC)	KGA576
48.5000	Washington Gas & Light	(Washington DC)	KXB435
47.9000	Washington Gas-Light	(Rockville MD)	KGA578
48.3800	Washington Suburban -F1 North	(Forestville MD)	KUN369
48.3800	Washington Suburban -F1 North	(Hyattsville MD)	KGD574
48.3800	Washington Suburban -F1 North	(Laurel MD)	KGS436
48.3800	Washington Suburban -F1 North	(Potomac MD)	KAW942
48.5400	Washington Suburban -F2 South	(Brown's Corner MD)	KOU833
451.4500	Western Union	(Catonsville MD)	
151.9850	Western Union	(Elkton MD)	KDT950
151.9850	Western Union	(Severn MD)	KDT947
461.1000	Western Union	(Silver Spring MD)	KNBF553
451.3000	Western Union	(Washington DC)	KJZ480

Transportation

Frequency	Name	Location	Callsign
461.3750	Admiral Limousine	(Washington DC)	KIQ626
27.4700	Aid Van	(Alexandria VA)	KSA777
499.2375	Aid Van	(Alexandria VA)	KB5414
464.5000	American Public Transit	(Washington DC)	
155.2350	B & B Bus Lines	(Linthicum MD)	KIG699
155.2350	B&B Bus Lines	(Linthicum MD)	
161.4750	Baltimore Region Rapid Transit	(Baltimore MD)	WSH550
151.5650	Baltimore Region Rapid Transit	(Baltimore MD)	(WSH550)
494.6875	Beltway Limo	(Silver Spring MD)	
816.4875	Bethany Limousine	(Washington DC)	
851.4875	Blue Line Sightseeing	(Fairfax VA)	
151.6550	Blue Ribbon Bus Rental	(Washington DC)	KSR615
43.0000	Boole's Personal Auto Svc.	(College Park MD)	
155.2350	Brooks Transport	(Pasadena MD)	KJF907
43.8400	Capitol Bus	(BWI Airport MD)	WZX683
43.8400	Capitol Bus	(Baltimore MD)	KIB829
43.8400	Capitol Bus	(Washington DC)	KIB816
499.6875	Carons Delivery	(Alexandria VA)	KB4758
499.2875	Classic Vans	(Alexandria VA)	WFV820
35.1000	Clydes Charter Bus	(Glen Burnie MD)	KDF884
46.0000	Compton Bus	(Port Tobacco MD)	WXB873
463.8000	Cotter Limousine	(Washington DC)	
464.3000	Creative Bus Tours	(Washington DC)	KNBK539
461.3500	Cumberland Limousine	(Midland MD)	KNCD786
463.8000	D & J Bus Lines	(Baltimore MD)	WSW593
851.7125	Damita Bus	(Wheaton MD)	WQP302
151.9250	Dillons Bus	(Millersville MD)	WYB506
155.2800	Dillons Bus	(Millersville MD)	WSY238
45.9200	Duffy Bus	(Waldorf MD)	WSW732
154.5400	Evans Bus	(Warwick MD)	KNFE621
464.1000	Executive Limousine	(Bethesda MD)	WQI419
464.1750	Fay Radcliffe Bus	(Annapolis MD)	KNCX689
462.0000	Frederick Limo	(Braddock Hgts. MD)	
160.7400	Fruit Growers Express	(Alexandria VA)	KLW312
46.0400	Hedges Bus Service	(Bryans Road MD)	KWV611
47.5800	Highview Bus	(Capitol Hgts. MD)	
155.2350	Indian Creek School	(Crownsville MD)	KGX928
464.2250	Ironsides Transportation	(Bethesda MD)	KKU801
816.9612	Jim's Bus Service	(Temple Hill MD)	
463.2000	Joy Bus Svc.	(Arlington VA)	WQD274
31.1600	Kenwood Bus	(Baltimore MD)	KZD468
463.3000	Magsmens Bus	(Baltimore MD)	KNAM878
31.0000	McMichael School Bus	(Oxon Hill MD)	KRZ683
496.7875	Merit Transportation	(Millersville MD)	
47.5000	Montgomery Retired Citizens	(Silver Spring MD)	
154.5400	National Airport Shuttle Bus	(Arlington VA)	

452.6500	Ocean City Transport	(Ocean City MD)	WZX480
461.1750	Panda Transport	(Baltimore MD)	WSH298
463.2500	RFK Mini Bus	(Baltimore MD)	
31.2400	Ridgeway Motor Coach	(Baltimore MD)	KWT350
155.2200	Shaw Bus	(Baltimore MD)	
495.5625	Strand Limo Service	(Alexandria VA)	
463.5500	Suggs Transportation	(Arlington VA)	WXX329
464.2250	Suggs Transportation	(Washington DC)	WQR551
464.4500	Tara Lines	(McLean VA)	KNCH253
35.8800	Taxi Limousine	(Annapolis MD)	WXF351
464.7000	Thompsons Bus Service	(Annapolis MD)	KNFD269
461.8750	Transportation Science	(Arlington VA)	KCC872
464.1500	Urban Rural Transport	(Ellicott City MD)	KNCM365
151.8950	V I P Transport	(Baltimore MD)	KNCY574
463.2000	Victory Van	(Arlington VA)	
44.4800	Washington Metropolitan	(Silver Spring MD)	KIB754
452.6750	Washington Metropolitan	(Washington DC)	KIB325
462.0250	Watergate Limousine	(Washington DC)	WQR364
460.7850	Western Maryland Railroad	(Owings Mills MD)	KLY772
462.0000	White House Sightseeing	(Silver Spring MD)	WXJ270
151.9250	Wilson Bus Svc.	(Pasadena MD)	KGG375
461.1750	Yellow Bus Lines	(Washington DC)	WSY892

Marine

466.7000	Allens Hatchery	(Seaford DE)	WBL946
156.4250	Anchor Away, Inc.	(Galesville MD)	KUZ450
156.5000	Anchorage Launch	(Milford DE)	WXZ263
156.4500	Ann-Bay Launch Co.	(Annapolis MD)	WQB574
156.5750	Annapolis Boat Rental	(Annapolis MD)	WQZ323
156.4500	Annapolis City Marina	(Annapolis MD)	KGA480
156.6000	Atlantic Cement	(Sparrows Point MD)	WHF845
156.5000	Atlantic Marine Construction	(Bethany Beach DE)	KGA607
463.8000	B & M Harbor Service	(Dundalk MD)	
156.5000	Baker Whiteley Towing	(Baltimore MD)	KLU805
156.7000	Baker Whiteley Towing	(Baltimore MD)	KLU805
156.5000	Baltimore Gas & Electric	(Baltimore MD)	WQB630
156.6000	Baltimore Gas & Electric	(Baltimore MD)	WQB630
464.8500	Baltimore Launch	(Towson MD)	KNBZ549
156.4500	Baltimore Launch Svc.	(Baltimore MD)	WQB891
156.4500	Bethlehem Steel	(Baltimore MD)	KGC339
156.4500	Bethlehem Steel	(Sparrows Point MD)	WQB334
156.4750	Breakwater Marine	(Lewes DE)	KVY615
157.2500	C & P Mariphone	(Baltimore MD)	KDO769
157.3000	C & P Mariphone	(Baltimore MD)	KDO769
161.8500	C & P Mariphone	(Bodkin Point MD)	KGD518
161.9000	C & P Mariphone	(Bodkin Point MD)	KGD518
162.0000	C & P Mariphone	(Cambridge MD)	KRS907
157.3000	C & P Mariphone	(Salisbury MD)	KSK391
157.4000	C & P Mariphone	(Salisbury MD)	KKS391
161.9000	C & P Mariphone	(West Ocean City MD)	KSK223
156.4250	Calvert Marina	(Solomons MD)	WQB849
156.4500	Cape & Carribbean	(Annapolis MD)	WRV525
156.4250	Castle Marine	(Chester MD)	KVE877
156.6000	Cataneo Line Service	(Baltimore MD)	WHF823
156.7000	Cataneo Line Service	(Baltimore MD)	WHF823
464.2750	Cataneo Line Service	(Baltimore MD)	KDJ339
464.3750	Chesapeake Container	(Baltimore MD)	WXC664
156.9000	Chesapeake Marine	(Annapolis MD)	WQZ375
35.9000	Chester River Boats	(Millington MD)	WSW591
156.6500	City of Baltimore	(Baltimore MD)	KVY616
463.4750	Coastal Pile Driving	(Falls Church VA)	KXT539
31.8800	Coastal Supply	(Dagsboro DE)	KUI287
461.4250	Conval Port	(Baltimore MD)	KBD206
156.3500	Curlis Construction	(Edgemere MD)	WHF730
156.4500	Delaware Bay Launch	(Lewes DE)	KWS607
156.4500	Delaware Bay Launch	(Slaughter Beach DE)	KZV695
156.7000	Delaware Bay Launch	(Slaughter Beach DE)	KZV695
156.3500	Delaware River & Bay	(Lewes DE)	KEN781
157.3500	Diamond State Marine Telephone	(Lewes DE)	KBP379
161.9500	Diamond State Marine Telephone	(Lewes DE)	KVF855
156.4250	Dorchester County	(Cambridge MD)	KZM670
151.8350	El Paso Marine	(Solomons MD)	WXP990
156.4500	Exxon	(Baltimore MD)	WDT521
461.1000	Fager's Island Ltd.	(Ocean City MD)	
156.9500	Food Coop of America	(Lewes DE)	KQU392
151.7150	General Ship Repair	(Baltimore MD)	KAI320
156.9250	Gibson Island Yacht	(Gibson Island MD)	KSK352
156.5000	Great Lakes Dredge	(Baltimore MD)	KZE942
156.4500	Gunpowder Cove Marina	(Joppa MD)	KBK469
156.4250	Havre de Grace Marina	(Havre de Grace MD)	KTR919
156.5000	ITT Telecommunications	(Baltimore MD)	KTD482
156.4250	Indian Creek Inlet	(Beach Haven MD)	WXY955
156.4500	Indian Creek Inlet	(Beach Haven MD)	WXY955
156.5000	International Marine Transport	(Annapolis MD)	WQX605
156.9000	Isle of York	(Ocean City MD)	WXF622
156.9000	Jack Pot, Inc.	(Ocean City MD)	WHF945
156.4250	Kent Island Yacht	(Chester MD)	KGA390
156.9000	Kristen Leigh Inc.	(Ocean City MD)	KJA934

156.4250	L & L Marine	(West Ocean City MD)	WRD835
156.9000	L & L Marine	(West Ocean City MD)	WRD835
154.6000	Maersk Line	(Baltimore MD)	
156.4250	Marinas International	(Stevenville MD)	WQA331
461.8750	Marine Container	(Baltimore MD)	WRM317
463.6000	Marine Engineering	(Washington DC)	KGE347
464.6000	Marine Service Co.	(Baltimore MD)	KNBI662
464.1750	Marine Service Company	(Annapolis MD)	KNBI662
461.7750	Marine Structural	(Manassas VA)	KNCL572
156.4250	Maryland Capital Yacht	(Annapolis MD)	WQB599
156.9000	Maryland Shipbuilding	(Baltimore MD)	KGA563
156.4500	Maryland Tours	(Baltimore MD)	WQZ242
156.3500	McLean Contracting	(Baltimore MD)	KWS658
156.4250	Metropolitan Police	(Washington DC)	KUF703
157.0250	Metropolitan Police	(Washington DC)	KUF703
157.0750	Metropolitan Police	(Washington DC)	KUF703
156.8000	Metropolitan Police	(Washington DC)	KUF703
156.4250	Metropolitan Yacht Club	(Washington DC)	KZN550
156.4250	Murray's Bait & Tackle	(Ocean View DE)	WQA326
461.4000	New Star Ship Supply	(Baltimore MD)	WSV522
156.4250	New White Marlin Marine	(Ocean City MD)	KBP578
156.4500	Oxford Food Svc.	(Oxford MD)	WQX714
156.3250	Pax-Tropix Corp.	(Lexington Park MD)	WQA312
156.5400	Pax-Tropix Corp. -& 156.900	(Lexington Park MD)	WQA312
156.7000	Pilot's Assn. -also .725,.925	(Lewes DE)	KUF842
156.4750	Pilot's Association	(Lewes DE)	KUF842
156.4250	Piney Narrows Marina	(Chester MD)	KUZ443
156.2750	Puerto Rico Marine	(Baltimore MD)	KEB599
156.9750	Puerto Rico Marine	(Baltimore MD)	KEB599
162.0000	Radio Communications mariphone	(Bethesda MD)	KTA453
156.4500	Raytheon Service	(Glen Burnie MD)	KZV781
464.0500	Ring Maritime	(Towson MD)	KNAP433
154.6000	Rukert Marine	(Baltimore MD)	WQE369
157.0250	Savage Fisheries	(Berlin MD)	WDT525
156.8000	Savge Fisheries	(Berlin MD)	WDT525
156.4250	Scheibles Fishing	(Ridge MD)	WRS921
156.6750	Scheibles Fishing	(Ridge MD)	WRS921
157.0250	Scheibles Fishing	(Ridge MD)	WRS921
461.6000	Sea Horse Marine	(Annapolis MD)	KNCB687
462.1750	Sea Horse Marine	(Baltimore MD)	KNCB687
151.6550	Sea Watch Council	(Ocean City MD)	WSP854
156.4500	Selby Bay Yacht	(Edgewater MD)	WQZ440
156.4500	Severn River Marina	(Severna Park MD)	KZA979
151.7450	Shoreline	(Willards MD)	WXC582
156.5000	Smith Brothers	(Galesville MD)	WDT549
156.4250	Solomons Marine	(Solomons MD)	WQB363
156.9000	Sonat Marine	(Baltimore MD)	KVL869
156.9000	Sonat Marine	(Milford DE)	WRD834
156.4250	South Shore Marina	(Bethany Beach DE)	KZN585
156.5500	State of Maryland	(Baltimore MD)	WQB495
156.4500	Steamship Service	(Sparrows Point MD)	KCE329
156.9000	Steuart Transportation	(Crisfield MD)	KZJ317
30.8800	Surf Clams	(West Ocean City MD)	WSE710
156.4750	Texas Instruments	(Grasonville MD)	WQB552
156.9250	Tidewater Marina	(Havre de Grace MD)	WQZ419
156.4250	Tolchester Marina	(Chestertown MD)	KTR917
156.4500	United Radio Svc.	(Glen Burnie MD)	WXY981
156.5500	University of Delaware	(Lewes DE)	KTD423
156.4500	University of Maryland	(Solomons MD)	WRS974

Taxis

152.4200	A & H A P Taxi	(Odenton MD)	KGC429
152.3900	A B C Cab	(Frederick MD)	KGH827
152.3300	Ace Cab	(Frederick MD)	KQO235
152.3450	Action Cabs	(Edgewood MD)	WXP540
152.4350	Alexandria Diamond Cab	(Alexandria VA)	KCQ759
152.3000	Alexandria Yellow Cab	(Alexandria VA)	KIB336
152.3000	Alexandria Yellow Cab	(Fairfax VA)	KIB336
152.3900	All American Cab	(Alexandria VA)	KIH683
33.1600	Allied Cab	(Salisbury MD)	KSN537
154.5150	Andy's Cab	(Bel Air MD)	KUN661
152.2850	Anne Arundel Cab	(Fort Meade MD)	WSC517
152.4350	Arbutus Taxicab	(Baltimore MD)	WRB368
496.2125	Area Wide Delivery	(Washington DC)	
452.4000	Arlington Yellow Cab	(Arlington VA)	KIA639
152.3150	Arrow Cab Co.	(Baltimore MD)	KYV209
452.3000	Assadollah Malekzade	(Rockville MD)	WSQ363
152.4200	Assoc. of Independents	(Baltimore MD)	KGA428
152.4500	Assoc. of Independents	(Baltimore MD)	KGA428
151.7450	Associated Cab	(Glen Burnie MD)	KGL301
152.2700	Astor Cab	(Cumberland MD)	KGA345
452.1500	Atwater Cab	(Dundalk MD)	KDB764
152.3450	B & L Cab	(Brooklyn Park MD)	KGD764
452.1000	Barwood	(Washington DC)	KXR791
152.3000	Barwood of Silver Spring	(Bethesda MD)	KLU391
157.5650	Barwood of Silver Spring	(Bethesda MD)	
452.0500	Barwood of Wheaton	(Rockville MD)	KLU391
452.0500	Barwood of Wheaton	(Wheaton MD)	KLU391

151.7750	Black Top Cab	(Aberdeen MD)	WYT458
152.3300	Blue & Gray Cab	(Baltimore MD)	KGC367
152.3900	Blue Bird Cab	(Cheverly MD)	KGA943
42.9600	Blue Diamond Cab	(Annapolis MD)	KQM230
152.3750	Blue Star Taxi	(Annapolis MD)	WSC507
152.2700	Bull Run Cab	(Manassas VA)	KZV212
152.2700	C &PS Taxicab	(Annapolis MD)	KNFC564
152.4500	Capitol Cab	(Bowie MD)	KLG514
152.4500	Capitol Cab	(Coral Hills MD)	KLG514
452.4500	Capitol Cab	(Washington DC)	KGB339
452.5000	Capitol Cab	(Washington DC)	KGB339
151.9250	Cecil's Taxi	(Easton MD)	KNFQ348
152.3150	Central Cab	(Capital Hgts. MD)	KVU749
496.7625	Charles County Cab	(Waldorf MD)	KNM947
151.9250	City Cab	(Cambridge MD)	KNCZ305
152.3900	City Cab	(Dover DE)	KNAH358
152.3900	City Cab	(Dover DE)	
152.3300	Clinton Taxi	(Clinton MD)	KNCZ384
152.4350	Colonial Cab	(Annapolis MD)	WSW378
152.2850	Community Cab	(Cecilton MD)	KNBD684
152.4050	Crown & Diamond Cab	(Annapolis MD)	WSE497
462.1000	Davis Yellow Cab	(Willards MD)	WXM521
151.8650	Dennis Taxi	(Ocean City MD)	KSV327
152.3600	Dial Cab	(Washington DC)	KGT338
452.2000	Dial Cab	(Washington DC)	KGT338
495.7875	Diamond Cab	(Arlington VA)	KXC227
496.3625	Downtown Cab	(Washington DC)	KBY792
496.3875	Downtown Cab	(Washington DC)	KBY792
151.7150	Econocab	(Salisbury MD)	WRU475
152.3900	Edgewood Taxi	(Edgewood MD)	WYC659
152.4500	Elkton Cab	(Elkton MD)	KDA538
462.7250	Falls Church Yellow	(Falls Church VA)	KAD3484
152.2700	Fritz Taxi	(Brunswick MD)	KBZ859
152.4200	G & H Taxi	(Pasadena MD)	KNAJ330
152.4200	G B Taxi	(Odenton MD)	KGX554
152.3000	GI Veterans Taxicab	(Baltimore MD)	KNFD535
152.3900	Gene's Taxi	(Salisbury MD)	KNCE383
452.2750	Independent Taxi Owners	(Washington DC)	KGA818
452.1500	Independent Taxi Owners	(Washington DC)	KGA818
152.3900	Jakes Taxi	(Elkton MD)	KGG358
452.4000	Jimmy's Cab	(Towson MD)	KGB542
452.5000	Ken's Cab	(Essex MD)	KGB595
154.5400	Kerfoot Livery	(Hagerstown MD)	KWQ251
33.1600	Leesburg Taxi	(Leesburg VA)	KRN513
152.3300	Lofthus Transportation	(Alexandria VA)	WYG281
152.4500	Louden Yellow Cab	(Leesburg VA)	WRJ388
152.4500	Manassas Taxi	(Manassas VA)	KIF715
152.2700	Metro Cab	(Alexandria VA)	KZE583
152.3300	National Cab	(Alexandria VA)	KIB336
452.1000	National Cab	(Alexandria VA)	WSI526
151.9550	New City Cab	(Columbia MD)	KVG466
151.9250	New City Cab	(Columbia MD)	
152.3900	New Eastern Cab	(Essex MD)	KGB612
151.9550	Norris Cab	(Frederick MD)	KJ0919
152.3600	P G County Cab	(Coral Hills MD)	KNAX367
152.3900	Patuxent Cab	(Lexington Park MD)	KGC871
152.3300	Peninsula Cab	(Salisbury MD)	WQJ962
452.2250	Red Top Cab	(Arlington VA)	KGI584
452.3500	Red Top Cab	(Arlington VA)	KGI586
462.6000	Red Top Cab	(Arlington VA)	KAA4883
152.4050	Reston Cab	(Reston VA)	
157.6650	Reston-Herndon Transport	(Reston VA)	WRE305
152.3900	Robert's Taxi	(Easton MD)	KGB414
152.2700	Royal Cab Association	(Baltimore MD)	KTL641
152.4500	Salisbury Taxi	(Salisbury MD)	KBA416
152.4500	Salisbury Taxi	(Salisbury MD)	WQS973
151.8050	Seaford Taxi	(Seaford DE)	WRN865
152.4500	Seaford Taxi	(Seaford DE)	KJZ901
152.2700	Silver Spring Taxi	(Silver Spring MD)	KGA258
31.2400	Smith's Taxi	(Berlin MD)	KSN924
461.4000	Smyrna Clayton Cab	(Harrington DE)	WQM826
152.4200	Springfield Yellow Cab	(Springfield VA)	KB08844
452.0500	Sun Cab	(Baltimore MD)	KGC544
452.4500	Sun Cab	(Baltimore MD)	
152.4050	Sykesville Taxi	(Sykesville MD)	
152.3300	Takoma Langley Taxi	(Silver Spring MD)	KGA579
152.2700	Turners Taxi	(Hagerstown MD)	KRG717
152.3450	Valley Cab	(Pikesville MD)	
152.2700	Valley Cab	(Pikesville MD)	KLR429
152.4500	Victory Cab	(Frederick MD)	WZX365
152.4200	Weaver Cab	(Silver Spring MD)	WRY821
152.3900	West End Cab	(Elkton MD)	KRL382
152.3300	Westminster Cab	(Westminster MD)	KGC670
152.2700	White Top Cab	(Alexandria VA)	KZM864
452.2250	Yellow Cab	(Baltimore MD)	
152.3600	Yellow Cab	(Baltimore MD)	KGC556
152.3750	Yellow Cab	(Baltimore MD)	KGC556
152.3900	Yellow Cab	(Baltimore MD)	KGC556
152.3300	Yellow Cab	(Baltimore MD)	
152.4200	Yellow Cab	(Silver Spring MD)	KGA385
452.0000	Yellow Cab	(Washington DC)	KGH203
452.2500	Yellow Cab	(Washington DC)	KGH203

152.2700	Yellow Cab	(Wilmington DE)	
152.3300	Yellow Checker Cab	(Annapolis MD)	KBL234
152.3900	Yellow Top Cab	(Cumberland MD)	KGB486

Disposal Services

463.3500	AAA Disposal	(McLean VA)	KZA561
463.3250	ARA Services	(Washington DC)	KNCK396
464.1250	Aesop Refuse	(Rockville MD)	KG0483
159.8550	Alexander's Trash	(Baldwin MD)	WYR324
494.7625	Alexandria Sanitation	(Alexandria VA)	KNT344
463.2500	All Rite Rubbish	(Woodside DE)	KWN666
43.2000	American Trash	(Aberdeen MD)	
43.0000	American Trash	(Lutherville MD)	KIW472
31.2400	American Trash	(Bel Air MD)	KRK298
33.1600	Annapolis Trash	(Annapolis MD)	KXY555
496.8625	B & K Trucking	(Mt. Airy MD)	KNR852
461.0750	Big H Refuse	(Falls Church VA)	KGD888
151.9550	Bowen Trash	(Silver Spring MD)	WRP497
154.5150	Bowman Trash	(Washington DC)	KZL610
463.9000	Browning Ferris	(Oakland MD)	
463.2750	Browning Ferris	(Falls Church VA)	KRI425
30.9200	Browning Ferris	(Springfield VA)	KJG730
44.4200	Browning Ferris	(Glen Burnie MD)	KOH708
159.7200	Browning Ferris	(Silver Spring MD)	KAZ609
461.5500	Browning Ferris	(Silver Spring MD)	KQV401
464.1250	Browning Ferris	(Towson MD)	KNBP687
851.9375	Browning Ferris	(Towson MD)	WQ0906
462.0500	Bryan's Trash	(Towson MD)	KNCL843
463.2500	Bryan's Trash	(Cockeysville MD)	
851.7875	Callahan Refuse	(Falls Church VA)	KRT326
151.7450	Candy Kitchen Shoppes	(Ocean City MD)	WZF416
463.4000	Carter's Trash	(Washington DC)	WZF843
463.5000	Clarke Refuse	(Baltimore MD)	KV0270
33.1600	Cooley's Trash	(McLean VA)	KTI348
461.3250	D F Lawson Trash	(Falls Church VA)	KUL497
495.5125	Don Dawes Refuse	(Silver Spring MD)	
461.8500	Drapers Refuse	(Pen Mar MD)	KKI835
461.5750	Eastern Disposal	(Aberdeen MD)	KNFQ354
31.2400	Eastern Disposal	(Aberdeen MD)	KNBG7343
464.2250	Eastern Transit-Waste	(Washington DC)	KUE914
461.2750	Econo Waste Trash	(Silver Spring MD)	KXK925
461.8500	Fred Reitz Trash	(Baltimore MD)	WYE700
463.7750	Germantown Refuse	(Rockville MD)	WRZ416
151.9250	Gobrecht Trash	(Reisterstown MD)	WXA528
159.6450	Haden Trash	(Boring MD)	WSH701
461.9250	Harford Sanitation	(Aberdeen MD)	KRC525
463.7000	Harris Trash	(Churchville MD)	KMD364
461.5500	Hodges Refuse	(Towson MD)	KUV402
464.1750	Hondo Trash	(Annapolis MD)	WSG882
463.2500	Hughes Trash	(Manchester MD)	KKU983
461.4500	Hunt Trash	(Falls Church VA)	WSJ672
496.2375	Hunt Trash	(Falls Church VA)	KNR731
496.2125	Industrial Disposal	(Rockville MD)	KXY630
463.9500	James Taylor	(Washington DC)	WQL739
464.1000	Jeffrey's Trash	(Baltimore MD)	WRZ848
160.1100	Jones Express	(Washington DC)	KJB937
44.4400	K & K Trash	(Severn MD)	KYN481
464.0250	Kent Sanitation	(Church Hill MD)	KNAM228
464.7000	Leon's Dumpsters	(Falls Church VA)	WYM472
151.8050	Mall Management	(Salisbury MD)	WSC908
151.7450	Mason Dixon Recycling	(Silver Spring MD)	WSY595
159.6300	Modern Trash	(Baltimore MD)	KNBB272
496.3875	Montgomery County Refuse	(Rockville MD)	KAZ515
151.7150	Montgomery County Refuse	(Rockville MD)	KAZ515
463.4000	Prince George's Trash	(Oxon Hill MD)	KAT993
461.7750	Prince William Trash	(Manassas VA)	KGN764
44.2000	Propst Refuse	(White Hall MD)	KTA877
461.9500	Racz Refuse	(Church Hill MD)	KSA658
461.7000	Racz Refuse	(Smithville MD)	KFS405
461.1500	Red Line Disposal	(Bethesda MD)	KXA810
496.0125	Refuse Removers	(Birdville MD)	KKE813
496.8125	Refuse Removers	(Patuxent MD)	KKE813
496.8125	Refuse Removers	(Waldorf MD)	KKE813
461.6000	S & T Trash Removal	(Falls Church VA)	KNFE548
154.5150	Sanitary Disposal	(Williamsport MD)	KXN521
496.0625	Sanitation Specialists	(Annapolis MD)	KNS291
152.4800	Sawyer Sanitation	(Hazlettville DE)	WQP680
44.0000	Schuman Trash	(White Marsh MD)	KLI300
151.6850	Seaford Disposal	(Seaford DE)	KJU679
461.0750	Simms Trash	(Baltimore MD)	WRK518
463.8500	Stuart Refuse	(McLean VA)	KJM939
496.9875	Titus Trash	(Dickerson MD)	KB4497
462.1000	Unified Refuse	(Washington DC)	WXK831
461.5000	W C Trash	(Silver Spring MD)	KNAX260
30.9200	Waldorf Sanitation	(Waldorf MD)	KTF822
464.1250	Warreners Trash	(Towson MD)	KGB891
466.3250	White Line Disposal	(Oak Orchard DE)	WSS581

Towing

461.9750	A & B Auto Truck	(Bethesda MD)	KSG711
150.8450	A & B Towing	(Baltimore MD)	KDY420
462.5750	A & B Towing	(Silver Spring MD)	KAD0267
463.2250	A & B Towing	(Waldorf MD)	WQE682
154.5150	A J Towing	(Rockville MD)	KBT279
31.1600	A&D 24hr. Towing	(Mount Airy MD)	KNBZ912
31.1600	A&D 24hr. Towing	(New Windsor MD)	KNBZ912
461.0750	A-1 Discount Towing	(Fairfax VA)	
33.1600	A-1 Towing	(Baltimore MD)	WRT300
150.8600	A-1 Towing	(Hyattsville MD)	KIA924
461.3250	ABC Mobile Brake	(Annapolis MD)	KBK906
461.0750	ABC Mobile Brake	(Falls Church VA)	KZP756
35.9200	AMP Auto Parts	(Manassas VA)	KAV678
461.7750	Ace Towing	(Silver Spring MD)	WRK904
151.6550	Ace Wrecking	(Flint MD)	
461.2250	Action Auto Delivery	(Baltimore MD)	
31.0400	Adams Towing	(Washington DC)	KXS959
150.8150	Air Brakes & Control	(Bladensburg MD)	KBU908
35.9000	Al's Service	(Baltimore MD)	KIS923
31.2400	Alger Tire	(Rising Sun MD)	KUD295
461.6750	Allens Arco	(Washington DC)	KXR307
150.9050	American Auto Assn.	(Arlington VA)	WZT846
452.5500	American Auto Assn.	(Falls Church VA)	WZT849
452.5750	American Auto Assn.	(Falls Church VA)	WXY454
452.6000	American Auto Assn.	(Rockville MD)	WZT850
452.5250	American Auto Assn.	(Silver Spring MD)	KLS515
150.9650	American Auto Assn.	(Washington DC)	WZT846
150.9500	American Auto Assn.	(Washington DC)	
151.7450	Anacostia Auto	(Washington DC)	KLE557
461.1000	Angelos Towing	(Silver Spring MD)	WYB887
151.8050	Annapolis Radiator	(Annapolis MD)	KBS722
35.1800	Annapolis Service	(Annapolis MD)	WRU275
462.5750	Anytime Towing	(Silver Spring MD)	KAC7926
461.0250	Archway Motors	(Baltimore MD)	KWS728
464.0500	Arlington Auto Service	(Baltimore MD)	WSX429
462.7250	Arundel Diesel Engine	(Baltimore MD)	KAD2968
496.8375	Aspen Hill Chevron	(Rockville MD)	KNR578
452.5500	Auto Emergency	(Falls Church VA)	WRM833
154.5400	Auto Salvage & Parts	(Hagerstown MD)	KTK333
464.2500	B & P Towing	(Arlington VA)	KNFQ409
464.0500	Baltimore Auto Recovery	(Bethesda MD)	KNBB381
496.2375	Banks Auto Parts	(Falls Church VA)	KNR910
461.5500	Barkers Brake	(Arlington VA)	KKN646
463.2250	Barnes Towing	(Westminster MD)	WXM404
461.2500	Beahm's Towing	(Wheaton MD)	WXV886
461.3500	Bel Air Gulf	(Midland MD)	WRM413
150.8450	Belle Haven Amoco	(Alexandria VA)	KQL959
43.0000	Beltway Mobil	(Springfield VA)	KWC616
150.8750	Beltway Sunoco	(Baltimore MD)	KVT578
150.8150	Berman's	(Baltimore MD)	KXV505
33.1600	Bernard West Towing	(Beltsville MD)	KET210
31.0000	Berwyn Shell	(College Park MD)	WSX430
157.4700	Bethesda Shell Service	(Bethesda MD)	KCY789
35.9800	Biddle Towing	(Dover DE)	KNAE540
154.5150	Bill's Radiator	(Gaithersburg MD)	WYF504
35.9200	Bill's Towing	(Ellicott City MD)	KLH290
150.8150	Bill's Towing	(Wheaton MD)	WYG430
150.8600	Bill's Towing	(Wheaton MD)	WYG430
496.0125	Billy's Towing	(Washington DC)	
150.8150	Bob's Towing	(Hyattsville MD)	KQP460
150.8150	Bobby's Crane Svc.	(Kensington MD)	KRP828
495.7125	Bogle Tire	(Falls Church VA)	KNT492
157.5000	Boulevard Gulf	(Washington DC)	WSQ786
461.6500	Bowden Sunoco	(Baltimore MD)	KNCL611
463.8000	Brakes'n Parts	(Baltimore MD)	WSA469
462.1250	Briggs Towing	(Arlington VA)	KNQ429
461.6500	Briggs Towing	(Rockville MD)	WXD868
464.1250	Brooks-Huff Tire	(Towson MD)	KAL644
463.3750	Bunting Garage	(Dagsboro DE)	
851.2875	C & D Auto	(Silver Spring MD)	KRW408
496.8375	C & L Mobile Car Care	(Rockville MD)	KNQ612
150.8450	C & R Towing	(Seabrook MD)	KMA318
496.2375	C & S Towing	(Falls Church VA)	KNR630
30.9600	C & S Towing	(Reston VA)	KXP592
461.2750	C&C Automotive	(Silver Spring MD)	KNCT964
150.8900	Caltrider Amoco	(Finksburg MD)	KFQ799
157.4700	Campbell's Garage	(Washington DC)	KDQ898
31.0400	Campus Hills Citgo	(Towson MD)	KGD280
463.7000	Capital Tire	(McLean VA)	KNCM396
462.7000	Capitol Hill Gulf	(Washington DC)	KAC6167
464.4000	Car Care	(Williamsburg MD)	KXP714
150.8750	Carney Towing	(Baltimore MD)	KEM809
150.8300	Cathedral Exxon	(Baltimore MD)	WQI277
496.7125	Catlett's Amoco	(Birdville MD)	KNR495
31.0000	Cavanaugh Motors	(Salisbury MD)	WQR977
154.5150	Central Auto Parts	(Glen Burnie MD)	KYK281
30.9600	Ceresville Motor	(Frederick MD)	KGF667
150.8750	Chadwick Towing	(Baltimore MD)	WZX427
461.8500	Champion Ford Sales	(Baltimore MD)	KWC580
150.8750	Check Point Foreign Auto	(District Hghts. MD)	KGY773
496.0875	Chevy Chase Towing	(Bethesda MD)	KZN979
496.9625	Christian Tire	(Baltimore MD)	KNP549
151.7150	City & County Towing	(Baltimore MD)	KNBR381
461.4000	City & County Towing	(Baltimore MD)	WRH810
496.0625	Coale's Service	(Crownsville MD)	
31.1600	Coles American	(Silver Hill MD)	KLR649
35.1200	Collins GMC Olds	(Cumberland MD)	WSU837
463.8250	Colonial Auto Supply	(Annapolis MD)	KWS747
463.5750	Colonial Dodge	(Rockville MD)	KNFQ238
157.4850	Colonial Sunoco	(Waldorf MD)	KEG676
463.3500	Colonial Towing	(Towson MD)	WS0317
461.0250	Columbia Auto	(Randallstown MD)	
851.5625	Columbia Mobil	(Dayton MD)	KNBX924
154.5150	Conaway Motors	(Georgetown DE)	KKJ305
462.1750	Connecticut Ave. Amoco	(Washington DC)	
496.2875	Connecticut Ave. Tow	(Rockville MD)	KNQ609
151.8950	Cooks Towing	(Washington DC)	WRJ931
462.1500	County Towing	(Towson MD)	KNBX584
851.1875	Courtesy Towing	(Bethesda MD)	KMK490
461.3250	Crossroads Auto Radiator	(Falls Church VA)	KRG942
35.9000	Cullums Towing	(Aberdeen MD)	
463.5500	D & R Towing	(Silver Spring MD)	KNAS517
464.9000	D&D Tire	(Silver Spring MD)	KET924
464.6250	Dales Sunoco	(Wheaton MD)	KYE821
31.2000	Damascus Shell	(Damascus MD)	WRK308
461.7250	Dansicker Body Shop	(Towson MD)	KNCL562
151.7150	Darden VW & Foreign Auto	(Annapolis MD)	KNBQ550
463.3500	Dawkins Mobile Auto	(McLean VA)	WRI714
461.9250	Day's Gulf Service	(Bethesda MD)	KQ0986
151.7750	Dist. Hgts. Shell	(District Hgts. MD)	
154.5150	Dixon Chevrolet	(Waldorf MD)	KUN698
150.8750	Dolly's	(Baltimore MD)	KJZ933
461.1250	Don's Sunoco	(McLean VA)	KNBS501
463.7500	Dover Exxon	(Hazlettville DE)	KNCD619
461.4250	Down's Auto-Truck	(Fairfax VA)	
151.8650	Downtown Exxon	(Baltimore MD)	KRB785
150.8300	Dual Highway Exxon	(Hagerstown MD)	WSU440
35.7200	Duffey's Ford	(Wye Mills MD)	KZ0501
150.8750	Durbin Auto	(Hagerstown MD)	KGG232
150.8150	Dutchman's Auto	(Baltimore MD)	KT0565
150.8900	Eastern Boulevard	(Baltimore MD)	WYK350
150.8600	Easton Shell	(Easton MD)	WRJ395
464.8500	Eddie's Towing	(Waldorf MD)	WYK871
463.8250	Edsall Road Mobil	(Falls Church VA)	WRR436
463.9750	Els Tire	(Elkton MD)	WXX647
30.8000	Erzine Truck Tire	(Baltimore MD)	KRV701
27.3900	Eudy's American	(Alexandria VA)	KG0501
150.8900	Exxon Travel Center	(Millersville MD)	KGX460
851.7125	F & F Towing	(Wheaton MD)	WXM574
31.0000	Fairfax City Shell	(Fairfax VA)	
150.8450	Ferndale American	(Glen Burnie MD)	KRI541
150.8450	Firestone	(Dover DE)	KNCV399
462.5750	Fleetwood Towing	(Towson MD)	WYS681
35.1800	Fletchers Amoco	(Olney MD)	KTW373
31.1600	Forrestville Towing	(Forrestville MD)	
461.5000	Fort Lincoln New Tow	(Washington DC)	WYD901
150.8600	Fowblesburg Motors	(Upperco MD)	WQS479
151.7750	Franconia Towing	(Alexandrai VA)	KIL951
157.4700	Franconia Towing	(Alexandria VA)	KNFD562
463.2000	Frank's 24 hr. Towing	(Arlington VA)	WSR779
150.8300	Frank's Exxon	(Linthicum MD)	WQF438
157.5150	Frank's Towing	(Arlington VA)	WXT772
157.4700	Frank's Towing	(Rockville MD)	KYF384
495.7625	Frankford Towing	(Baltimore MD)	KDB371
35.0800	Frantzs Auto	(Fairfax VA)	KEF657
151.7150	Frederick Tire Mart	(Frederick MD)	

Frequency	Name	Location	Callsign
463.3000	Friends Tire	(Bethesda MD)	KJK828
151.6550	Frostburg Auto	(Frostburg MD)	KYY488
150.8600	Furlows Garage	(Cumberland MD)	KUK588
463.5250	G & G Gulf	(Silver Spring MD)	WQK518
151.8950	G & J Towing	(Washington DC)	KNCG726
154.5400	Gary's 66 Service	(Cambridge MD)	WSA943
150.8450	Gastrocks Garage	(Essex MD)	KGF665
151.7750	Gastrocks Towing	(Baltimore MD)	KXY300
463.3000	Geddes Towing	(Bethesda MD)	KNCY537
31.0400	Gelhaus Motor Parts	(Annapolis MD)	KER510
461.8750	Gemps Garage	(Cantonsville MD)	KII674
150.8900	Gene's Towing	(Silver Spring MD)	WXK633
461.8500	General Tire	(Salisbury MD)	KUR263
464.1250	General Tire	(Towson MD)	WYB860
463.4000	George's Auto	(Oxon Hill MD)	KNBL575
464.8500	Gerbers Garage	(Towson MD)	KTH932
150.8750	Gerst Sunoco	(Millersville MD)	WQJ978
464.4500	Goodyear Tire	(Catonsville MD)	KTZ771
462.1750	Goodyear Tire	(Wheaton MD)	KQX269
150.8750	Govan's Shell	(Baltimore MD)	KNCX346
30.9600	Greenbelt Road Shell	(Berwyn Heights MD)	KJE609
463.2500	Greens Garage	(Manchester MD)	KNAA513
496.9625	Greff's Exxon	(Baltimore MD)	KNR961
462.6500	Gregory's Towing	(Washington DC)	KAC7933
496.1875	Grimes Towing	(Frederick MD)	KAJ743
464.9500	Guy Motors	(Waldorf MD)	KNBN970
464.6000	H & R Towing	(Bethesda MD)	WQG747
463.5500	Hams 24 hr. Towing	(Arlington VA)	WXU517
463.9500	Harps BP	(Hagerstown MD)	KFT316
157.5000	Harry's Towing	(Glen Burnie MD)	KGX361
461.7250	Heineck Motors	(Towson MD)	KGG705
461.1750	Henderson Tire	(Washington DC)	WQT365
461.4500	Henry's Wrecker	(Falls Church VA)	KUU901
496.0875	Herson Auto Parts	(Bethesda MD)	KZG752
157.4700	Hillcrest Crane	(Forestville MD)	KSQ794
157.5000	Hitt Towing	(Washington DC)	
150.8450	Hollenshades	(Towson MD)	KGH356
463.4000	Hopkins Sunoco	(Oxon Hill MD)	KMM332
157.4700	Hughes Texaco	(Lutherville MD)	KLS485
461.2000	Hurlock Sunoco	(Williamsburg MD)	WQJ553
151.7150	Impala Towing	(Washington DC)	WXM801
157.4700	Impala Towing	(Washington DC)	
151.8950	International Motors	(Rockville MD)	KNBM721
461.0250	Intl. Truck Tire	(Baltimore MD)	WXT948
30.7600	Iron Gate Arco	(Manassas VA)	KVG442
496.7625	J & R Truck Tire	(Waldorf MD)	KYK909
461.8000	Jerry's Chevrolet	(Towson MD)	KXH391
496.7875	Jerry's Texaco	(Annapolis MD)	KNR428
469.2250	John's Towing	(Berwyn Heights MD)	WCA420
464.2250	John's Towing	(Bethesda MD)	KCB943
463.5500	Johnny's Towing	(Arlington VA)	WYW524
463.5000	Johnson's Texaco	(Washington DC)	KMJ333
464.8000	Jumps Recycled Auto	(Midland MD)	WQE295
461.8500	Keefers Gulf	(Hagerstown MD)	KOI251
150.8750	Keithley Bros. Garage	(Edgewood MD)	KGF654
150.8150	Ken Porter's Amoco	(Glen Burnie MD)	KBU906
154.5400	Kenny's Wholesale Tire	(Germantown MD)	KAU485
150.8450	Kensington Town Svc.	(Kensington MD)	KNBX723
43.0000	Kenway Exxon	(Bladensburg MD)	KGI341
151.7450	Kersey Motor	(Millsboro DE)	KNFJ781
462.0250	Key Bridge Towing	(Washington DC)	KNCT846
151.8350	Kimmel Automotive	(Baltimore MD)	KJU493
461.1000	Kimmel Automotive	(Baltimore MD)	WYH894
463.2500	Kimmel Tire	(Bethesda MD)	KQF348
157.5000	King Motor	(Washington DC)	KBN574
461.7250	Kings Towing	(Towson MD)	KRW569
35.1200	Kunkel Tire	(Baltimore MD)	KNBB435
463.4000	L & L Towing	(Oxon Hill MD)	KNBK397
151.6550	LB&W Amoco	(Oxon Hill MD)	WS0501
498.5625	LWH Towing	(Beltsville MD)	WIB354
496.5625	LWH Towing	(Silver Spring MD)	KNQ289
461.6000	Lakeview Exxon	(Kitzville MD)	WSI472
464.8500	Langley Park Texaco	(Rockville MD)	KNFD295
152.4800	Larry's Amoco	(Hazlettville DE)	WXG568
461.9500	Larry's Amoco	(Hazlettville DE)	WYP644
464.1250	Leatherwood Citgo	(Towson MD)	WYY289
463.5250	Leatherwood Motor	(Silver Spring MD)	KNBG350
464.6000	Leatherwood Motor Co.	(Baltimore MD)	KNBG350
150.8150	Lee's American	(Annapolis MD)	KS0644
463.8250	Lesters Towing	(Falls Church VA)	KSC466
463.6000	Linhard's Towing	(Baltimore MD)	WQT328
152.3000	Little Heaven Auto	(Little Heaven DE)	KZN697
461.8500	Littons Amoco	(Hagerstown MD)	KKY453
461.5750	Locks Garage	(Birdville MD)	KKT207
150.8450	Looper Servicenter	(Rockville MD)	
462.1750	Lustine Chevrolet	(Silver Spring MD)	KXK577
31.0000	MDL Auto & Truck	(Thurmont MD)	
43.0000	Manassas Mall Exxon	(Manassas VA)	KNCT852
461.5000	Marions Texaco	(Midland MD)	KNCV478
157.5000	Martins Towing	(Washington DC)	KZR655
150.9050	Maryland Auto Club	(Baltimore MD)	KNBV983
150.9200	Maryland Auto Club	(Baltimore MD)	KCT862
150.9350	Maryland Auto Club	(Baltimore MD)	KCJ261
452.5750	Maryland Auto Club	(Baltimore MD)	KCE416
452.5750	Maryland Auto Club	(Baltimore MD)	KGE416
150.9200	Maryland Auto Club	(Cantonsville MD)	KCT862
150.9200	Maryland Auto Club	(Columbia MD)	KLE659
150.9350	Maryland Auto Club	(Frederick MD)	WRR694
150.9350	Maryland Auto Club	(Hagerstown MD)	WXF951
150.9350	Maryland Auto Club	(Salisbury MD)	WYG385
150.9350	Maryland Auto Club	(Taneytown MD)	KXF701
150.9200	Maryland Auto Club	(Vienna MD)	KFR425
150.8300	Maryland Service Center	(Berlin MD)	WRN817
461.1500	Master Mobile Tune-up	(Cantonsville MD)	KWH241
33.1600	Mathias Servicenter	(Gaithersburg MD)	WXX464
157.5000	May's Brake	(Washington DC)	KBT244
157.5000	McArthur Service	(Washington DC)	KLE887
151.8650	McBees Towing	(Hanover MD)	WSX642
157.4700	Mel's Tow	(Baltimore MD)	KD0931
461.7500	Merchant's Tire	(Bethesda MD)	KSX463
463.8250	Merchants Tire	(Falls Church VA)	KSX463
42.9600	Middletown Ford	(Middletown MD)	KQC932
851.8875	Midtown Towing	(Towson MD)	WXB604
462.1500	Mikie's 24hr. Towing	(Falls Church VA)	KNCP931
31.0000	Miller Motors	(Baltimore MD)	KNFT382
151.8350	Millersville Auto	(Millersville MD)	
150.8900	Millersville Exxon	(Millersville MD)	WQJ978
151.7750	Millersville Shell	(Millersville MD)	KII244
35.4000	Milton Service Center	(Milton DE)	WXN573
461.4500	Mobile Car Care	(Falls Church VA)	KZK536
461.5500	Mobile Service	(Arlington VA)	KNBM447
30.9600	Modern Body Shop	(Wheaton MD)	KNAQ286
30.9600	Modern Body Shop	(Wheaton MD)	KNBC352
461.2500	Moneys Towing	(Wheaton MD)	KNBA841
462.1750	Montgomery Tire	(Baltimore MD)	KNBU323
150.8750	Mort's Sunoco	(Baltimore MD)	KJZ849
496.2375	Mt. Washington Auto	(Baltimore MD)	KNS346
151.8950	Mueller Auto	(Monkton MD)	KIF889
464.2500	Murphy's Towing	(Arlington VA)	KAZ325
463.6500	My O Tire	(Midland MD)	WRJ797
464.4000	Myersville Exxon	(Frederick MD)	WSD490
151.8650	N & C Auto Supply	(Glen Burnie MD)	KDK692
150.8150	N & N Towing	(Temple Hills MD)	KOB553
463.3500	National Automobile	(McLean VA)	KZO701
151.7150	National Car Rental	(Baltimore MD)	KNCL252
851.7125	National Tire	(Wheaton MD)	KSV818
461.0750	Neals Auto Repair	(Falls Church VA)	KZN717
461.5000	Nelsons Body Shop	(Williamsburg MD)	KNCH931
464.2750	New Carrollton Shell	(Arlington VA)	KCH640
463.3250	New Carrolton Shell	(Silver Spring MD)	KDN956
150.8750	Norman Towing	(Pikesville MD)	WYR802
463.5750	Normans Towing	(McLean VA)	WSF549
463.3500	Northeast Auto Clinic	(Towson MD)	WSS600
461.1750	Oakley Trailer Repair	(Baltimore MD)	
157.5000	Oaklleigh Towing	(Baltimore MD)	KKV851-2
464.2250	Orems Garage	(Towson MD)	KNCF359
464.6250	Orlando Towing	(Silver Spring MD)	WRI362
463.7500	Owings Mill Shell	(Owings Mill MD)	
463.9750	Oxon Hill Shell	(Waldorf MD)	WSN317
463.5500	Palmer Ford	(Silver Spring MD)	KNBS290
461.4250	Park Road Auto	(Silver Spring MD)	KSH324
461.6750	Park Road Auto Parts	(Washington DC)	KAP433
495.7625	Pasadena Motors	(Glen Burnie MD)	
35.1200	Patrick's Body Shop	(Chestertown MD)	KVG301
464.2500	Perfect Radiator	(Baltimore MD)	KLQ500
461.0500	Performance Towing	(Bethesda MD)	KEI768
461.6750	Pikeway Towing	(Towson MD)	WRJ905
820.7125	Piney Branch Sunoco	(Silver Spring MD)	
466.7750	Pocomoke Gulf	(Pocomoke City MD)	WDM499
43.0000	Pooles Personal Auto	(College Park MD)	KTF276
154.5150	Poolesville Motor	(Poolesville MD)	KAL807
461.7250	Precision Alternator	(Falls Church VA)	WYN470
463.7500	R & F Auto	(North Linthicum MD)	
463.8250	R & R Auto	(Wheaton MD)	WSN526
468.6750	Raley's Emergency Road	(Capitol Hgts. MD)	WJE94
463.6750	Raleys Emergency Svc.	(Silver Spring MD)	KTL871
157.5000	Ralph Cates Towing	(Rockville MD)	KEX514
151.8350	Ray's Auto Body	(Vienna VA)	KMG988
461.7250	Ray's Auto Service	(Falls Church VA)	
35.0800	Ray's Towing	(Bowie MD)	KBP211
463.5750	Ray's Towing	(Rockville MD)	WXW779
462.6500	Reaves Towing	(Washington DC)	KAC8336
157.4850	Redmonds Towing	(Pasadena MD)	KBV904
495.4875	Reliable Tire	(Baltimore MD)	
150.8300	Reliable Towing	(Glen Burnie MD)	KNAV728
151.7450	Reston Gulf	(Reston VA)	KVK712
463.4500	Rhine Towing	(Towson MD)	WSA321
35.7000	Rice Motors	(Lewes DE)	WQH756
35.1800	Rich BP	(Annapolis MD)	KTL987
463.4000	Rich's Towing	(Washington DC)	KBD911
151.8050	Ridgely Repair	(Ridgely MD)	KBO469
31.2400	Rober Minners Wrecker	(Milford DE)	KKJ201
157.5150	Roberts Repair	(Bethany Beach DE)	KNBH423
150.8750	Rockdale Towing	(Woodsboro MD)	KRJ636

Freq	Name	Location	Call
463.3750	Rockville Towing	(Silver Spring MD)	WZW567
157.5150	Rolling Road Exxon	(Baltimore MD)	WSQ357
150.8300	Rose Hill Shell	(Baltimore MD)	WSO304
157.4700	Ruxton	(Baltimore MD)	KFR909
464.3500	S & K Towing	(McLean VA)	KAZ973
463.2000	Schulte Ford Sales	(Cantonsville MD)	KUE905
461.9750	Scotties Auto Sales	(Baltimore MD)	WSX821
495.9125	Scotty's Texaco	(Manassas VA)	KGA760
464.4500	Sears Towing	(Catonsville MD)	KNCC691
461.3500	Security Ford Tractor	(Baltimore MD)	
463.5500	Service Station Main	(Baltimore MD)	KIZ969
150.8450	Severna Park Shell	(Severna Park MD)	KNAK409
42.9600	Shireys Auto Sales	(Milford DE)	WYV379
151.8350	Silver Spring Tow	(Silver Spring MD)	KLG448
150.8900	Simpson Towing	(Salisbury MD)	KWV717
464.3250	Skidmore Auto	(Midlothian MD)	KNAD665
464.9000	Skyhill Shell	(Arlington VA)	KAZ357
464.4500	Smitty's Auto Radiator	(McLean VA)	KNCM487
157.4700	Snooks Auto	(Elkton MD)	KRG656
31.1600	Spicklers Garage	(Hagerstown MD)	KUW382
463.6500	Sponaugle Towing	(Midland MD)	WYS280
463.2000	Springfield Gulf	(Arlington VA)	WRQ897
151.8650	Starting Gate Shell	(Laurel MD)	KTG992
462.1750	Sterling Auto Radiator	(Baltimore MD)	KNAJ458
35.7200	Steve's Towing	(Clinton MD)	KMH447
150.8750	Stevens Forest Exxon	(Columbia MD)	KRY929
463.7750	Stickley Towing	(Rockville MD)	WXE313
464.6000	Stidman Tire	(Bethesda MD)	KFU205
461.0250	Sundance Towing	(Wheaton MD)	WXY317
462.1750	Swans Tire	(Smithville MD)	KTH708
461.4250	Swartz & Bowie Towing	(Silver Spring MD)	KNCG361
463.9500	T & R Tire	(Hagerstown MD)	WYC321
151.8950	TNT Towing	(Washington DC)	WSI945
151.8950	TNT Towing	(Washington DC)	WSI945
151.9250	Taubers Services	(Linthicum MD)	KGC705
463.8500	Ted Britt Ford	(McLean VA)	KIQ756
44.0600	Ted's Towing	(Baltimore MD)	KLU449
496.0875	Teddy's Towing	(Bethesda MD)	KDN658
150.8900	Ten Oaks Auto	(Dayton MD)	KLX321
157.5000	Tenleytown Service	(Washington DC)	KBQ341
461.9000	The Maryland Tire	(Baltimore MD)	KES506
464.2750	Tidewater Auto	(Easton MD)	
464.1250	Timonium Mobil	(Towson MD)	WYF662
464.9000	Timonium Texaco	(Timonium MD)	
464.8500	Timonium Texaco	(Towson MD)	KYE776
851.9125	Tiny & Dukes Towing	(Silver Spring MD)	WQP336
463.8000	Tom's Car & Truck	(Baltimore MD)	WXW684
495.8875	Touch of Class Road Service	(Washington DC)	
35.0600	Towing by Nick	(Laurel MD)	KNAY783
461.5750	Tri-County Tire	(Black Horse MD)	KNBH479
151.7450	Tucker's Exxon	(Annapolis MD)	KNAT487
495.8125	Union 76 Auto Truck	(Frederick MD)	
150.8150	United Towing	(Harwood MD)	WQE965
463.5500	Valley Towing	(Baltimore MD)	WZS717
157.4700	Varsity Auto Repair	(Catonsville MD)	KCX683
463.8500	W R W Auto Parts	(Silver Spring MD)	KNCX232
461.2250	Wadkins Garage	(Milford DE)	
30.7600	Walt Seymore Towing	(Rockville MD)	KJB427
461.0500	Warrens Auto	(Towson MD)	KNCB426
151.6550	Weber Tire	(Fairfax VA)	KEP794
463.8500	Wertz Garage	(Manchester MD)	KNCA871
461.1750	West Boulevard 66	(Columbia MD)	
30.7600	Whitehall Sunoco	(Annapolis MD)	KNAR698
30.7600	Whitehall Sunoco	(Edgewater MD)	KNAR698
31.1600	Wildwood Towing	(Gaithersburg MD)	KNBV221
463.7750	Wildwood Towing	(Rockville MD)	KNCY575
499.8125	Wilson's Exxon	(Washington DC)	WIB743
496.8125	Wilsons Exxon	(Silver Spring MD)	KNQ637
157.4850	Windsor Services	(Baltimore MD)	KGN434
30.7600	Winslow's Sunoco	(Annapolis MD)	KXF469-0
464.4500	Wrecking Corp. of America	(McLean VA)	KNBW540
461.1750	Y Standard Service	(Excelsior Springs MD)	
150.8450	Yeakles Towing	(Big Pool MD)	KTY983
150.8750	Zappardino Auto	(Baltimore MD)	KBT247
461.9250	Tri-County Tire	(Aberdeen MD)	KNBH479

Trucking

Freq	Name	Location	Call
464.1500	A & B Trucking	(Baltimore MD)	
462.6500	A A Minuteman Delivery	(Washington DC)	KAD0619
461.1750	A-1 Courier	(Washington DC)	KNFF384
159.8400	Able Messenger	(Laurel MD)	WSN400
463.2000	Able Messenger	(Silver Spring MD)	WRX528
461.9000	Ace Delivery	(Washington DC)	WRI943
43.9600	Acme Delivery	(Baltimore MD)	KEP727
463.2250	Action Courier	(Washington DC)	KNBF337
495.7375	Action Couriers	(Arlington VA)	KNR286
464.2750	Acuity Traffic	(Arlington VA)	KCH812
159.7650	Acuity Traffic Courier	(Arlington VA)	WZY424
27.4700	Aid Van	(Alexandria VA)	KSA777
464.6250	Air Cargo Express	(Silver Spring MD)	WQY464
159.9000	Air Couriers Int'l	(Silver Spring MD)	KXX650
452.6500	Air Transit	(Arlington VA)	KWM940
463.6500	Airborne Air Freight	(Cantonsville MD)	KTF505
160.0800	Airborne Freight	(Falls Church VA)	KSK963
42.9600	Al's Hauling	(Hagerstown MD)	WQL764
151.7150	Albatross Container	(Baltimore MD)	KNFJ765
463.5750	Alert Delivery	(Rockville MD)	KLH829
44.2800	Allegheny Freight	(Baltimore MD)	KCL359
452.7500	Allstate Messenger	(Arlington VA)	KY0395
452.8000	Allstate Messenger	(Arlington VA)	KGC689
462.6000	Allstate Messenger	(Arlington VA)	KAB4145
463.3250	Alpha Messenger	(Washington DC)	
44.0200	Amerco Field Office	(Baltimore MD)	KBV713
159.8700	American Messenger	(Baltimore MD)	KEV994
452.8750	Amid-Atlantic Air Freight	(Baltimore MD)	WSW270
151.8050	Anchor Motor Freight	(Baltimore MD)	KKB901
159.8100	Anchor Motor Freight	(Jessup MD)	WSH501
851.7375	Annapolis Message	(Baltimore MD)	WZZ517
160.0050	Area Wide Courier	(Bethesda MD)	KED427
464.4500	Arrow Delivery	(Fairfax VA)	
159.9750	Atkinson Freight	(Baltimore MD)	KDC249
151.9550	Attkisson Truck	(Manassas VA)	KZ0590
464.4500	Atwood Gold Line	(Washington DC)	KEM795
43.7000	Atwoods Gold Line	(Bladensburg MD)	KOM403
462.1750	Avis Truck Rental	(Washington DC)	KYW733
159.5400	B & E Hauling	(Baltimore MD)	KSM977
806.1625	B & W Air Freight	(Baltimore MD)	WDH749
851.1625	B W Air Freight	(Baltimore MD)	KQR416
461.6000	BWA Triangle Parcel	(Annapolis MD)	KQK750
461.9500	Bakers Messenger	(Washington DC)	KVH432
462.1750	Bee-line Delivery	(Silver Spring MD)	WQH926
461.1250	Beltway Delivery	(McLean VA)	KNFF387
461.0500	Beltway Movers	(Bethesda MD)	KRR614
461.3250	Beltway Trucking	(Falls Church VA)	KQX223
463.4750	Benton Trucking	(Falls Church VA)	WYE888
43.8600	Blue Diamond Corp.	(Baltimore MD)	KES863
44.4400	Brinks	(Bethesda MD)	KJK651
159.4950	Brinks	(Bethesda MD)	
461.7750	Butler Jones Air Freight	(Eden MD)	WXD553
463.4000	C & C Delivery	(Washington DC)	KUN347
159.7950	Call-A-Messenger	(Silver Spring MD)	KNFE827
452.8250	Capitol Hill Cycle	(Washington DC)	WRB371
159.8550	Capitol Messengers	(Wheaton MD)	KXL349
461.3250	Carey Diesel	(Dover DE)	
461.1250	Carey Diesel	(Dover DE)	
160.0050	Carl Messenger	(Towson MD)	KYW910
160.0050	Carl's Messenger	(Baltimore MD)	KRJ788
159.6750	Carolina Freight	(Baltimore MD)	KEX522
496.6875	Caron's Delivery	(Falls Church VA)	KNQ546
464.1000	Cary Diesel -461.125, 461.325	(Dover DE)	
159.5850	Central Delivery	(Baltimore MD)	KFR623
160.1250	Central Delivery	(Bethesda MD)	KFB424
159.7500	Central Delivery	(McLean VA)	KFB424
160.0650	Central Delivery	(Silver Spring MD)	KFB424
160.1250	Central Delivery	(Silver Spring MD)	KFB424
151.8350	Chesapeake Transport	(Havre de Grace MD)	WXG805
159.6600	Choice Courier	(Washington DC)	
461.7500	Choice Delivery	(Bethesda MD)	KIM221
159.6900	City Wide Trucking	(Washington DC)	KCV860
464.2500	Classic Delivery	(Arlington VA)	WXV868
461.1500	Clay's Delivery	(Bethesda MD)	KCN469
461.6500	Clem Miller Trucking	(Baltimore MD)	
44.3800	Coale Truck Tractor	(Aberdeen MD)	
153.0500	Continental Container	(Baltimore MD)	KSO749
463.4750	Continental Parcel	(Baltimore MD)	KNCQ528
464.0750	Continental Parcel	(Silver Spring MD)	KNCQ528
43.8800	Contractor's Transport	(Alexandria VA)	KFR750
43.8800	Contractors Transport	(Alexandria VA)	KFR750
159.5700	Creative Air Courier	(Takoma Park MD)	KIU273
461.1000	Creative Expediting	(Bethesda MD)	KKN297
151.7750	Crouthamels Auto	(Baltimore MD)	KIW205
159.6600	Crown Queen Equipment	(Alexandria VA)	KBJ554
851.4375	Cully Cartage	(Towson MD)	WQO999
159.7950	Davidson Transfer	(Baltimore MD)	KEN644
495.9625	Devilbiss Trucking	(Westminster MD)	KNQ611
495.7125	Direct Courier	(Alexandria VA)	
452.3750	Direct Courier	(Washington DC)	WRJ381
159.8250	Dunbar Armored	(Washington DC)	
160.2000	Eagle Messenger	(Baltimore MD)	WQV712
461.4000	East Coast Air Freight	(Washington DC)	
35.9400	East Trucking	(Jessup MD)	KNBL711
159.5400	Ebong Express	(Oxon Hill MD)	KBP876
851.1125	Edgewater Truck	(Birdville MD)	KEV922
496.9375	Edmondson Courier & Messenger	(Baltimore MD)	KNS580
461.5500	Edwards Trucking	(Arlington VA)	KSG376
461.7000	Elliott Bros. Trucking	(Smithville MD)	KZK738
452.3250	Emery	(Arlington VA)	WSL990
452.3250	Emery	(Arlington VA)	
463.7750	Enight Trucking	(Baltimore MD)	KOH939

Freq	Name	Location	Call
464.8500	Executive Delivery	(Rockville MD)	WQM710
461.4000	Expeedite Services	(Washington DC)	KNBD778
159.7050	Expressway Messenger	(Baltimore MD)	KGL829
159.6000	Expressway Messenger	(Washington DC)	KVA368
462.5750	Fast Trucks	(Salisbury MD)	
159.8250	Federal Armored	(Baltimore MD)	KAS451
159.8250	Federal Armored	(Fairfax VA)	KXZ295
159.8250	Federal Armored	(Washington DC)	KGQ227
851.8125	Federal Express	(Baltimore MD)	KXK763
461.2750	Federal Express	(Hagerstown MD)	WSH789
852.1875	Federal Express	(Washington DC)	KNFU732
851.4125	Federal Express	(Washington DC)	KXN493
496.1625	Federal Express	(Washington DC)	
159.7650	Federal Messenger	(Washington DC)	KUN573
452.4250	Fitzgerald & Johnson	(Washington DC)	WSE381
807.2875	Five Star Courier	(Alexandria VA)	
463.4250	Flying Eagle Delivery	(Silver Spring MD)	KNAY796
463.2250	Fort Washington Trucking	(Oxon Hill MD)	
461.4250	GMS Corporate Courier	(Silver Spring MD)	WRY669
151.8950	Gaithersburg Hauling	(Gaithersburg MD)	KWL829
496.1125	Gelco Courier	(Silver Spring MD)	KYW549
462.1750	Glenair Freight	(Baltimore MD)	KNBQ574
463.5500	Gopher Service	(Baltimore MD)	WRI349
851.1875	Grace Courier	(Bethesda MD)	WQA571
43.9000	Green's Express	(Baltimore MD)	WQQ544
159.7350	Greenwood's Garage	(Baltimore MD)	KRG693
461.2750	H & P Hauling	(Silver Spring MD)	KMJ362
160.0350	H J Kane Delivery	(Bethesda MD)	KTZ830
160.0350	H.J. Kane Delivery	(Baltimore MD)	KTZ830
44.3000	Hahn Transportation	(New Market MD)	KCK355
44.3600	Hall's Motor Transport	(Baltimore MD)	KGG994
159.9300	Hall's Motor Transport	(Washington DC)	KCO680
151.8650	Harrelson Transportation	(Baltimore MD)	KWD492
151.8950	Haul it All	(Rockville MD)	KNAW308
160.1700	Hemingway Transport	(Baltimore MD)	KGG997
852.1375	Hemingway Transport	(Washington DC)	KNAX775
462.1000	Hills Transportation	(Towson MD)	WRQ259
463.5250	Howell Trucking	(Cumberland MD)	KNBD801
463.5250	Howell Trucking	(Midland MD)	KNBD801
461.2750	Hub City Express	(Hagerstown MD)	WZQ296
49.5200	Hudson Transfer	(Harbeson DE)	KBY410
452.6750	I G Expediting	(Washington DC)	KNFR282
464.2250	Ironsides Transport	(Washington DC)	WCX654
929.8375	John Matthews Fuel & Trucks	(Washington DC)	]
154.5400	Johnny Mattthews Truck	(Washington DC)	KAF418
462.1500	Johnny Unitas Air Freight	(Towson MD)	KWB448
160.0500	Joseph Dignan & Sons	(Ardwick MD)	KDX790
160.0500	Joseph Dignan & Sons	(Baltimore MD)	KDD506
151.8950	Kane Delivery	(Baltimore MD)	KNCU682
151.8950	Kane Delivery	(Bethesda MD)	KNCU6822
160.0350	Kane Delivery	(Rehoboth Beach DE)	WSO210
160.0350	Kane Delivery	(Washington DC)	
461.1250	Key Warehouse Service	(Baltimore MD)	KQJ544
151.4900	King Trucking	(Laurel MD)	KCD521
461.7250	Knight Trucking	(Towson MD)	KFK905
461.3500	L & N Hauling	(Midland MD)	WSS275
495.9625	L & R Messenger	(Falls Church VA)	KZK591
498.9625	L & R Messenger	(Springfield VA)	WBN664
44.1600	Laurel Trucking	(Laurel MD)	KBL251
464.1250	Lees Delivery	(Towson MD)	KEY501
30.9600	Leydig Trucking	(Midland MD)	WSC278
159.7650	M & M Messenger	(Bethesda MD)	
31.1600	M & M Truck	(Finksburg MD)	KTY550
151.6850	Mack Trucks	(Hagerstown MD)	WXE685
44.4400	Marvaco	(Silver Spring MD)	KIZ700
159.9150	Maryland Messenger	(Baltimore MD)	KGV747
464.0750	Maryland Metro Truck	(Silver Spring MD)	WSX529
159.6000	Mason & Dixon Lines	(Alexandria VA)	KBF768
159.6000	Mason & Dixon Lines	(Baltimore MD)	KBJ601
464.2750	McCall Trucking	(Baltimore MD)	
851.1625	McCall Trucks	(Baltimore MD)	WZU965
43.9800	McLean Trucking	(Baltimore MD)	KGE241
806.3875	Metro Truck & Tractor	(Beltsville MD)	WFK327
851.3875	Metro Truck & Tractor	(Bethesda MD)	WYL714
160.1850	Metropolitan Messenger	(Washington DC)	KNAU392
159.4950	Michael's Courier	(Washington DC)	KXA332
461.4250	Mickey's Dump Truck	(Baltimore MD)	WRU372
452.8750	Mid Atlantic Air Freight	(Falls Church VA)	WSH503
461.7750	Miller Trucking	(Manassas VA)	KMJ319
461.6750	Minority Truckers	(Washington DC)	WYA730
464.7250	Moore Trucking	(Cooksville MD)	KNAZ783
151.8350	Morrisey Bros. Transfer	(Baltimore MD)	KON682
159.7650	Mr. Messenger	(Washington DC)	WRN823
44.1200	Norfolk Baltimore	(Baltimore MD)	KZE618
461.4250	Nova Courier	(Fairfax VA)	KAC8221
461.4250	Nova Courier	(Falls Church VA)	WRE760
464.1000	Nu-Car Carriers	(Baltimore MD)	WQN654
452.8500	Official Couriers	(Washington DC)	KKR483
159.6900	Omni of Washington	(Washington DC)	KMK445
496.2625	Overland Courier	(Baltimore MD)	KNR492
496.7625	Overland Courier	(Waldorf MD)	KNR493
159.5250	Overnite Transport	(Baltimore MD)	KWY464
159.5250	Overnite Transport	(Silver Spring MD)	KVX731
159.6450	PDQ Delivery	(Arlington VA)	
44.0200	Pacific Intermountain	(Camp Springs MD)	WRM845
44.0000	Pacific Intermountain	(Jessup MD)	KLB714
44.3200	Palmer Heavy Hauling	(Washington DC)	KBV711
463.9500	Parcel Express	(Hagerstown MD)	
463.9500	Parcel Express	(Hagerstown MD)	KJU428
159.6450	Paul Henry Air Freight	(Hagerstown MD)	KFO589
464.6500	Peninsula Trucking	(Elk Neck MD)	WYL243
44.3600	Penn Yan Express	(Baltimore MD)	KNBU843
496.7675	Perry Transfer	(Baltimore MD)	KNP961
44.2000	Phillip's Bros. Warehouse	(Baltimore MD)	KGF684
461.8500	Phillips Trucking	(Salisbury MD)	WRH362
463.8250	Pittmans Freight	(Wheaton MD)	KNAZ950
44.0000	Pollard Delivery	(Arlington VA)	KGF696
44.0000	Pollard Delivery	(Glen Burnie MD)	KGG675
807.3375	Poole Air Couriers	(Laurel MD)	
461.4000	Port East Transfer	(Baltimore MD)	KIH726
461.4000	Potomac Industrial Truck	(Washington DC)	KNAS493
463.3500	Powells Transport	(Towson MD)	KME391
463.8000	Presidential Express	(Washington DC)	
160.1550	Preston Trucking	(Ardmore MD)	KEQ762
44.0400	Preston Trucking	(Baltimore MD)	KGG366
44.1000	Preston Trucking	(Dover DE)	KGG365
44.1000	Preston Trucking	(Preston MD)	KGG363
44.1000	Preston Trucking	(Salisbury MD)	KGG364
159.5850	Preston Trucking	(Winterthur DE)	KUY873
462.1750	Prettyman Trucking	(Smithville MD)	KIQ840
463.3500	Price Trucking	(Towson MD)	KWA917
160.1400	Purolator Armored	(Baltimore MD)	KGG245
160.1400	Purolator Armored	(Oxon Hill MD)	KIU589
452.6250	Purolator Courier	(Baltimore MD)	KSZ761
452.6250	Purolator Courier	(Falls Church VA)	KTE411
463.6000	R&M Delivery	(Washington DC)	WSC377
495.9375	R.M. Call Trucking	(Manassas VA)	KNQ426
461.5250	Ray's Hauling	(Cantonsville MD)	KNFE543
461.1750	Red Line Transport	(Cantonsville MD)	WYE876
44.0800	Red Star Express	(Baltimore MD)	WRD950
44.2200	Red Star Express	(Silver Hill MD)	KNCT665
43.9400	Reisch Trucking	(Crofton MD)	WRP538
159.6450	Reliable Delivery	(Bethesda MD)	KUK359
31.0000	Rentals Unlimited	(Rockville MD)	
462.6500	Repete Paper Pushers	(Washington DC)	KAD0988
463.4750	Rick's Delivery	(Falls Church VA)	KTU968
461.8750	Road Runner Delivery	(Cantonsville MD)	KEF273
463.8250	Roadrunner Delivery	(Falls Church VA)	KVF278
452.7250	Roadway Express	(Catonsville MD)	KTC948
452.7000	Roadway Express	(Washington DC)	KGF964
42.9600	Ryder Truck	(Hagerstown MD)	WYS491
30.9600	S T C Trucking	(Midland MD)	KNFA542
159.5400	Shayne Brothers	(Washington DC)	KGH363
159.6300	Shayne Brothers	(Washington DC)	KAX616
43.1800	Shipley Transfer	(Jonestown MD)	KEX533
495.5125	Skippy's Trucking	(Fairfax VA)	KNR780
159.7350	Smith & Soloman	(Baltimore MD)	KIT865
159.9000	Smith's Transfer	(Arlington VA)	KAS490
44.1400	Smith's Transfer	(Baltimore MD)	KGF486
461.3000	Sparkle Trucking	(Washington DC)	KNBW567
159.8850	Speed Service	(Washington DC)	KJP288
461.5250	Speed Service	(Washington DC)	KNFE301
464.2250	Speed Service	(Washington DC)	WRR937
463.5250	Spurgeon Trucking	(Frederick MD)	KNBZ791
462.1250	Star Courier	(Arlington VA)	WRP980
463.8250	Sterling Trucking	(Falls Church VA)	WRF569
49.5800	Steuart Transportation	(Piney Point MD)	KNFK582
816.9875	Steves Trucking	(Manassas VA)	
452.6750	Superior Transfer	(Baltimore MD)	KSI615
462.6750	Ted Top Cab	(Washington DC)	KAA7172
461.4000	Thomas Hauling	(Washington DC)	KBD461
44.2200	Tidewater Inland Express	(Baltimore MD)	KQU249
464.1750	Todd Van & Storage	(Gaithersburg MD)	
159.9600	Trans Urban Courier	(Washington DC)	KDD505
31.2000	Trapp Truck	(Linthicum MD)	KRN494
463.7750	Truck Brokerage Corp.	(Washington DC)	WSK790
464.1500	Twin Trucking & Warehouse	(Baltimore MD)	
461.3750	Two-Way Radio	(Cumberland MD)	
31.2000	Tysons Corner Transport	(Vienna VA)	KAP527
853.7625	U.S. Express	(Washington DC)	
463.9250	US Delivery	(Bethesda MD)	KNBD766
151.6550	United Parcel Service	(Arbutus MD)	KTC418
467.7500	United Parcel Service	(Laurel MD)	
467.8000	United Parcel Service	(Laurel MD)	
496.7625	Valentine Trucking	(Baltimore MD)	KNP429
160.0050	Vast Horizon Courier	(Arlington VA)	WYF474
44.0400	Waldorf Transportation	(La Plata MD)	KTG753
44.3800	Washington Cartage	(Bladensburg MD)	KXQ853
159.5700	Washington Express	(Landover Hills MD)	
463.2000	Washington Freightliner	(Silver Spring MD)	WQR854
461.9000	Washington Transport	(Washington DC)	WZN920
463.4500	Wayne Courier	(Washington DC)	WST502
159.7500	Webb Trucking	(Silver Hill MD)	KDA482

461.2500 Whitfield Hauling	(Wheaton MD)	KQR734
44.0600 William H. Bissell	(Baltimore MD)	KNBU598
44.2600 Wiser Brothers	(Fairfax VA)	KFM593
461.1500 World Wide Delivery	(Bethesda MD)	KNAD460
462.0250 World Wide Delivery	(Bethesda MD)	
461.1500 Yale Industrial Trucks	(Bethesda MD)	KSO435
461.1500 Yale Industrial Trucks	(Cantonsville MD)	KLY702

Farms

31.0400 ABC Farm Equipment	(Easton MD)	KEP283
47.5200 Agrico Chemical	(Hurlock MD)	KDY621
464.2000 Agway	(Easton MD)	
153.0050 Albeck Farms	(Rising Sun MD)	KWN430
452.1750 Allens Hatchery	(Federalsburg MD)	KZH502
461.3750 Arden Farm	(Churchville MD)	WXA459
461.3250 Arundel Nurseries	(Annapolis MD)	KNBK354
466.4750 Azalea Acres Nursery	(Clifton VA)	WFU342
151.6850 Banks Dairy Market	(Salisbury MD)	KDH843
157.6200 Baxter Farms	(Georgetown DE)	WXV325
35.8000 Beilers Crop Service	(Massey MD)	KJI310
461.3500 Bell Farms	(Frederick MD)	WSM306
35.1200 Blackwater Farms	(Cambridge MD)	KCF376
496.6375 Blanchfield Nursery	(Birdville MD)	KNP826
154.5700 Bonita Farms	(Bel Air MD)	
464.1750 Bountiful Farms	(Smithville MD)	WXJ569
464.1750 Bradleys Meadow	(Smithville MD)	KNAV389
451.8500 Brendel Farms	(Woodbine MD)	KNFH792
466.8500 Bromley Orchards	(Smithsburg MD)	WFP217
151.8650 Bunting Nurseries	(Selbyville DE)	KCQ681
151.8050 Carter Nurseries	(Sykesville MD)	KUE960
158.4600 Char Mar Farm	(Burkittsville MD)	KNAP874
463.2750 Chesapeake Nurseries	(Salisbury MD)	KXI348
461.6250 Clear Brook Farms	(Seaford DE)	KNBH463
466.6250 Clear Brook Farms	(Seaford DE)	KNBH462
152.9750 Clear Meadow Farm	(White Hall MD)	KNAM628
152.9150 Coldspring Farms	(New Windsor MD)	KZN455
461.6250 Conaway Farms	(Georgetown DE)	
35.8400 Country Pride Foods	(Hurlock MD)	KWB313
35.8400 Country Pride Foods	(Preston MD)	KYZ844
152.3000 Curtis W. Steen Farms	(Dagsboro DE)	KIQ707
151.6550 Dailey Tobacco	(Hanover MD)	KRL647
47.6000 Danner Farms	(New Windsor MD)	WQT568
31.4400 Dear Bought Farm	(New Windsor MD)	KCX633
461.0250 Delmarva Poultry	(Eden MD)	WXJ712
466.0250 Delmarva Poultry	(Laurel DE)	WDV381
151.6250 Diamond Farms	(Gaithersburg MD)	
464.1750 Dutch Ayr Farms	(Smithville MD)	KUD875
462.1750 Earlview Farms	(Smithville MD)	KGB956
30.8800 Egypt Farm	(White Marsh MD)	KWP870
151.8950 Elgin Farm	(Worton MD)	KIP964
152.9900 Elgin Farm	(Worton MD)	WXY846
151.8050 Ewing Farms	(Smyrna MD)	KSP797
462.0250 Fair Hill Farms	(Church Hill MD)	KAO951
152.3600 Fairview Orchards	(Hancock MD)	
33.1600 Farm Landscaping Constr.	(Annapolis MD)	KWD345
151.7450 Farmer's Supply	(Frederick MD)	KAU919
151.5500 Farmers & Planters	(Salisbury MD)	KBW553
461.1250 Fifer Orchards	(Woodside DE)	KNFM341
152.4650 Fletcher Farms	(Snow Hill MD)	WSP713
151.7150 Flower Barn	(Pasadena MD)	WRP961
463.6500 Fort Pleasant Farms	(Midland MD)	KNAO565
461.4250 Good Hope Farms	(Kennedyville MD)	KNFS408
151.5500 Goosehill Farm	(Chestertown MD)	WYQ682
461.8500 Guy Farms	(Salisbury MD)	KNAQ256
35.1400 H & L Farms	(Laurel DE)	WYU276
461.7000 Hab-Hab Farm	(Smithville MD)	WRH400
152.9150 Hank Spies Farm	(Cordova MD)	KGD317
31.3600 Harvey Bros. Farm	(Deer Park MD)	KIP416
463.8500 Haugen Farms	(Portland MD)	WSQ660
31.6400 Hepburn Orchards	(Hancock MD)	KXH965
151.5500 Hepburn Orchards	(Hancock MD)	KKL243
43.0600 Hexton Farms	(Cecilton MD)	KTU458
464.7250 Hoffman Farms	(Cooksville MD)	KNFM490
35.7200 Holly Farms Poultry	(Snow Hill MD)	KLI683
461.2000 Hubbert Farms	(Williamsburg MD)	KNBH557
44.0600 James Way Farms	(Cambridge MD)	KNBT552
461.1250 Jarrell Farms	(Clayton DE)	
30.9200 Ken Hales Farm	(Salisbury MD)	KIS375
151.5500 Langdon Farms	(Sherwood MD)	WSF451
152.9450 Lewis Orchards	(Cavetown MD)	WZV259
35.9400 Mac Farms	(Rhodesdale MD)	KCZ986
151.8050 Maxalea Nurseries	(Baltimore MD)	KRL665
464.3500 Meadows Farms	(McLean VA)	KZY200
463.5750 Merrifield Garden Cntr.	(McLean VA)	WXC346
31.6000 Merry Wood Farm	(Brookeville MD)	KNFP752
851.9125 Metropolitan Poultry	(Silver Spring MD)	WQA642
43.4800 Meyers Fertilizer	(Mount Airy MD)	KWN339
464.1750 Mid City Poultry	(Smithville MD)	WRL332

456.9000 Mighty Fine Farms	(Rhodesdale MD)	WDF735
151.7450 Moore Sod Farm	(Ocean City MD)	WZF908
158.4600 Mountaire Farms	(Delmar DE)	KGH313
158.4600 Mountaire Farms	(Selbyville DE)	KGH313
30.9600 Nanticoke Homes Farms	(Greenwood DE)	KWK721
461.3000 North Yarmouth Farms	(Williamsburg MD)	KNCX2032
151.5650 Oak Bluff Farm	(Woodsboro MD)	WYG700
152.8850 Oatland Farms	(Olney MD)	KNFM631
151.8650 Oswald Nurseries	(Smithsburg MD)	KKI506
461.4250 Pahlman Farms	(Easton MD)	KNCN911
47.6400 Perdue Farms	(Bridgeville DE)	KLD505
461.1500 Perdue Farms	(Eden MD)	KKE672
47.6400 Perdue Farms	(Georgetown DE)	
47.6400 Perdue Farms	(Salisbury MD)	KLD499
47.6400 Perdue Farms	(Salisbury MD)	
35.7200 Picketts Nursery	(Woodbine MD)	KTK982
31.6000 Pleasant Valley Farm	(Brookeville MD)	KYL455
151.8050 Pleasant View Farm	(Braddock Hts. MD)	KNAW528
464.0250 Pondview Farms	(Church Hill MD)	KNCW494
151.5950 Price Farms	(Kennedyville MD)	KSO747
151.8050 Pulte Franklin Farms	(Herndon VA)	
31.2800 Rayner Farms	(Salisbury MD)	KDW482
461.5000 Reliance Farms	(Williamsburg MD)	WSP269
463.5750 Rokeby Farms	(McLean VA)	WRK584
43.3600 Savage Farms	(Mount Airy MD)	WRS243
466.4750 Seawood Farms	(Lewes DE)	WGG445
461.4750 Seawood Farms	(Milford DE)	WRH865
35.1800 Showell Farms	(Showell MD)	KGG460
464.8000 Smithville Farm	(Smithville MD)	WSU823
464.6750 Snow Farms	(Smyrna DE)	KNCJ342
158.3850 Soil Service	(Denton MD)	WZB425
498.7125 Springfield Nursery	(Fairfax VA)	KB6411
495.7125 Springfield Nursery	(Falls Church VA)	KNS842
151.5800 Star Farms	(Magnolia DE)	WZM574
35.4400 Starkey Farms	(Galena MD)	KVD803
463.5250 Stegmaier Orchards	(Midland MD)	KNFE428
464.7250 Sunset Hill Farm	(Cooksville MD)	KNBW764
27.4500 T.E. Wood Farms	(Clinton MD)	
464.2750 Talbot Grain	(Cordova MD)	
464.2750 Talbot Grain	(Cordova MD)	
152.9450 Ten Oaks Nursery	(Clarksville MD)	KWN442
461.9500 Townsend Grain Farms	(Hazlettville DE)	KWO271
47.6000 Walnut Hill Farms	(Hurlock MD)	WQC968
151.5200 Wilcom Farm	(Ijamsville MD)	KYS560
151.5200 Wilcom Farms	(Frederick MD)	WXZ698
466.2000 Willin Farms	(Seaford DE)	WDP833
461.2000 Willin Farms	(Williamsburg MD)	WXB578
463.9750 Windfields Farms	(Elkton MD)	KQC887
152.9750 Windridge Farm	(Germantown MD)	KUW949
451.9000 Wings Landing Farm	(Preston MD)	
463.3000 Woodley Hill Farm	(Fairplay MD)	

Mobilephone - RCC - Paging

152.2400 Advanced Radio Commnications	(Washington DC)	KUO649
152.1500 Advanced Radio Communications	(Alexandria VA)	KLF495
152.2400 Advanced Radio Communications	(Alexandria VA)	KUO649
454.2000 Advanced Radio Communications	(Falls Church VA)	KQZ755
454.3000 Advanced Radio Communications	(Falls Church VA)	KQZ755
152.1500 Advanced Radio Communications	(Washington DC)	KLF495
454.2000 Advanced Radio Communications	(Washington DC)	KQZ755
454.3000 Advanced Radio Communications	(Washington DC)	KQZ755
454.3500 Advanced Radio Communications	(Washington DC)	KQZ755
152.0900 Airsignal Int'l	(Dover DE)	KGC591
152.0300 American Radio-Telephone	(Baltimore MD)	KGA249
152.0900 American Radio-Telephone	(Baltimore MD)	KGA249
152.2400 American Radio-Telephone	(Baltimore MD)	KUO650
152.2400 American Radio-Telephone	(Bethesda MD)	KUO651
454.1000 American Radio-Telephone	(Bethesda MD)	KGA248
454.2500 American Radio-Telephone	(Cantonsville MD)	KGA249
454.0250 American Radio-Telephone	(Catonsville MD)	KGA249
454.0500 American Radio-Telephone	(Catonsville MD)	KGA249
454.1500 American Radio-Telephone	(Catonsville MD)	KGA249
152.2400 American Radio-Telephone	(Oxon Hill MD)	KUO650
152.2400 American Radio-Telephone	(Rockville MD)	KUO650
152.2400 American Radio-Telephone	(Towson MD)	KUO650
152.0300 American Radio-Telephone	(Washington DC)	KGA248
152.2400 American Radio-Telephone	(Washington DC)	KUO651
454.1500 American Radio-Telephone	(Washington DC)	KGA248
152.1800 American Radio-Telephone	(Westminster MD)	KGA249
152.6600 Armstrong Telephone	(Rising Sun MD)	KGH873
152.8400 C & P Telephone	(Alexandria VA)	KCG590
152.8400 C & P Telephone	(Arlington VA)	KGC590
454.3750 C & P Telephone	(Arlington VA)	KGA586
454.4250 C & P Telephone	(Arlington VA)	KGA586
454.4750 C & P Telephone	(Arlington VA)	KGA586
454.5250 C & P Telephone	(Arlington VA)	KGA586
454.5500 C & P Telephone	(Arlington VA)	KGA586
454.5750 C & P Telephone	(Arlington VA)	KGA586

454.6250 C & P Telephone	(Arlington VA)	KGA586
454.6500 C & P Telephone	(Arlington VA)	KGA586
152.8400 C & P Telephone	(Baltimore MD)	KWH310
152.5100 C & P Telephone	(Baltimore MD)	KGA587
152.8400 C & P Telephone	(Baltimore MD)	KWH310
152.8400 C & P Telephone	(Bethesda MD)	KGC590
152.5400 C & P Telephone	(Charlotte MD)	KGC600
152.7200 C & P Telephone	(Havre de Grace MD)	KGH866
152.5400 C & P Telephone	(Midland MD)	KGC592
454.6750 C & P Telephone	(Washington DC)	KGC405
454.9500 C & P Telephone	(Washington DC)	KGC405
35.2200 Contact, Inc.	(Aberdeen MD)	KGA807
35.2200 Contact, Inc.	(Annapolis MD)	KGA807
35.2200 Contact, Inc.	(Baltimore MD)	KGA807
43.5800 Contact, Inc.	(Baltimore MD)	KGA807
35.2200 Contact, Inc.	(Bel Air MD)	KGA807
35.2200 Contact, Inc.	(Crofton MD)	KGA807
35.2200 Contact, Inc.	(Glen Burnie MD)	KGA807
43.5800 Contact, Inc.	(Oxon Hill MD)	KGA806
43.5800 Contact, Inc.	(Rockville MD)	KGA806
35.2200 Contact, Inc.	(Washington DC)	KGA806
152.6600 Continental Telephone	(Manassas VA)	KIY597
152.6900 Diamond State Telephone	(Dover DE)	KGH864
152.7500 Diamond State Telephone	(Dover DE)	KGH864
152.6000 Diamond State Telephone	(Georgetown DE)	KGH865
152.7800 Diamond State Telephone	(Georgetown DE)	KGH865
152.8400 Diamond State Telephone	(Milford DE)	KGA473
454.1250 Dover Radio Page	(Dover DE)	WRV241
152.2400 Dover Radio Page	(Hazlettville DE)	WRV242
152.1500 Hawkins Communications	(Arbutus MD)	KGA250
454.2750 Hawkins Communications	(Baltimore MD)	KUD232
494.0125 Hawkins Communications	(Baltimore MD)	WXS470
494.0375 Hawkins Communications	(Baltimore MD)	WXS470
494.0625 Hawkins Communications	(Baltimore MD)	WXS470
494.0875 Hawkins Communications	(Baltimore MD)	WXS470
494.1125 Hawkins Communications	(Baltimore MD)	WXS470
494.1375 Hawkins Communications	(Baltimore MD)	WXS470
494.1625 Hawkins Communications	(Baltimore MD)	WXS470
494.1875 Hawkins Communications	(Baltimore MD)	WXS470
494.2125 Hawkins Communications	(Baltimore MD)	WXS470
494.2375 Hawkins Communications	(Baltimore MD)	WXS470
494.2625 Hawkins Communications	(Baltimore MD)	WXS470
494.2875 Hawkins Communications	(Baltimore MD)	WXS470
454.0750 Hawkins Communications	(Catonsville MD)	KGA250
152.2400 Hawkins Communications	(Hagerstown MD)	WQZ680
454.0750 Hawkins Communications	(Towson MD)	KGA250
454.0750 Hawkins Communications	(Washington DC)	KUD232
454.2750 Hawkins Communications	(Washington DC)	KUD232
43.2200 Hawkins Communications	(Westminster MD)	KWU226
463.5000 Kwik Kall	(Fort Ritchie MD)	KNBT960
929.7625 MCI Airsignal	(Baltimore MD)	
929.7625 MCI Airsignal	(Washington DC)	
454.1250 Maryland Mobile Phone	(Baltimore MD)	KKB567
454.3250 Maryland Mobile Phone	(Baltimore MD)	KKB567
929.9875 Millicom Information	(Washington DC)	
929.8875 Mobilcomm of DC	(Baltimore MD)	
929.8875 Mobilcomm of DC	(Washington DC)	
152.2400 Modern Communications	(Cumberland MD)	KGC402
152.2400 Modern Communications	(Hagerstown MD)	WXR909
929.9375 Page America	(Washington DC)	
494.0125 Phone Depots	(Baltimore MD)	WXS468
494.0375 Phone Depots	(Baltimore MD)	WXS468
494.0625 Phone Depots	(Baltimore MD)	WXS468
494.0875 Phone Depots	(Baltimore MD)	WXS468
494.1125 Phone Depots	(Baltimore MD)	WXS468
494.1375 Phone Depots	(Baltimore MD)	WXS468
494.1375 Phone Depots	(Baltimore MD)	WXS468
494.1625 Phone Depots	(Baltimore MD)	WXS468
494.1875 Phone Depots	(Baltimore MD)	WXS468
494.2125 Phone Depots	(Baltimore MD)	WXS468
494.2375 Phone Depots	(Baltimore MD)	WXS468
494.2625 Phone Depots	(Baltimore MD)	WXS468
494.2875 Phone Depots	(Baltimore MD)	WXS468
152.1800 Professional Bureau	(Woodside DE)	KTS240
494.0125 RCC of Virginia	(Baltimore MD)	WXS408
494.0375 RCC of Virginia	(Baltimore MD)	WXS408
494.0625 RCC of Virginia	(Baltimore MD)	WXS408
494.0875 RCC of Virginia	(Baltimore MD)	WXS408
494.1125 RCC of Virginia	(Baltimore MD)	WXS408
494.1375 RCC of Virginia	(Baltimore MD)	WXS408
494.1625 RCC of Virginia	(Baltimore MD)	WXS408
494.1875 RCC of Virginia	(McLean MD)	WXS408
494.2125 RCC of Virginia	(Baltimore MD)	WXS408
494.2375 RCC of Virginia	(Baltimore MD)	WXS408
494.2625 RCC of Virginia	(Baltimore MD)	WXS408
494.2875 RCC of Virginia	(Baltimore MD)	WXS408
152.2400 Rad-Com	(Washington DC)	KWU293
152.0600 Radio Broadcasting Co.	(Dover DE)	WRD394
152.1200 Radio Communications	(Annapolis MD)	KGC583
454.1250 Radio Communications	(Baltimore MD)	KKB643
454.2000 Radio Communications	(Baltimore MD)	KKB643
454.3250 Radio Communications	(Baltimore MD)	KKB643

454.3500 Radio Communications	(Baltimore MD)	KKB643
152.0600 Radio Communications	(Bethesda MD)	KGC594
152.2100 Radio Communications	(Bethesda MD)	KGC587
152.2400 Radio Communications	(Bethesda MD)	KUD652
152.2100 Radio Communications	(Cambridge MD)	KWU413
43.2200 Radio Communications	(Frederick MD)	KKB683
152.1800 Radio Communications	(Hagerstown MD)	WDZ590
43.2200 Radio Communications	(La Plata MD)	KGI277
43.2200 Radio Communications	(Upper Marlboro MD)	KGI277
152.0600 Radio Communications	(Upper Marlboro MD)	KGC594
35.2200 Radio Phone	(Arlington VA)	KAD516
152.1800 Radio Phone	(Arlington VA)	KMM684
454.2500 Redi-Call	(Georgetown DE)	KUS359
158.7000 Redi-Call	(Milford DE)	KSU368
152.0600 Redi-Call	(Millsboro DE)	KUS359
152.2100 Redi-Call	(Oak Orchard DE)	KUS359
454.2500 Redi-Call	(Oak Orchard DE)	KUS359
158.7000 Redi-Call	(Rehoboth Beach DE)	KUS363
152.4500 Redi-Call	(Seaford DE)	KUS359
464.4500 Redi-Call	(Washington DC)	
152.2400 Salisbury Mobile Tel	(Ocean City MD)	WXR994
152.2400 Salisbury Mobile Tel	(Pocomoke City MD)	WXR994
152.0900 Salisbury Mobile Tel	(Salisbury MD)	KGH868
152.2400 Salisbury Mobile Tel	(Salisbury MD)	WXR994
454.1000 Salisbury Mobile Tel	(Salisbury MD)	WXR994
152.1500 Salisbury Mobile Tel	(Willards MD)	KGH868
152.2400 Salisbury Mobile Tel	(Williamsburg MD)	WXR994

Communications

461.7250 Advanced Communications	(Falls Church VA)	KRF754
464.8000 Allied Communications	(Midland MD)	WSN476
464.8000 Allied Mobile Communications	(Cumberland MD)	WSN473
461.0750 Alpha Communications	(Falls Church VA)	KCC257
464.8500 Antenna Site Locaters	(Rockville MD)	KNBU565
461.4750 Arlington Telecommunications	(Arlington VA)	KSG579
462.7000 BCD Electronics	(Dundalk MD)	KAB1345
464.0500 Baltimore Communications	(Towson MD)	KIW405
35.9000 Blanton Antenna	(Annapolis MD)	KSX619
35.9000 Blanton Antenna	(Severna Park MD)	KNFC241
498.5625 Business Radio Communications	(Beltsville MD)	KB4478
463.4250 Business Radio Communications	(Silver Spring MD)	WZF975
495.5625 Business Radio Communications	(Silver Spring MD)	KNQ224
461.8000 CES Corporation	(Towson MD)	WXH254
461.4500 Caldabaugh Communications	(Salisbury MD)	KRP318
496.7375 Calvert Telecommunications	(Baltimore MD)	KNS892
464.4000 Capitol Radio	(Alexandria VA)	
462.6000 Capitol Radio Communications	(Alexandria VA)	
852.3375 Capitol Radio Communications	(Falls Church VA)	KNBX890
462.7000 Catoctin Communications	(Frederick MD)	KAB2163
151.8050 Catonsville Communications	(Catonsville MD)	KQQ694
151.7150 Coaxial Communications	(Reston VA)	KVI721
151.9250 Comm Center	(Laurel MD)	KSJ691
0.0000 Commercial Communications	(Arlington VA)	
461.4000 Communication Services	(Hagerstown MD)	
463.8500 Communications Electronics	(Manchester MD)	KKO651
462.0500 Communications Electronics	(Towson MD)	KZR887
463.8000 Communications Engineering	(Arlington VA)	KCO274
0.0000 Communications Engineering	(Fairfax VA)	
852.4875 Communications Engineering	(Silver Spring MD)	KNFU784
852.4875 Communications Engineering	(Upper Marlboro MD)	KNFU784
464.3000 Communications Engineers	(Upper Marlboro MD)	
461.9250 Communications Facilities	(Leonardtown MD)	KNCD963
463.8000 Communications, Inc.	(Manassas VA)	KCO274
461.4500 Community Antenna	(Salisbury MD)	KJD649
495.7125 Community Communications	(Falls Church VA)	KYC491
466.4000 Conks Communications	(Dover DE)	WDX319
461.4000 Conks Communications	(Harrington DE)	KAO786
462.5500 Consolidated Radio	(Smyrna DE)	KAC1361
154.5150 County Communications	(Forest Hill MD)	KUW251
496.7625 Crawford Communications	(Falls Church VA)	KNS807
464.4500 Crawford Communications	(McLean VA)	KNAU872
151.8650 Curtis Antenna	(Street MD)	KNAE230
151.7150 Custom Antenna	(Rockville MD)	KCV349
461.4000 E J Electronics	(Harrington DE)	WYH778
463.7500 E J Electronics	(Hazlettville DE)	KKY794
0.0000 E.F. Johnson	(Arlington VA)	
0.0000 Electronic Communications	(Silver Spring MD)	
461.2250 Eastern Walkie-Talkie	(McLean VA)	KNBH516
461.5500 Ebbitt Green Electronics	(Arlington VA)	KNCT915
461.2000 Ecker Communications	(Towson MD)	KZL454
151.9250 Elctronic Technical Radio	(Alexandria VA)	
464.8500 Electronic Communications	(Rockville MD)	WSU206
461.4250 Electronic Communications	(Silver Spring MD)	WSD448
462.5750 Electronic Services	(Oxon Hill MD)	KAB6162
451.5250 Ford Communications	(Dearborn MD)	
151.8050 Ford Communications	(Hagerstown MD)	KLA412
464.7500 Ford Communications	(Hagerstown MD)	WQF412
462.3750 General Electric	(Columbia MD)	

464.8750 General Electric	(Rockville MD)	KUW263	
464.0750 General Electric	(Silver Spring MD)	KQZ431	
464.5000 General Electric	(Springfield VA)		
464.9250 General Electric	(Springfield VA)		
464.5500 General Electric	(Springfield VA)		
461.7250 General Electric	(Towson MD)	KBS860	
461.5000 General Electric	(Waldorf MD)	KWM538	
461.7000 General Electric	(Washington DC)	KRG567	
495.6625 General Electric	(Washington DC)	KNQ432	
33.1400 General Electric	(Washington DC)	KD4394	
461.0500 General Electric	(Willards MD)	KNFM921	
463.3000 Global Telecommunications	(Hagerstown MD)	KNFQ353	
464.9250 Grace Communications	(Columbia MD)	KBS811	
463.7000 Hankeys Communications	(Frederick MD)	KWM492-3	
151.8350 Hankeys Radio	(Frederick MD)	KDX913	
151.8050 Harvey Communications	(Frederick MD)	KYW681	
43.2200 Hawkins Communications	(Arbutus MD)	KDS979	
463.3000 Interstate Communications	(Hagerstown MD)	KNBV464	
461.8250 Jerry's Communications	(Churchville MD)	KQX341	
462.6500 Joe's Communications	(Ocean City MD)	KAB8081	
463.6750 Jones Communications	(Deal Island MD)	WZV960	
461.9750 Kwik Kall	(Baltimore MD)	WQV513	
461.9750 Kwik Kall	(Laurel MD)		
462.1000 Kwik Kall	(Silver Spring MD)	WRV745	
464.2750 Kwik Kall	(Silver Spring MD)	KXT793	
464.3000 LCA Tower	(Temple Hills MD)		
151.8050 Liberty Radio	(Randallstown MD)	WRY907	
464.7250 Lloydel Electronics	(Bellefonte DE)	KNAB568	
461.0250 M & J Communications	(Wheaton MD)	WXY316	
154.5400 Magothy Communications	(Pasadena MD)	KXN850	
154.5150 Marine Communications	(Annapolis MD)	KKM680	
156.4250 Marine Communications	(Annapolis MD)	KYU825	
156.4500 Marine Communications	(Annapolis MD)	KSK348	
461.3250 Maryland Communications	(Annapolis MD)	KXL431	
852.0125 Maryland Communications	(Baltimore MD)	WQP474	
461.3750 Maryland Communications	(Churchville MD)	KXL432	
464.7250 Maryland Communications	(Cooksville MD)	WSW202	
851.2375 Maryland Communications	(Hagerstown MD)	KNCZ506	
462.0000 Maryland Communications	(Silver Spring MD)	KZL217	
851.2875 Maryland Communications	(Silver Spring MD)	WQZ928	
0.0000 Maryland Communications	(Towson MD)		
151.8950 Mel Comm Electronics	(Frederick MD)	KDS939	
461.2250 Merrymount Communications	(White Hall MD)		
464.2250 Metro Communications	(Towson MD)	WRY857	
461.3000 Metrocom	(Washington DC)	KXI371	
929.7625 Metromedia	(Baltimore MD)		
929.7625 Metromedia	(Washington DC)		
483.5375 Midcities Communications	(Arlington VA)	KB5826	
464.8000 Mills Communications	(Manchester MD)	WSO636	
35.0800 Mills Communications	(Westminster MD)	KGF765	
463.2250 Mills Communications	(Westminster MD)	WSO555	
464.6000 Mobile & Marine Communica.	(Baltimore MD)	WZF69	
464.7500 Mobile & Marine Communications	(Forest Hill MD)	WSB454	
461.0750 Mobile Communications	(Falls Church VA)	KNCC915	
461.4250 Mobile Radio Communications	(Falls Church VA)	WRC202	
151.7150 Mobile Radio Svc.	(Chestertown MD)	KTV471	
463.8750 Mobile Radio System	(Washington DC)		
461.9250 Mobile Radio Systems	(Washington DC)	KNCG223	
461.4500 Moore's Radio Svc.	(Hazlettville DE)	WYF670	
462.6500 Motorola	(Camp Springs MD)	KAB9479	
464.2000 Motorola	(Catonsville MD)	KNBJ273	
851.0125 Motorola	(Catonsville MD)	KWH949	
463.9000 Motorola	(Church Hill MD")	WYH870	
463.9000 Motorola	(Eden MD)	WYH869	
462.6500 Motorola	(Falls Church VA)	KAB2055	
463.9000 Motorola	(Ocean City MD)	WYH867	
851.0125 Motorola	(Towson MD)	WQO911	
462.6500 Motorola	(Washington DC)	KAB9481	
464.2000 Motorola	(Washington DC)	WBX690	
851.0125 Motorola	(Washington DC)	KWH948	
462.0500 Motorola	(Washington DC)		
153.2750 Motorola	(Washington DC)		
461.8750 Motorola	(Washington DC)		
811.0375 Motorola	(Washington DC)		
463.9000 Motorola	(Williamsburg MD)	WYH868	
33.1600 Northeast Communications	(Elkton MD)		
154.5400 Page Communications	(Vienna VA)	WSZ644	
461.3750 Phase II Telecommunications	(Washington DC)	KNCN637	
464.2500 Radio Communications	(Arlington VA)	KZT323	
463.9750 Radio Relay Leasing	(Millsboro DE)	WYT253	
464.7250 Rice Communications	(Jackson MD)	WSK848	
154.5400 Scan Communications	(Washington DC)	KNCG996	
30.9200 Severn Communications	(Pasadena MD)	KSH747	
0.0000 Southern MD Communications	(White Plains MD)		
464.8500 Suburban Communications	(Fenton MD)	KNBU566	
464.8500 Suburban Communications	(Rockville MD)	KNBU566	
463.3750 Superior Radio	(Silver Spring MD)	KYV842	
929.7875 TRS Communications	(Towson MD)		
463.7500 Talbot Communications	(Hazlettville DE)	KSD436	
461.7000 Talbot Communications	(Smithville MD)	KZM512	
461.6000 Talbot Communications	(Willards MD)	KSD439	
851.3375 Ted Britt Communications	(McLean VA)	WZS444	

462.0750 Two Way Communications	(Washington DC)	KGU938	
461.3750 Two Way Radio	(Midland MD)	KFU292	
464.1250 Virginia Communications	(Alexandria VA)	KKE410	
154.5700 WFG Communications	(Baltimore MD)		
157.6800 Wes Mar Communications	(Midland MD)	KDJ751	
151.9250 Westinghouse	(Annapolis MD)	KSO531	
496.0625 Westinghouse	(Annapolis MD)	KAX935	
495.9375 Westinghouse	(Baltimore MD)	KAX942	
496.0625 Westinghouse	(Baltimore MD)	KAX940	
495.9375 Westinghouse	(Elkridge MD)	KY2259	
461.3000 Westinghouse	(Jonestown MD)	WSD942	
496.1125 Westinghouse	(Silver Spring MD)	KNT400	
464.1250 Westinghouse	(Towson MD)	WYM823	
461.6750 Westinghouse	(Towson MD)	WZG717	
855.3125 Westinghouse	(Washington DC)		
496.0375 Westinghouse -security	(Baltimore MD)	KNFH850	
464.4000 Wilmers Communications	(Birdville MD)	WRP841	

Manufacturing

151.7450 7 up Bottling	(Cantonsville MD)	KQY332	
461.7000 7-up Bottling	(Smithville MD)	KID596	
151.7750 A.B. McKee	(Silver Springs MD)		
807.2875 Achievement, Inc.	(Kensington MD)		
151.6850 Acutex International	(Fairfax VA)	KNAW826	
464.3000 Acutex International	(Fairfax VA)	KNCD744	
35.0600 Alcrymat Corp.	(Landover MD)	WRR701	
851.8875 Allegheny Pepsi	(Towson MD)	KNCE730	
451.5250 American Seamless	(Baltimore MD)	KNCY320	
464.7000 Anarex Inc.	(Annapolis MD)	KDR670	
151.9250 Andrew Beck Company	(Bethany DE)	KNBR989	
153.1250 Armco	(Baltimore MD)	KWW961	
462.2500 Armco Steel	(Baltimore MD)	KXS490	
151.7450 Armor Elevator	(Ocean City MD)	KWT977	
154.5400 Arrow Manufacturing	(Randallstown MD)	KTK351	
153.1700 Atlantic Research	(Alexandria VA)		
153.3200 Atlantic Research	(Alexandria VA)		
463.5000 Auto Data Processing	(Baltimore MD)	KTP238	
463.2000 Auto Data Processing	(Silver Spring MD)	KTP500	
35.9600 Baltimore Elevator	(Baltimore MD)	KTN788	
461.1000 Baltimore Envelope	(Silver Spring MD)	WRJ203	
461.7250 Baltimore Envelope	(Towson MD)	WRJ204	
851.7125 Bartley Corporation	(Silver Spring MD)		
851.7125 Bartley Corporation	(Wheaton MD)	WRG669	
151.7450 Bayshore Enterprises	(Lewes DE)	KVZ940	
462.8250 Bendix Corporation	(Towson MD)	WSV555	
462.4500 Bethlehem Steel	(Baltimore MD)	KGA264	
153.1400 Bethlehem Steel	(Sparrows Point MD)	KGG547	
158.2800 Bethlehem Steel	(Sparrows Point MD)	KGC383	
158.4300 Bethlehem Steel	(Sparrows Point MD)	KGD298	
451.2250 Bethlehem Steel	(Sparrows Point MD)	KGS758	
451.6750 Bethlehem Steel	(Sparrows Point MD)	KGH425	
462.5000 Bethlehem Steel	(Sparrows Point MD)	KJJ278	
154.5700 Bethlehem Steel	(Sparrows Point MD)		
462.3000 Bethlehem Steel	(Sparrows Point MD)		
462.4500 Bethlehem Steel	(Sparrows Point MD)		
151.9550 Black & Decker	(Easton MD)	KNCP447	
153.0500 Black & Decker	(Easton MD)	KNCP827	
462.2000 Black & Decker	(Hampstead MD)	WZZ881	
151.6850 Black & Decker	(Hampstead MD)		
151.6850 Black & Decker	(Towson MD)		
151.6850 Black & Decker	(Towson MD)	KCG451	
151.9250 Cabot Cabot & Forbes	(Washington DC)	KNBU912	
151.6850 Cargill Corporation	(Harbeson DE)	WXQ724	
158.4150 Carling Brewery	(Baltimore MD)	KNBJ257	
158.3450 Carr Lowrey Glass	(Baltimore MD)	KTE906	
152.3600 Cavalier Energy Co.	(Salisbury MD)	KDA480	
464.3250 Ceres Terminals	(Baltimore MD)	KNCK384	
464.4750 Ceres Terminals	(Baltimore MD)	KNCK384	
464.1500 Coca Cola Bottling	(Annapolis MD)	KRK488	
153.1100 Coca Cola Bottling	(Baltimore MD)	KGY885	
462.5250 Coca Cola Bottling	(Baltimore MD)	WYH207	
464.0250 Coca Cola Bottling	(Church Hill MD)	KML843	
464.0250 Coca Cola Bottling	(Easton MD)		
461.3000 Coca Cola Bottling	(Easton MD)		
461.4750 Coca Cola Bottling	(Silver Spring MD)	KRW834	
461.2750 Coca Cola Bottling	(Towson MD)	KWN906	
153.0650 Coldwater Seaford	(Cambridge MD)	WZS899	
463.3500 Combustioneer Corp.,	(Washington DC)	KQW956	
154.5400 Communications Satellite	(Clarksburg MD)	KXR637	
464.8000 Computer Data Systems	(Bethesda MD)	WSG221	
151.9250 Computer Sciences Co.	(Falls Church VA)	KRN992	
463.8250 Comsat	(Annapolis MD)	KAD800	
464.0750 Comsat	(Silver Spring MD)	KAD800	
151.7450 Comsat	(Washington DC)		
151.7450 Comsat	(Washington DC)		
462.0500 Comsat Corp.	(Wheaton MD)	KRC227	
153.2900 Conoco Communications	(Baltimore MD)	KFU709	
496.2625 Control Data	(Baltimore MD)	KNQ495	

462.5750	Control Data	(Silver Spring MD)	KAD3699
495.8375	Control Data	(Silver Spring MD)	KNQ496
865.3625	Control Data	(Towson MD)	
151.9550	Crown American	(Frederick MD)	WRT841
461.1750	Crystal Industries	(Washington DC)	WYF489
464.3750	Davco Corp.	(Baltimore MD)	WYH751
463.4500	Delaware Coca Cola	(Harrington DE)	KNBP775
31.9600	Delta Mining	(Grantsville MD)	KXH851
496.6875	District Associates	(Falls Church VA)	KNP788
153.1550	Dresser Industries	(Jennings MD)	KFD759
463.7000	Dualco	(McLean VA)	WRI558
151.6250	Dynalectric	(Wilmington DE)	
467.3000	E I Du Pont	(Seaford DE)	WYQ284-5
151.5800	Eastern Mining	(Mt. Savage MD)	WRW843
851.2375	Eastland Corporation	(Fort Meade MD)	WSB565
153.0800	Ei Du Pont	(Seaford DE)	WXS536
463.8250	Equality Enterprises	(Annapolis MD)	KBH693
153.2600	F M C	(Baltimore MD)	KYD637
153.3800	F M C	(Baltimore MD)	KGR619
153.2150	F. Bowie Smith	(Baltimore MD)	KLE706
153.0500	Fairchild Industries	(Germantown MD)	KLR571
153.0800	Fairchild Industries	(Germantown MD)	KLR571
153.1250	Fairchild Industries	(Germantown MD)	KXH587
466.2250	Fairchild Industries	(Germantown MD)	KLH87
153.0950	Fairchild Industries	(Hagerstown MD)	WXH839
464.6500	Fairmac Corporation	(Arlington VA)	KJF632
153.3200	Family Research Service	(Baltimore MD)	KQR625
462.2000	Family Research Service	(Baltimore MD)	KQR625
158.2800	Fedders	(Frederick MD)	KWR540
463.4000	Firestone Tire & Rubber	(Baltimore MD)	
153.1400	General Electric	(Columbia MD)	KTW741
151.8350	General Foods	(Dover DE)	
151.8350	General Foods	(Dover DE)	KFK475
153.2600	General Foods	(Dover DE)	KCG946
153.7600	General Foods	(Dover DE)	
153.3200	General Motors	(Baltimore MD)	KDC383
462.2250	General Motors	(Baltimore MD)	KRF619
462.2500	General Motors	(Hanover MD)	WRG365
496.1875	Georgia Pacific	(Baltimore MD)	KVY259
153.1100	Gould, Inc.	(Glen Burnie MD)	KTX946
462.4000	Grace	(Baltimore MD)	KUW745
35.7200	Gull Corporation	(Leesburg VA)	KGP912
158.3100	Harbison-Walker	(Baltimore MD)	KGX925
463.3000	Hobart Corp.	(Baltimore MD)	KVC207
461.0500	Holston Brothers	(Bethesda MD)	
154.5150	Honeywell	(Mclean VA)	
462.2750	Hughes Aircraft	(Arlington VA)	WXF509
158.2800	Huntington Creek	(Baltimore MD)	KLY353
462.7750	IBM	(Arlington VA)	KVK796
462.9000	IBM	(Baltimore MD)	KWM463-7
154.5150	IBM	(Bethesda MD)	KXO296
157.7400	IBM	(Bladensburg MD)	KRO467
462.8500	IBM	(Bladensburg MD)	WXP705
462.7750	IBM	(Falls Church VA)	KTM246
151.9250	IBM	(Gaithersburg MD)	KLI644
462.7750	IBM	(Manassas VA)	KRT399
157.7400	IBM	(McLean VA)	KLC766
152.4800	IBM	(Myersville MD)	KLC764
462.7750	IBM	(Reston VA)	KXK568
157.7400	IBM	(Rockville MD)	KIK295
462.8500	IBM	(Rockville MD)	KWW797
462.8500	IBM	(Silver Spring MD)	
152.4800	IBM	(Towson MD)	KYN695
157.7400	IBM	(Washington DC)	KLH725
462.7750	IBM	(Washington DC)	KLR207
462.9250	IBM	(Washington DC)	KEO658
151.6250	Instrucom	(Silver Springs MD)	
154.5150	J & D Manufacturing	(Severn MD)	WRH450
463.5500	J & L Industries	(Baltimore MD)	WYA809
464.4500	Janmar Corporation	(McLean VA)	KNCS738
463.6000	Johnson Controls	(Washington DC)	KNAR654
153.0800	Kelly Springfield	(Cumberland MD)	WYP734
153.3050	Kelly Springfield	(Cumberland MD)	KDZ608
35.0800	Kennecott Communications	(Marley Neck MD)	KQK669
153.0500	Kennecott Communications	(Marley Neck MD)	KGG819
153.3200	Kennecott Communications	(Marley Neck MD)	KGG819
153.1700	Koppers	(Baltimore MD)	KUE368
153.0500	L.D. Caulk Company	(Milford DE)	
463.8250	Law Investments Co.	(Annapolis MD)	WZR767
462.2250	Lehigh Portland Cement	(Union Bridge MD)	KDM536
158.3250	Lenmar Laquers	(Baltimore MD)	KDG632
461.4500	Litton Bionetics	(Falls Church VA)	KZO595
153.3500	Locke Radio	(Baltimore MD)	KCK313
151.8650	Locust Industries	(Baltimore MD)	KTT756
461.1000	MCI Communications	(Arlington VA)	
461.6750	MCI Communications	(Washington DC)	
461.5250	MCI Communications	(Washington DC)	
461.3000	MCI Communications	(Washington DC)	
35.0600	Marriott Corporation	(Arlington VA)	KXI509
173.2100	Martin Marietta	(Bethesda MD)	WBW221
153.2450	Martin Marietta	(Bethesda MD)	
35.0800	Martin Marietta	(Boonesboro MD)	KTG902

153.2000	Martin Marietta	(Middle River MD)	KGG289
35.8000	Martin Marietta	(Williamsport MD)	KTG904
151.5950	Martins Elevator	(Hagerstown MD)	WQH520
461.7750	Marx Corp.	(Baltimore MD)	KBL574
158.2950	Maryland Bedding	(Baltimore MD)	KLB360
153.3650	Maryland Cup Corp.	(Owings Mills MD)	KEE214
462.2750	Maryland Shipbuilding	(Baltimore MD)	KJT865
461.2750	Maryland Shipbuilding	(Baltimore MD)	
154.6000	Maryland Shipbuilding	(Baltimore MD)	
461.1250	Mashs Hams	(Baltimore MD)	KLH222
158.3850	Maugansville Elevator	(Maugansville MD)	KZH679
451.4250	McCormick Co.	(Baltimore MD)	WSE232
464.7000	Medallion Industries	(Annapolis MD)	KCG710
469.0750	Medallion Industries	(Bowie MD)	WBZ887
469.7000	Medallion Industries	(Bowie MD)	WBZ887
153.1550	Monsanto	(Havre de Grace MD)	KBU998
463.5000	Nelco	(Baltimore MD)	KTF290
463.5000	Nelco	(Washington DC)	KZK471
151.7450	Occidental Chemical	(Perryville MD)	KTC448
153.0650	Occidental Chemical	(Perryville MD)	KNCE786
461.7250	Oliver Mining	(Midland MD)	KNBP806
151.7450	Otis Elevator	(Ocean City MD)	WZF912
151.7450	Otis Elevator	(Willards MD)	WXB480
153.3800	PPG Industries	(Cumberland MD)	KGE345
158.2950	Pabin Corporation	(Cresaptown MD)	KUS304
154.5150	Page Beechcraft	(Manassas VA)	KNAT623
496.1625	Paragon Corporation	(Falls Church VA)	KNR850
461.0750	Pax-Tromix	(Leonardtown MD)	KZU689
461.8500	Penco Corp.	(Salisbury MD)	WZP740
463.8500	Pepsi Cola Bottling	(Annapolis MD)	KCW972
464.9000	Pepsi Cola Bottling	(Falls Church VA)	KGG701
464.4000	Pepsi Cola Bottling	(Williamsburg MD)	KYT519
463.2500	Pepsi Cola Bottling	(Woodside DE)	WXD753
153.2750	Pierce Associates	(Alexandria VA)	KNCQ904
462.7000	Plymouth Company	(Washington DC)	KAC8333
451.5750	Proctor & Gamble	(Baltimore MD)	KNBY391
466.1250	RCA -also 466.975	(College Park MD)	WDB885
496.2875	Radiation Physics	(Rockville MD)	KNR728
463.9750	Random House	(Westminster MD)	
158.3100	Reichhold Chemicals	(Cheswold DE)	KLF684
463.6000	Rite Aid	(Baltimore MD)	WXX448
43.5200	Robert Hay Mining	(Grantsville MD)	WRB656
33.1600	Royal Crown Bottling	(Hagerstown MD)	KLP539
153.1700	SCM	(Baltimore MD)	KJB901
463.5750	Salisbury Coca Cola	(Whaleysville MD)	WZG894
464.4250	Salus Corporation	(Arlington VA)	KNBQ641
496.0125	Seaboard Service	(Washington DC)	KUI904
30.7600	Sheridan Advertising	(Salisbury MD)	KEP519
496.0875	Southern Management	(Bethesda MD)	KNA438
462.1250	Southern Maryland Co.	(Arlington VA)	KEY508
153.0950	Sperry	(Reston VA)	KNFB757
464.1000	Sperry Univac	(McLean VA)	KNBW440
151.6850	Stargen Industries	(Annapolis MD)	KZG639
464.4250	State Farm Mutual	(Frederick MD)	
464.4250	State Farm Mutual	(Frederick MD)	WXE731
462.2250	Syntonic Tech	(Baltimore MD)	
462.3000	TRW	(McLean VA)	KNY841
462.3000	TRW	(McLean VA)	KRY841
464.8000	The Haight Corp.	(Bethesda MD)	KNBW468
463.8500	The Macke Company	(Washington DC)	KJY301
461.1250	The Standard Elevator	(Baltimore MD)	WSW600
153.2600	Thiokol Corporation	(Elkton MD)	WYK230
495.7375	Toledo Scale	(Arlington VA)	KNQ551
496.2625	Toledo Scale	(Baltimore MD)	KNQ552
496.7625	Toledo Scale	(Waldorf MD)	KNQ551
462.5250	US Gypsum Company	(Baltimore MD)	
468.7500	Union Labor Life Insurance	(Washington DC)	
461.3250	United Enterprises	(Annapolis MD)	KKE505
467.0500	Virginia Beef Co.	(Herndon VA)	WYK57
461.8250	Washington Coca Cola	(Bethesda MD)	KQO621
462.5750	Waverly Press	(Easton MD)	KAC7067
153.1100	Westavco	(Luke MD)	KJA443
153.3200	Westavco	(Luke MD)	KZL788
462.2000	Westavco	(Luke MD)	WXN514
151.6850	Western Electric	(Baltimore MD)	KVK711
153.0800	Western Electric	(Baltimore MD)	KBF751
462.3500	Western Electric	(Baltimore MD)	KSR756
153.0800	Western Electric	(Baltimore MD)	
153.1800	Westinghouse	(Baltimore MD)	KUR992
152.4800	Wiley Manufacturing	(Port Deposit MD)	KED943
151.7150	Wiley Manufacturing	(Port Deposit MD)	KBD943
151.8650	Wise, Inc.	(Columbia MD)	KBE428
158.2800	Wyoming Block	(Wyoming DE)	KCW836
462.1500	Xerox	(Leesburg VA)	KXL448

Construction

464.4000	A & H Excavating	(Frederick MD)	KMD955
496.0625	A & M Roofing	(Annapolis MD)	KNS211
464.1250	Accent Builder	(Rockville MD)	WYB413
31.9200	Admix Concrete	(Laurel MD)	KJQ280
496.7125	Adnil General Contractors	(Leesburg VA)	
496.9375	Alanzo Ours Construction	(Falls Church VA)	KNS894
153.0200	Alban Tractor	(Baltimore MD)	KGH321
461.2500	All Purpose Construction	(Wheaton MD)	KUL299
30.8000	Allstate Building	(Salisbury MD)	WXT438
30.8800	Allstate Building	(Timonium MD)	KTC628
461.1250	Alumisteel Systems	(Baltimore MD)	KWG880
851.5625	American Asphalt Paving	(Dayton MD)	WRG650
495.7375	American Backhoe	(District Hgts. MD)	KB5720
31.7600	American Concrete	(Washington DC)	WQQ783
461.4250	American Contractors	(Silver Spring MD)	WXU932
35.1200	American Excavating	(Fairfax VA)	WZG565
35.3200	American Excavating	(Fairfax VA)	WXD394
43.3600	American Paving	(Salisbury MD)	KWJ523
35.9800	Andrew Building	(Lutherville MD)	KLW644
451.9500	Annandale Asphalt	(Manassas VA)	KVW294
463.9000	Annapolis Construction	(Annapolis MD)	
152.9600	Apollo Paving	(Baltimore MD)	KBC694
463.9250	Apollo Paving	(Towson MD)	KBS963
816.1875	Araby Concrete	(Frederick MD)	
463.4750	Arlington Asphalt	(Falls Church VA)	KTY308
498.5625	Artisan Contractors	(Beltsville MD)	WIB284
495.5625	Artisan Contractors	(Silver Spring MD)	KNQ286
153.0200	Arundel Asphalt	(Forrestville MD)	
153.0200	Arundel Asphalt	(Silver Spring MD)	KQJ962
153.0200	Arundel Engineers	(Waldorf MD)	KQJ962
496.0625	Arundel Contractors	(Annapolis MD)	KNS656
851.1125	Arundel Structures	(Birdville MD)	KJV889
47.5200	Ashland Construction	(Chantilly VA)	KIU576
461.8000	Asphalt Construction	(Bethesda MD)	KDD736
43.3600	Asphalt Service	(Glen Burnie MD)	KUU688
463.6000	Atlantic Building	(Baltimore MD)	KNCF268
154.6000	Atlantic Rigging	(Baltimore MD)	
851.2875	Atlantic Rigging	(Silver Spring MD)	KNBG922
496.7625	Atlas Mobile Concrete	(Baltimore MD)	KNR490
496.7625	Atlas Mobile Concrete	(Silver Spring MD)	KNR491
30.9200	Austin Asphalt	(Waldorf MD)	KXD545
35.9600	B & C Paving	(Mitchellville MD)	KNFP719
31.7600	B & J Contracting	(Baltimore MD)	WRL870
464.7250	B & S Contracting	(Cooksville MD)	WRR946
851.5625	B L O Contracting	(Dayton MD)	WRH210
464.1750	BG's Crane	(Annapolis MD)	WRI511
464.2750	Bailey-Marine Construction	(Easton MD)	
462.0000	Baldi Construction	(Silver Spring MD)	WQT896
851.2125	Baltimore Asphalt	(Baltimore MD)	KJW854
154.5400	Baltimore Rigging	(Baltimore MD)	KIP822
464.2500	Banner Masonry	(Baltimore MD)	KTH929
463.2000	Bashioum Concrete	(Arlington VA)	WSX432
461.8500	Bateman Contracting	(Falls Church VA)	KNAZ690
851.7875	Beacon Masonry	(Falls Church VA)	KJT777
152.9450	Bel Air Excavating	(Bel Air MD)	WRN457
464.1000	Beltsville Construction	(Bethesda MD)	WRK401
464.1750	Benfield Builders	(Annapolis MD)	WXB574
462.0750	Bensky Construction	(Baltimore MD)	
461.0500	Benson Construction	(Baltimore MD)	
461.7250	Benson Construction	(Towson MD)	KTW407
461.1000	Bergstrom Construction	(Sherwood MD)	WZG257
43.0600	Better Roads Corp.	(Baltimore MD)	KDA996
463.2250	Bicentennial Builder	(Westminster MD)	KEF274
151.7150	Biero Construction	(Alexandria VA)	KMM408
461.3500	Big Boys Rigging	(Baltimore MD)	KVC851
495.6875	Billy's Crane Service	(Bethesda MD)	KDL317
33.1600	Bite Way Construction	(Alexandria VA)	KAD548
49.5400	Bituminous Construction	(Baltimore MD)	KGC864
31.4400	Bloomingdale Construction	(Queenstown MD)	KTB941
464.2250	Bob Grill General Contractor	(Washington DC)	WZV665
463.7000	Bohemia Contractors	(Churchville MD)	KDR764
43.0800	Brandywine Sand & Gravel	(Davidsonville MD)	WRT786
43.0800	Brandywine Sand & Gravel	(Herndon VA)	WRT787
461.6500	Brenfield Builders	(Baltimore MD)	WQT894
851.2625	Brigham & Day Paving	(Bethesda MD)	WZF948
851.5875	Brigham & Day Paving	(Bethesda MD)	WZF948
816.9625	Brookeville Turnpike	(Rockville MD)	
495.9125	Brookfield Builders	(Glen Burnie MD)	KZN993
464.8500	Brookhill Construction	(La Plata MD)	KKY627
464.0750	Brothers Construction	(Rockville MD)	KAI602
463.5250	Brown Construction	(Frederick MD)	KNBK831
35.9200	Browning Construction	(Germantown MD)	KFP542
35.9200	Browning Construction	(Monrovia MD)	KUY967
463.3750	Bruffey Contracting	(Rockville MD)	KYY979
461.9250	Buenos Aires Construction	(Hyattsville MD)	461.925
464.8500	Built Rite Builders	(Rockville MD)	KNBJ385
464.6250	Built Rite Builders	(Silver Spring MD)	WSK839
30.8800	Bunting Construction	(Selbyville DE)	KWF440
464.1000	Burman Construction	(Baltimore MD)	WSY797
464.0750	Buzzell Building	(Gaithersburg MD)	WXE995
464.0750	Buzzell Building Corp.	(Silver Spring MD)	WXE993
464.8000	C & E Construction	(Smithville MD)	KNCF372
464.6250	C & E Construction	(Willards MD)	KNCF372
461.3000	C D C Concrete	(Fairfax VA)	KEQ295
35.0800	C P S Contractors	(Vienna VA)	KKP390
30.5800	C W Wright Construction	(Bethany Beach DE)	KRT982
30.5800	C W Wright Construction	(Frederick MD)	WYL843
30.5800	C W Wright Construction	(Seaford DE)	KKH867
495.9375	Cable Constructors	(Manassas VA)	KWU675
461.2500	Capitol Building	(Wheaton MD)	KNFB537
49.5400	Capitol Concrete	(Dover DE)	KCJ696
463.2250	Caples Concrete	(Westminster MD)	WZJ643
464.0750	Cardinal Concrete	(Falls Church VA)	KKD608
462.1000	Carpex Construction	(Washington DC)	KNAU721
30.8000	Carroll Builders	(Sykesville MD)	
461.2250	Carroll Contractors	(Earleigh Heights MD)	KNBR402
463.9250	Carroll Engineering	(Towson MD)	KUG266
461.2500	Carvin Contractors	(Wheaton MD)	KTC566
464.1000	Cast Construction	(Baltimore MD)	WQD610
496.1875	Cearfoss Construction	(Catonsville MD)	KNS808
463.7500	Cement Contracting	(Woodside DE)	KLG766
151.6250	Centennial Contractors	(Springfield VA)	
461.3000	Centerville Concrete	(Fairfax VA)	WXE333
466.3750	Central Atlantic Construction	(Aberdeen MD)	WAF295
461.3750	Central Atlantic Construction	(Churchville MD)	KWK584
461.3000	Certified Concrete	(Minquadale DE)	KNAX988
461.2250	Certified Construction	(Bethesda MD)	WXE743
31.2160	Chantilly Construction	(Chantilly VA)	KJV841
810.9375	Charles City Concrete	(Waldorf MD)	
463.3000	Charley's Crane Svc.	(Bethesda MD)	KTP213
151.6250	Chase Construction	(Annapolis MD)	
461.8500	Chason Engineers	(Baltimore MD)	WSD837
31.8800	Cherry Hill Sand	(Jessup MD)	KQV689
461.7250	Ciambro	(Landover MD)	
30.6000	City Concrete	(Baltimore MD)	KJP501
452.0750	City Contractors	(Wheaton MD)	KRZ758
463.8250	Clauss Construction	(Annapolis MD)	KWN871
461.6250	Coastal Crane	(Baltimore MD)	KSX857
461.1750	Collins Contracting	(Manassas VA)	KQI788
463.3750	Collinson Construction	(Whaleyville MD)	
31.6000	Colonial Concrete	(Delmar DE)	KBO507
464.1750	Colonial Masonry	(Washington DC)	KTT428
461.4250	Community Roofing	(Falls Church VA)	KNFJ575
151.7150	Complete Builders	(Annapolis MD)	KAP643
463.6500	Complete Building Svc.	(Washington DC)	WRW465
463.3750	Concrete General	(Silver Spring MD)	KII421
496.1125	Concrete Services	(Beltsville MD)	KB6295
496.1125	Concrete Services	(Silver Spring MD)	KNS704
462.1250	Concrete Walls	(Arlington VA)	WSO395
816.0375	Consolidated Home Builder	(Columbia MD)	
151.6850	Consolidated Masonry	(Towson MD)	
463.8250	Construction Co.	(Falls Church VA)	KVU953
461.9200	Construction Materials	(District Hghts. MD)	WGJ381
31.9200	Contee Sand & Gravel	(Baltimore MD)	KOF237
49.5200	Contee Sand & Gravel	(Laurel MD)	air
463.7750	Contemporary Builders	(Baltimore MD)	KOI789
151.8050	Continental Block	(Farnhurst DE)	KNCM497
151.8050	Cooley Construction	(Clarksburg MD)	WYB900
469.7250	Coplay Cement -& 469.925	(Frederick MD)	
463.9250	Cornett Excavating	(Bethesda MD)	KUH338
43.1800	Cosle Contractors	(Baltimore MD)	KSS701
851.1625	Cossentino Construction	(Baltimore MD)	WSB490
461.4250	Crane Rental	(Baltimore MD)	WSK239
464.0500	Crane Rental	(Bethesda MD)	KVT347
461.1750	Creative Builders	(Manassas VA)	WZF509
47.5200	Crest Contracting	(Cockeysville MD)	KGC503
35.5200	Crouse Construction	(Street MD)	KUJ833
154.5400	Cumberland Cement	(Midland MD)	KFV362
154.4900	Cumberland Cement	(Midland MD)	KSK837
151.8950	Cunningham Crane	(Bethesda MD)	WXX351
35.8000	Curtis Bay Paving	(Baltimore MD)	KEP878
43.1400	Davis Concrete	(Aberdeen MD)	
43.1400	Davis Concrete	(Bel Air MD)	WZT514
43.1400	Davis Concrete	(Joppa MD)	WZV252
463.8250	Davis Roofing	(Falls Church VA)	WQU657
463.3000	De Jam Contracting	(Baltimore MD)	KBC213
47.5200	Dean Construction	(California MD)	KUO810
43.0800	Deer Park Paving	(Finksburg MD)	KNBK281
30.7600	Degarmo Construction	(Upperco MD)	KDU305
35.1000	Delaughter Construction	(Frederick MD)	WXQ522
461.2500	Demolition of DC	(Alexandria VA)	
464.0750	Demory Construction	(Silver Spring MD)	KLA756
496.2125	Deneau Construction	(Rockville MD)	KNQ229
464.2750	Design & Construction	(Towson MD)	KNBQ705
35.1400	Dewco Homes	(Hampstead MD)	KVZ788]
462.0750	Diggers, Inc.	(Baltimore MD)	KKR812
851.3875	Dimeglio Construction	(Bethesda MD)	KDM595
851.2375	Dimeglio Construction	(Fort Meade MD)	KNCE864
852.4625	District Concrete	(Silver Hill MD)	KNFT728
463.5250	Dream Contractors	(Frederick MD)	KNBC218
151.5950	Duma Construction	(Silver Spring MD)	KDG465
33.1600	Dunlap Homes	(Edgemere MD)	KLT945
461.1000	Dypsky Bros. Construction	(Selbyville DE)	
461.3000	E & G Contractors	(Washington DC)	KBO419
463.6000	E B Warren Company	(Washington DC)	KFI997
464.1000	E J Heskett Construction	(Bethesda MD)	KLK837

461.7750	E.W. Evans Construction	(Eden MD)	KNCB991q
463.8500	Eagle Concrete	(Mclean VA)	KTG274
31.0400	Eagle Ltd. Construction	(Manassas VA)	KUE952
154.4900	East Coast Builders	(Woodlawn MD)	KZP342
461.1500	Eastern Concrete	(Bethesda MD)	KNAT329
35.4800	Econo Crete Construction	(Hagerstown MD)	KVR524
498.7625	Eighty Eight Construction	(Alexandria VA)	WID983
42.9600	Eldreths Construction	(Conowingo MD)	KSC739
495.5125	Elliott Construction	(Burtonsville MD)	
464.7000	Empire Construction	(Annapolis MD)	KKZ701
461.1250	Empire Construction	(Baltimore MD)	KKJ652
463.5250	Excavation Construction	(Rockville MD)	WYW228
30.6400	Excavation Construction	(Washington DC)	KNAT810
463.5250	Excavation Construction	(Washington DC)	KIM553
30.6200	Explosive Engineers	(Butler MD)	WXU733
30.6200	Explosive Engineers	(Sparks MD)	KGY620
44.4000	F.O. Day	(Washington DC)	
47.4400	Faith Construction	(Washington DC)	KBJ379
152.8850	Faith Excavating	(Clear Spring MD)	KZI613
158.3850	Falls Road Corp.	(Baltimore MD)	KVX297
461.3250	Federal Builders	(Annapolis MD)	WSV563
31.0000	Felix Construction	(Reston VA)	WZV800
463.2750	Fidelity Engineering	(Towson MD)	KTW908
35.9000	Finnegan Builders	(Delaware City DE)	
451.8750	Flintkote Stone	(Catonsville MD)	KQY946
463.4750	Flippo Construction	(Baltimore MD)	WYQ637
464.0250	Flippo Construction	(Silver Spring MD)	KTL931
31.4800	Fooks Concrete Sand	(Hurlock MD)	KEY479
461.6250	Fort Myer Construction	(Arlington VA)	KYN653
464.6500	Fox Contracting	(Baltimore MD)	
483.4875	Francesco Excavating	(Boston MD)	KNS468
495.9125	Fred Newton Paving	(Fairfax VA)	KXD654
496.0625	Fred Pruitt Building	(Annapolis MD)	KXE830
496.6375	Fred Pruitt Building	(Birdville MD)	KXE830
463.8250	Free State Construction	(Annapolis MD)	KBE567
151.6550	Fuller Griffin Construction	(Washington DC)	KNAH214
463.8500	Furbush Construction	(McLean VA)	WRM916
151.6250	G & C Construction	(Tysons Corner MD)	
496.1625	G & M Construction	(Baltimore MD)	KNP924
461.6000	G T Construction	(Falls Church VA)	WFT393
464.6250	Gaithersburg Masonry	(Silver Spring MD)	WSD493
31.4400	General Paving	(Manassas VA)	KUA529
461.2000	Good Concrete Construction	(Falls Church VA)	KKE434
463.3000	Gossard Masonry	(Hagerstown MD)	KNBJ480
461.4750	Gray Concrete	(Arlington VA)	KNAM699
461.3500	Great Eastern Concrete	(Frederick MD)	WRK702
31.4800	Great Falls Excavating	(Herndon VA)	KRW517
461.8500	Green Contracting	(Baltimore MD)	KNBL909t
464.2500	Green Hill Contractor	(Baltimore MD)	KNCQ424
496.2375	Green Roofing	(Falls Church VA)	KNR341
461.0250	Greenbelt Homes	(Wheaton MD)	WYF468
461.5000	H & B Construction	(Silver Spring MD)	KNBK398
496.7875	H & H Construction	(Annapolis MD)	KNR343
461.1500	HMF Paving	(Bethesda MD)	KNBP240
463.3000	Haass & Broyles Excvating	(Bethesda MD)	KKN940
151.4900	Hagerstown Concrete	(Hagerstown MD)	KCD952
151.9550	Hagerstown Concrete	(Hagerstown MD)	KCX763
496.3625	Haines Excavating	(Rockville MD)	KNP829
463.7250	Haines Paving	(Manassas VA)	WSB973
463.2000	Halle Construction	(Silver Spring MD)	KTZ573
495.8625	Hamel Construction	(Arlington VA)	KNO303
495.8625	Hamel Construction	(Capitl Hgts. MD)	KB3166
498.6625	Harkless Construction	(Beaver Heights MD)	WID442
495.6625	Harkless Construction	(Laurel MD)	KNS417
43.2200	Hawkins Construction	(Washington DC)	KKB471
461.9000	Hayes Construction	(Baltimore MD)	KVV336
461.4250	Henry Mcnew Excavating	(Baltimore MD)	KNAM452
43.3200	Hercules Construction	(Chantilly VA)	con
461.6750	Hill & Ward Construction	(Towson MD)	WZG429
464.2250	Hillandale Crane	(Bethesda MD)	WZG652
464.2500	Hitchcock General Contractors	(Arlington VA)	KNAR974
461.8500	Hobson Excavation	(Falls Church VA)	KVK707
466.8500	Hobson's Excavation	(Vienna VA)	WSE92
464.3000	Homestead Builders	(Hazlettville DE)	KDP302
464.4000	Horncraft Builders	(Frederick MD)	KCT334
451.9500	Howat Concrete	(Washington DC)	KAT929
461.3750	Howes Construction	(Churchville MD)	WXC572
35.8800	Humberson Homes	(McHenry MD)	KUA282
461.5000	Hurlock Construction	(Williamsburg MD)	WST359
31.7600	Inland Construction	(Ocean City MD)	KCV310
49.5400	Insley Construction	(Mechanicsville MD)	WZE492
31.2800	Interstate Bridge Co.	(Frederick MD)	KVM782
461.6250	Irwin Construction	(Baltimore MD)	KCB942
461.6500	J & E Excavating	(Arlington VA)	WZA539
495.6125	J & S Paving	(Manassas VA)	
463.7500	J & W Contracting	(Bethesda MD)	WZP216
35.8800	J.F. Comoljak Concrete	(Annapolis MD)	KZC848
464.2500	JJ Gipson Asphalt	(Arlington VA)	KAE831
461.3000	James Roane Construction	(Washington DC)	KZI927
30.7600	James S. Ray Builders	(Annapolis MD)	KAI400
35.1000	James Webb Paving	(Wyoming DE)	KKU866
35.9200	Jarrettsville Builders	(Jarrettsville MD)	WRZ472
31.0400	Jennings Construction	(Fairfax VA)	KFM289
463.9500	Jeter Paving	(Hagerstown MD)	WYU311
461.9250	Jimmy Bean Excavating	(Leonardtown MD)	WRF594
496.0625	John Diamond Masonry	(Annapolis MD)	KNS703
464.8500	John's Crane	(Waldorf MD)	WXH444
496.0875	John's Crane	(Waldorf MD)	KNS466
35.9200	Jones Excavating	(Silver Spring MD)	KKI232
461.2000	Jones Roofing	(Falls Church VA)	WYJ397
31.8000	Joppa Paving	(Baltimore MD)	KQU880
464.2250	K & B Builders	(Hazlettville DE)	KNAC514
33.1600	K & B Builders	(Millington MD)	KWR256
463.2250	K & E Construction	(Westminster MD)	WYU749
31.0000	K & K Excavators	(Reston VA)	WZT371
31.0400	Kalb Contracting	(Millersville MD)	KED770
461.2750	Ken Mark Construction	(Silver Spring MD)	KNBZ269
496.1125	Ken-Mar Drywall	(Silver Spring MD)	KNS730
461.1250	Kent Construction	(Woodside DE)	KNCA504
152.9450	Keysers Black Topping	(Frederick MD)	KUR999
31.2400	Kibler Construction	(Eldersburg MD)	KUK850
47.6800	Kibler Construction	(Finksburg MD)	KON805
151.8950	Kimball Construction	(Towson MD)	KWR382
464.8750	King Sand	(Alexandria VA)	WXM922
463.5250	Knott Restoration	(Arlington VA)	WXM873
30.6200	L & H Construction	(Salisbury MD)	KTP671
464.3000	Lakewood Builders	(Hazlettville DE)	KSD453
851.1625	Lambert Paving	(Baltimore MD)	KTW869
464.3250	Lamberton Construction	(Dover DE)	KNBR494
30.9600	Lauer Bros. Excavating	(Baltimore MD)	KEN231
496.0625	Laurer Construction	(Annapolis MD)	KZP743
463.6000	Ledford Construction	(Washington DC)	KDR249
462.1500	Leesburg Builders	(Falls Church VA)	KNFT441
451.7250	Lehigh Portland Cement	(Union Bridge MD)	
463.8250	Libson Concrete	(Falls Church VA)	WSA723
47.4400	Liller Bros. Asphalt	(Midland MD)	KWB314
461.1250	Linder Steel Erecting	(Baltimore MD)	KVX500
464.8250	Linder Steel Erection	(Baltimore MD)	
462.0000	Linder Steel Erectors	(Silver Spring MD)	KVX500
461.1000	Loewer Construction	(Ocean City MD)	WSC809
463.2000	Lopez Construction	(Arlington VA)	KNAA717
466.0250	Lopez Construction	(Bladensburg MD)	WFE706
461.0250	Lopez Construction	(Wheaton MD)	KGB494
154.4900	Luck Stone	(Fairfax VA)	KQR637
462.1750	M & B Construction	(Silver Spring MD)	WRT424
30.6200	M & P Construction	(Silver Spring MD)	KTS426
461.3000	M B Paving	(Washington DC)	KNBG581
851.1625	M J Construction	(Baltimore MD)	WXK285
461.4250	M P K Mechanical Constr.	(Baltimore MD)	KNAN922
461.4250	M V Construction	(Silver Spring MD)	KQE651
47.6800	M.J. Grove Construction	(Washington DC)	
461.7500	Majestic Builders	(Bethesda MD)	KFU798
496.3125	Maloney Concrete	(Arlington VA)	KGD810
47.5600	Maloney Concrete	(Washington DC)	KUT409
461.0250	Marjak Paving	(Wheaton MD)	WZL364
851.3875	Marlboro Excavating	(Bethesda MD)	WYH498
35.7400	Marocco Construction	(Baltimore MD)	
35.7400	Marocco Construction	(Baltimore MD)	KDE551
461.1750	Marsh Construction	(Cantonsville MD)	KQW661
496.6625	Martens Contractors	(Silver Spring MD)	KNQ288
463.8000	Martic Construction	(Baltimore MD)	WXW486
153.0200	Martin Limestone	(Delmar DE)	KFZ407
43.3600	Maryland Equipment	(Beltsville MD)	WRX260
33.1600	Masonry Contractors	(Manchester MD)	KUF027
463.2500	Masonry Contractors	(Manchester MD)	WYW529
463.8500	Masonry Contractors	(Manchester MD)	
461.7250	Master Roofing	(Falls Church VA)	KEE865
152.9300	Mattingly Construction	(Midland MD)	KVR733
151.7450	Mattingly Excavation	(New Market MD)	KBK976
31.9600	Mclean Contracting	(Baltimore MD)	KEK457
461.6500	Mergentime Construction	(Baltimore MD)	KNBL488
33.1600	Merritt Construction	(Millville DE)	KDO436
35.9600	Messick & Gray Construction	(Bridgeville DE)	KLK377
30.6600	Metropolitan Concrete	(Beltsville MD)	KBU769
463.8000	Metropolitan Masonry	(Baltimore MD)	KDQ842
464.0750	Metropolitan Masonry	(Silver Spring MD)	KDQ861
461.2750	Mideast Builders	(Hagerstown MD)	WYU358
462.1750	Miller Bros. Masonry	(Smithville MD)	KJU448
467.1000	Miller Construction	(Berlin MD)	WDB774
461.3250	Millersville Construction	(Annapolis MD)	KUR437
462.7250	Mirabile Construction	(Baltimore MD)	KAD0995
152.9000	Mitten Construction	(Woodside DE)	KNFG392
851.3375	Mobile & Marine Communications	(Baltimore MD)	WSB455
462.1750	Mogavero & Son Builders	(Baltimore MD)	KNAW484
31.0000	Monrovia Construction	(Monrovia MD)	KFD786
151.8350	Monument Construction	(Arlington VA)	KNCL717
461.9500	Moon Construction	(Washington DC)	
461.8000	N & W Concrete	(Towson MD)	WZR885
30.5800	N.E. Taylor Contracting	(Easton MD)	KGF884
461.2750	Naham Construction	(Silver Spring MD)	KFG754
464.7000	National Asphalt	(Falls Church VA)	KRN587
464.1750	Nazario Construction	(Washington DC)	KTM745
464.1750	Nazario Construction	(Wheaton MD)	KTM475

463.6750	Neff Construction	(Aberdeen MD)	KNAQ534
463.8250	Nestorio Construction	(Wheaton MD)	KNAQ828
461.3000	Newington Concrete	(Fairfax VA)	WXE841
451.8500	Newton Asphalt	(Falls Church VA)	KIL843
496.0625	Norman Cully Excavating	(Annapolis MD)	KNR285
464.6000	North Star Construction	(Baltimore MD)	KNAQ866
158.3850	Northwood Builders	(Salisbury MD)	KUK735
461.6500	O H Lettman Contracting	(Arlington VA)	WXV606
463.4750	O'Meara Construction	(Baltimore MD)	KXG424
464.9000	Oak Mar Construction	(Silver Spring MD)	WZE313
464.1250	Oaklawn Homes	(Rockville MD)	KEU274
461.1250	Oakton Asphalt Paving	(McLean VA)	KNBH234
464.4250	Ohio Valley Construction	(Arlington VA)	KGB873
151.8950	Old Liberty Builders	(Mounty Airy MD)	WZH388
464.0750	Omeara Construction	(Rockville MD)	KXG423
154.5400	Omni Construction	(Washington DCV)	WZC234
855.8875	Opportunity Concrete	(Washington DC)	
151.5200	Orrie Contracting	(Midland MD)	KUW999
463.3750	Osprey Construction	(Whaleysville MD)	KNFR917
151.8950	Oxford Roofing	(Falls Church VA)	KBE981
461.6000	P & A Engineers	(Salisbury MD)	
461.2500	P & P Contractors	(Wheaton MD)	KNFB213
151.7750	Palmer & Baker Engineers	(Baltimore MD)	
461.4250	Pasarew Construction	(Baltimore MD)	KNAU734
464.2750	Paul Rice Engineering	(Towson MD)	WRU377
30.8800	Pavilion Construction	(Leesburg VA)	WZL2621
151.7450	Payne Sand & Gravel	(Ocean City MD)	WZG551
152.4800	Peninsula Communications	(Hazlettville DE)	WXC430
469.9500	Perini Construction	(Hagerstown MD)	
30.8000	Perry Contractors	(Baltimore MD)	KJN567
49.5800	Perry Engineering	(Leesburg VA)	KIH960
496.6625	Person Concrete	(Silver Spring MD)	KNP474
461.3250	Phelps Bros. Land Clearing	(Annapolis MD)	KWD666
35.0600	Philip Dadamo Construction	(Baltimore MD)	KCJ334
152.9600	Phillips Concrete	(Finksburg MD)	KNBE276
154.6250	Phoenix Construction	(Midland MD)	KYQ795
152.9150	Pilot Construction	(Silver Spring MD)	WXC923
495.6125	Pleasant Excavating	(Baltimore MD)	KYY765
495.6125	Pleasant Excavating	(Bethesda MD)	KYY781
495.6125	Pleasant Excavating	(Clarksburg MD)	WBH206
495.6125	Pleasant Excavating	(Mount Airy MD)	KNO658
152.9000	Plummer Construction	(Hagerstown MD)	KQL539
463.2500	Poor Richards Crane	(Washington DC)	WXX444
451.1250	Potomac Contractors	(Manassas VA)	KRZ772
464.4000	Potomac Engineering	(Deer Park MD)	WQM287
463.3250	Potomac Stone	(Silver Spring MD)	KNCX206
463.3500	Potter & Wolfe Concrete	(Cockeysville MD)	
30.8800	Pownall Builders	(Cumberland MD)	KTV585
463.3750	Precision Concrete	(Cantonsville MD)	KLM901
452.0000	Princemont Construction	(Silver Spring MD)	KGF716
800.0000	Pucillo & Storch Builders	(Seabrook MD)	
464.9500	Pulte Home	(Waldorf MD)	KNBE498
462.0250	Pulte Homes	(Silver Spring MD)	
463.2000	Pulte Homes	(Silver Spring MD)	KSK568
496.9375	Quality Crafters	(Baltimore MD)	
157.6800	Quality Homes	(Hagerstown MD)	KJO751
462.1500	R & K Contractors	(Towson MD)	WXJ257
463.5750	RC&B Construction	(Rockville MD)	WRH796
35.1400	RMK Contractors	(Whitehall MD)	KFK541
461.0750	Radisson Construction	(Baltimore MD)	WRH487
461.5500	Rapp Contracting	(Arlington VA)	KGD644
463.7000	Rays Contracting	(Churchville MD)	KFK606
496.7875	Reco Builders	(Annapolis MD)	KNQ428
35.8200	Reliable Contracting	(Millersville MD)	KGE808
464.8000	Resicon Building Corp.	(Bethesda MD)	WZP284
495.6625	Rhoades Paving	(Laurel MD)	KNS345
35.3600	Richard Marouse Excavating	(Clifton VA)	KWT447
463.3500	Richmarr Construction	(McLean VA)	WZA376
461.2750	Riders Contracting	(Hagerstown MD)	WZQ617
464.1750	Riverview Builders	(Smithville MD)	WXR451
495.9375	Robinson Construction	(Catonsville MD)	KNR430
498.9375	Robinson Construction	(Columbia MD)	WIC479
43.1000	Rockingham Construction	(Gaithersburg MD)	WYL894
43.1000	Rockingham Construction	(Upper Marlboro MD)	KLN328
35.1400	Rosemont Contractors	(Gaithersburg MD)	WXF517
464.8500	Rye Excavating	(Waldorf MD)	KXD800
461.9250	S & G Concrete	(Aberdeen MD)	KNCV822
463.6500	S & G Concrete	(Cantonsville MD)	KNFG597
816.2375	S & G Concrete	(Edgewood MD)	
461.1250	S & H Contracting	(Woodside DE)	KNBC587
461.1500	SNS Construction	(Eden MD)	KGA900
461.0500	Salisbury Brick	(Hazlettville DE)	WXE523
466.0500	Salisbury Brick	(Salisbury MD)	WAX918
461.1750	Salisbury Brick	(Smithville MD)	KYB236
461.6000	Salisbury Brick	(Willards)	WXE524
461.5000	Sante Fe Construction	(Silver Spring MD)	WST505
464.7000	Sargent Construction	(Annapolis MD)	WXX661
469.7000	Sargent Construction	(Arnold MD)	WFD282
35.5200	Schneider Construction	(New Market MD)	KSP446
461.1250	Seaboard Foundations	(Baltimore MD) F391	WR
461.1000	Seaboard Foundations	(Silver Spring MD)	WRF390
464.1500	Security Builders	(Baltimore MD)	

496.9125	Seminary Construction	(Arlington VA)	KNM242
463.8250	Service Asphalt	(Wheaton MD)	WYF467
31.4800	Sherman Contracting	(Glen Burnie MD)	KZV538
151.6250	Sigal Construction	(Washington DC)	KNCC693
151.8050	Sigal Construction	(Washington DC)	KNCC693
464.2750	Silver Hill Sand & Gravel	(Silver Hill MD)	KGH286
461.7750	Site Engineering	(Manassas VA)	KLJ767
151.8650	Slavinsky Contractor	(Catonsville MD)	KNCF474
154.5150	Smith Bros. Construction	(Sykesville MD)	KNCL930
154.6000	Somar Concrete	(Capitol Heights MD)	
466.4750	Southland Concrete	(Herndon VA)	WCM686
463.4500	Southwestern Contracting	(Towson MD)	KKO487
151.8650	Speck Construction	(Frederick MD)	KYR882
461.6750	Spel Construction	(Towson MD)	WZG833
151.6850	Spencer Construction	(Jarrettsville MD)	WSC551
153.0350	Springfield Sand & Gravel	(Springfield VA)	WSV837
495.9625	Stambaugh Excavating	(Westminster MD)	KNR284
461.3750	Stancills Excavating	(Churchville MD)	WZP290
461.7500	Stanley Halle Communications	(Bethesda MD)	KFV504
464.7000	Stocketts Excavating	(Annapolis MD)	KQV453
461.3250	Strathmore Concrete	(Falls Church VA)	KQD281
462.1000	Structural Preservation	(Washington DC)	KNCU592
31.2400	Stuller Construction	(Taneytown MD)	KLN282
43.0600	Sullivan Construction	(Parkville MD)	KGF212
43.0600	Super Concrete	(Cumberland MD)	KGE572
452.0250	Super Concrete	(Washington DC)	KGH243
47.6400	Sykesville Construction	(Sykesville MD)	KCZ398
851.1875	T E Norris Construction	(Bethesda MD)	WRE474
464.1500	T&A Excavating	(Baltimore MD)	
154.5150	TBC Contractors	(Baltimore MD)	WQL361
43.1200	Teal Construction	(Hazlettville DE)	KGE298
464.1750	Thompson Builders	(Smithville MD)	WSU823
31.9200	Thoro Goods Concrete	(Millsboro DE)	KGO836
464.3500	Thrasher Construction	(McLean VA)	WRP205
464.7000	Tidewater Builders	(Annapolis MD)	KEK229
461.3750	Tidewater Homes	(Waldorf MD)	WRJ861
462.0000	Tilcon Delaware	(Harrington DE)	WST232
43.0600	Tilcon Warren	(Dover DE)	KLN444
495.9625	Tonya Concrete	(Westminster MD)	KKC821
464.4500	Townshend Explosives	(Catonsville MD)	KUW319
496.6875	Traako Construction	(Baltimore MD)	KNP922
463.5000	Tracey Construction	(Baltimore MD)	KNBM963
464.7000	Traditional Homes	(Annapolis MD)	KES633
461.4250	Transit Concrete	(Easton MD)	WSS296
35.8400	Tri-County Asphalt	(Leesburg VA)	KDL340
35.9800	Tri-State Concrete	(Hagerstown MD)	KSA588
464.8000	Tri-State Roofing	(Midland MD)	KJT515
851.3875	Trible Construction	(Bethesda MD)	WZZ508
462.1500	Tricon Triangle Constr.	(Potomac MC)	WYN382
462.1500	Tricon Triangle Contracting	(Falls Church VA)	WYN383
47.5200	Tru-Mix Concrete	(Cambridge MD)	KTU315
463.7500	Tyroc Construction	(Bethesda MD)	KUD440
495.7625	United Building	(Frederick MD)	KED848
495.7625	United Concrete	(Frederick MD)	
464.6500	United Masonry	(Arlington VA)	KFX581
461.9250	Universal Construction	(Bethesda MD)	KZT239
496.1625	Universal Contractors	(Catonsville MD)	KNR345
464.1000	Urban Demolition Contractors	(Baltimore MD)	
461.6000	Utz Construction	(Annapolis MD)	KKU999
498.8125	Valley Concrete	(Buckeystown MD)	WIE389
463.2250	Valley Crest Builder	(Westminster MD)	KNAP774
152.4800	Vernon Pike	(Hazlettville DE)	WQP685
461.1000	Viking Contractors	(Silver Spring MD)	KNAJ866
451.8250	Virginia Concrete	(Falls Church VA)	KFC220
451.9250	Virginia Concrete	(Falls Church VA)	KLQ655
451.9750	Virginia Concrete	(Falls Church VA)	KIU531
35.4000	W & W Paving	(Frederick MD)	WYR459
461.6000	W Jennings Builder	(Falls Church VA)	KYJ773
463.6500	W. Godwin & Sons	(Arlington VA)	
152.4800	Walker Excavation	(Hazlettville DE)	WZG021
463.2750	Ward Contracting	(Churchville MD)	WRP387
462.0000	Ward Contracting	(Towson MD)	WRP387
463.2250	Warfel Construction	(Smithville MD)	KYR514
462.0500	Weidman & Son Construction	(Birdville MD)	KXA610
461.4500	Weiss Construction	(Falls Church VA)	KLT300
495.7625	Welsh Construction	(Baltimore MD)	KJY831
496.6275	Wes Construction	(Birdville MD)	KNP632
464.4000	Wes Mar Construction	(Midland MD)	KDJ751
462.1750	Wessels Contractors	(Silver Spring MD)	KNFE425
463.5500	Wexford Construction	(Prince Frederick MD)	
462.1000	White Construction	(Willards MD)	WQQ737
496.8125	White Oak Construction	(Silver Spring MD)	KNR677
43.0600	White Pine Contracting	(Finksburg MD)	KTG780
461.2250	White's Concrete	(Earleigh Hgts. MD)	WQR385
461.8250	Whiteford Construction	(Churchville MD)	WYN545
151.9250	Whiting Turner Construction	(Baltimore MD)	KIL565
463.8250	Whyte Construction	(Falls Church VA)	KBQ727
35.9600	Willett Construction	(White Plains MD)	KIK364
461.3250	William Porter Homes	(Annapolis MD)	KAI680
30.9600	Williams Crane	(Baltimore MD)	KDY922
35.8400	Wilson Construction	(Cumberland MD)	KDE537
43.1200	Wilson Contracting	(New Caste DE)	

Petroleum

152.9600 Adams Fuel	(Baltimore MD)	KRU459
43.0800 Adams Oil	(Seaford DE)	KGG422
35.8200 Aero Oil	(Frederick MD)	KGH585
47.5200 Agrico Chemical	(Chestertown MD)	KDY621
462.1250 Air Products & Chemical	(Baltimore MD)	KNBQ710
451.6250 Amoco Oil	(Baltimore MD)	KSD819
463.8750 Armstrong Oil	(Washington DC)	KEH873
152.9750 Arundel Gas & Water	(Edgewater MD)	WRR292
466.7000 Atlanta Heating	(Bridgeville DE)	WFJ645
464.0750 Atlantic Petroleum	(Rockville MD)	KCA979
464.1250 Atlantic Petroleum	(Towson MD)	KCA980
452.0000 B P Oil	(Baltimore MD)	KLU889
451.8750 B P Oil	(Washington DC)	KLT595
451.8750 B P Oil	(Washington DC)	KYO569
42.9600 Basore Oil	(Hagerstown MD)	WYS477
47.4800 Besche Oil	(Clinton MD)	WYW865
47.4800 Besche Oil	(Leonardtown MD)	KYV404
47.4800 Besche Oil	(Lexington Park MD)	KQL575
47.4800 Besche Oil	(Suitland MD)	KGS598
154.4900 Besche Oil	(Suitland MD)	WSX591
47.4800 Besche Oil	(Waldorf MD)	KLU980
461.0750 Billmeyer Oil	(Baltimore MD)	WRK385
31.4800 Bock Oil	(Hagerstown MD)	KUT431
42.9600 Bock Oil	(Hagerstown MD)	WYS478
151.5650 Boulden Oil	(Earleville MD)	KVK455
152.9900 Brices Oil	(Baltimore MD)	KNAM577
153.0350 Brock Fuel	(Catonsville MD)	KTI830
47.4400 Brunswick Oil	(Brunswick MD)	KKW505
47.6000 Burtonsville Fuel	(Burtonsville MD)	KCQ727
152.9900 Bynums Fuel	(Baltimore MD)	KZV629
47.5600 Care Petroleum	(Pasadena MD)	KRJ309
158.3850 Carter Fuel	(Washington DC)	WRL594
31.6000 Central Ice & Fuel	(Baltimore MD)	KJJ834
31.8000 Chesapeake Petrol	(Annapolis MD)	KCK385
461.0500 Chesapeake Petrol	(Bethesda MD)	KRU931
451.7500 Chevron	(Baltimore MD)	KTS420
451.7500 Chevron	(Baltimore MD)	KTU835
43.5200 Clark Oil	(Pheonix MD)	KBP660
461.3500 Clarke Coal	(Midland MD)	KNBS604
154.4900 Clinton Oil	(Clinton MD)	KGH490
35.5200 Cobra Fuel	(Oakland MD)	KNBK982
464.3000 Colonial Fuel	(Washington DC)	KFI270
33.3800 Columbia Gas	(Granite MD)	KGB250
33.3800 Columbia Gas	(Jacksonville MD)	KGD319
33.3800 Columbia Gas	(Rockville MD)	KGA614
33.3800 Columbia LNG	(Lusby MD)	KIX701
451.5500 Columbia LNG	(Lusby MD)	WZU83
451.6000 Columbia LNG	(Lusby MD)	KWN305
451.7000 Columbia LNG	(Lusby MD)	KIX882
496.7625 Community Fuel	(Baltimore MD)	KNQ436
47.6400 Corbin Fuel	(Bel Air MD)	KGO209
462.1500 County Fuel	(Towson MD)	WXE335
153.0200 Cox Oil	(Suitland MD)	KAQ501
31.5600 Creswell Oil	(Bel Air MD)	KJC635
30.7600 Croppers Oil	(Berlin MD)	KRN823
152.9600 Crown Central Petrol	(Baltimore MD)	KJZ478
463.8000 Crystal Oil	(Baltimore MD)	KDZ522
35.1800 D & H Fuel	(Eagle Rock MD)	KZL924
42.9600 Damascus Fuel	(Damascus MD)	KGH449
35.4800 Deep Creek Oil	(Kitzmiller MD)	KXQ358
150.9800 Delaware Bay Coop	(Lewes DE)	WSU991
158.4450 Delaware Bay Coop	(Lewes DE)	WSU991
47.4800 Delmarce Oil	(Pocomoke City MD)	WZW625
151.5350 Delmarva Oil	(Millsboro DE)	WRB567
151.5200 Delmarva Oil	(Salisbury MD)	KUI421
35.0600 District Line Fuels	(Washington DC)	WXV329
31.6400 Dodge City Coal	(Oakland MD)	KIP438
35.1400 Downing Oil	(Milford DE)	KVD205
47.4400 Eagle Oil	(Westminster MD)	KGG729
151.5950 Eastern Petroleum	(Annapolis MD)	WQC249
151.5950 Eastern Petroleum	(Glen Burnie MD)	WQC249
158.4600 Eastern Petroleum	(Glen Burnie MD)	KLM281
152.9000 Enterprise Fuel	(Baltimore MD)	KBT782
154.4900 Ewing Oil	(Frederick MD)	KRU428
154.4900 Ewing Oil	(Hagerstown MD)	KGZ455
460.7000 Exxon	(Baltimore MD)	KQM317
462.1250 Fischbach & Moore	(Baltimore MD)	WSV909
461.3750 Fischbach & Moore	(Washington DC)	KTY562
151.7450 Fischbach & Moore	(Landover MD)	KVS488
35.3200 Fleming Petroleum	(Sykesville MD)	KCD738
452.0750 Fred Cross Fuel	(Towson MD)	WYH408
152.8700 Fulton Petroleum	(Hancock MD)	KRV511
151.5950 G & M Oil	(Baltimore MD)	KYA319
151.9250 Garland Petroleum	(Midland MD)	WSQ805
31.2400 Granville Hooper	(Cambridge MD)	KEZ554
462.1250 Green Fuel	(Arlington VA)	WSY501
152.8850 Grier Oil Company	(Aberdeen MD)	
451.9250 Griffith Consumers	(Arbutus MD)	KDT484
851.5375 Gulf Oil	(Towson MD)	WZA764
462.1750 Heat & Power Corp.	(Baltimore MD)	KWD695
154.5150 Heating Services	(Baltimore MD)	KKJ841
152.9150 Highway Petroleum	(Hancock MD)	KZH731
31.2800 Homes Oil	(Washington DC)	KBN304
461.0250 Ideal Fuel	(Baltimore MD)	KQT958
461.3500 Ideal Fuel	(Baltimore MD)	KNCH984
462.7250 Ideal Fuel	(Baltimore MD)	KAD3064
152.8700 Jackson Oil	(Baltimore MD)	KKR901
31.5200 Kerr McGee Chemical	(Waldorf MD)	KCQ992
154.4900 Kustom Fuel	(Baltimore MD)	WXU644
464.1750 L C Parker Fuel	(Annapolis MD)	KNCD554
151.5650 Laurel Fuel	(Laurel MD)	KBNQ514
151.5650 Laurel Petroleum	(Laurel DE)	KFE292
35.7400 Liberty Gas	(Waldorf MD)	WQN349
152.9600 Liberty Oil	(Baltimore MD)	
152.9600 Liberty Oil	(Baltimore MD)	KTS8457
154.5150 Liberty Oil	(Baltimore MD)	KGP423
43.1400 Liberty Oil	(White Marsh MD)	KSP434
151.4900 Lincoln Fuel	(Lincoln DE)	
31.8400 Loac Coal	(Oakland MD)	KOK582
461.0250 Manassas Ice	(Manassas VA)	KJZ296
451.9000 McDowell Oil	(Williamsburg MD)	WXM262
451.9000 McMaham Oil	(Williamsburg MD)	KFB652
495.6375 Metropolitan Fuel	(Bethesda MD)	KZM689
43.0000 Middleburg Oil	(Leesburg VA)	KGR521
49.1000 Mobil Oil Company	(Washington DC)	
495.5625 Montague Fuel	(Silver Spring MD)	KNQ550
154.4900 Moody & Sons Fuel	(Baltimore MD)	KQX443
35.9000 Moore's Fuel	(Baltimore MD)	KOF630
151.5650 Moran Coal	(Westernport MD)	
464.2500 Mount Vernon Fuel	(Arlington VA)	KWJ697
35.2800 Mrohs Gas & Oil	(Crisfield MD)	KUQ475
33.1600 Palmer Petroleum	(Westminster MD)	KUC561
35.8800 Paradee Oil	(Dover DE)	KRO700
43.0200 Parker Fuel	(Ellicott City MD)	KCK868
31.6800 Payne Fuel	(Baltimore MD)	
152.9300 Peninsula Oil	(Harrington DE)	KUQ984
152.9300 Peninsula Oil	(Milford DE)	WXY678
152.9300 Peninsula Oil	(Selbyville DE)	KLQ912
463.3750 Petro Supply	(Silver Spring MD)	WYX899
851.1625 Petroleum Engineering	(Baltimore MD)	WRG721
152.9000 Phillips Oil	(Grasonville MD)	KBI349
152.8850 Riggins Oil	(Annapolis MD)	KZE254
463.9750 Right Oil	(Millsboro DE)	KQU536
35.8400 Rittenhouse Fuel	(Hampstead MD)	KAR392
35.8400 Rittenhouse Fuel	(Monkton MD)	KCW336
152.9900 Robert Shrevo	(Arlington VA)	
31.3600 Rockville Fuel	(Derwood MD)	KDJ895
461.7250 Roses Fuel	(Falls Church VA)	KRZ503
461.3500 Save on Fuel	(Baltimore MD)	KOH492
152.9750 Scarborough Oil	(Snow Hill MD)	WQG866
43.0600 Schagrin Gas	(Elkton MD)	KGG240
851.8875 Schwarzchild Oil	(Towson MD)	WQA498
463.9000 Scruggs Heating	(Birdsville MD)	KNBE908
35.7600 Sharpgas	(Georgetown DE)	KAU489
49.5800 Shore Fuel	(Salisbury MD)	KAZ742
158.3550 Skyline Terminal	(Baltimore MD)	WRZ796
151.9550 Sockriter Petrol	(Lewes DE)	KJT360
152.9450 Solliday Oil	(Hagerstown MD)	KTO628
31.2800 Southern Maryland Gas	(Waldorf MD)	KFK23
35.5200 Southern Maryland Oil	(Annapolis MD)	KGK513
35.5200 Southern Maryland Oil	(La Plata MD)	KGD783
43.0200 Speedee Oil	(Bryans Road MD)	KJU773
33.1600 Staats Gas Service	(Smyrna DE)	KZY263
49.5600 Steuart Petroleum	(Washington DC)	KAU789
156.8000 Steuart Petroleum	(Washington DC)	KUF610
156.9000 Steuart Petroleum	(Washington DC)	
49.5600 Steuart Petroleum	(Piney Point MD)	KAU789
35.1200 Stouter Oil	(Emmitsburg MD)	KAV315
463.8500 Suburban Fuel	(McLean VA)	WYD842
35.2800 T G & C Coal	(Midlothian MD)	KVI382
152.4650 T G & C Coal	(Midlothian MD)	KVI382
31.3200 Takoma Fuel	(Washington DC)	KFT789
152.8700 Taylor Oil	(Salisbury MD)	KIZ744
151.6850 Tenneco	(Chestertown MD)	KLK441
43.3200 Thrift Oil	(Leonardtown MD)	KUM202
48.7400 Transcontinental Gas	(Ellicott City MD)	KGB471
49.5200 Tri County Gas	(Salisbury MD)	KGF235
151.5800 Tri State Oil	(Snow Hill MD)	KNCY438
461.2000 Tri State Oil	(Denton MD)	
43.3200 Union Coal	(Barton MD)	KXP817
152.8700 Vienna Fuel	(Vienna VA)	KTK972
43.0200 Walsh Fuel	(Manchester MD)	KGE668

Business Notes

FREQUENCY ALLOCATION CHART

000.54-001.60	A.M. RADIO	330.00-370.00	SATELLITE BAND
001.60-001.80	UTILITIES	370.00-399.90	UHF AIR BAND (US GOV'
001.80-002.00	160 METER AMATEUR	400.00-420.00	U.S. GOVERNMENT
002.00-014.00	SHORTWAVE BAND	420.00-450.00	3/4 AMATEUR BAND
014.00-014.34	20 METER AMATEUR	450.00-470.00	LOC GOV'T/BUSINESS/GM
014.34-021.00	SHORTWAVE BAND	470.00-806.00	TV CHANNELS 14-84
021.00-021.45	15 METER AMATEUR	806.00-811.00	CONVENTIONAL PLM
021.45-025.02	SHORTWAVE BAND	811.00-816.00	NEW TRUNKED PLM
025.02-026.90	US GOV'T/BUSINESS	816.00-821.00	OLD TRUNKED PLM
026.95-027.40	CITIZENS BAND	821.00-825.00	MOB SATELLITE SVC
027.41-027.98	BUSINESS	825.00-835.00	CELLULAR RCC
028.00-029.70	10 METER AMATEUR	835.00-845.00	CELLULAR WCC
029.71-029.88	LOCAL GOVERNMENT	845.00-848.00	CELLULAR RCC (FUTURE)
029.90-030.55	U.S. GOVERNMENT	848.00-851.00	CELLULAR WCC (FUTURE)
030.58-031.98	LOCAL GOVERNMENT	851.00-856.00	CONVENTIONAL PLM
032.01-032.99	U.S. GOVERNMENT	856.00-861.00	NEW TRUNKED PLM
033.02-033.98	LOCAL GOVERNMENT	861.00-866.00	OLD TRUNKED PLM
034.01-034.99	U.S. GOVERNMENT	866.00-870.00	MOB SATTELITE SVC
035.02-035.98	BUSINESS	870.00-880.00	CELLULAR RCC
036.01-036.99	U.S. GOVERNMENT	880.00-890.00	CELLULAR WCC
037.02-037.98	LOCAL GOVERNMENT	890.00-893.00	CELLULAR RCC (FUTURE)
038.01-038.99	U.S. GOVERNMENT	893.00-896.00	CELLULAR WCC (FUTURE)
040.01-041.99	LOCAL GOVERNMENT	896.00-898.00	AIRCRAFT PHONES (AIR)
042.02-046.58	LOC GOV'T/BUSINESS	898.00-902.00	PRIVATE RCS
046.61-046.99	U.S. GOVERNMENT	902.00-912.00	AMATEUR / AVM
047.02-049.58	LOC GOV'T/BUSINESS	912.00-918.00	AMATEUR / ISM
049.71-049.99	U.S. GOVERNMENT	918.00-928.00	AMATEUR / AVM
050.00-054.00	6 METER AMATEUR	928.00-929.00	PLM
054.00-088.00	TV CHANNELS 2-6	929.00-932.00	PAGING
088.00-108.00	F.M. RADIO BAND	932.00-935.00	FIXED
108.00-118.00	AERONAUTICAL BAND	935.00-937.00	RESERVED
118.00-136.00	VHF AIRCRAFT BAND	937.00-941.00	PRIVATE RCS
136.00-138.00	SATELLITE BAND	941.00-943.00	AIRCRAFT PHONES (LAND
138.00-143.99	U.S. MILITARY BAND	943.00-946.00	FIXED
144.00-147.99	2 METER AMATEUR	946.00-947.00	RESERVED
148.00-150.75	U.S. GOVERNMENT	947.00-952.00	STUDIO TO XMTR LINK
150.78-162.00	LOC GOV'T/BUSINESS	952.00-953.00	PLM
162.03-173.98	U.S. GOVERNMENT	953.00-960.00	FIXED MICROWAVE SVC
174.00-216.00	TV CHANNELS 7-13	960.00-1215.0	AIRCRAFT RADIONAVAG.
216.00-220.00	UHF AIR (US GOV'T)	1215.0-1300.0	AMATEUR BAND
220.00-225.00	1 1/4 METER AMATEUR	1545.0-1559.0	SATELLITE
225.00-330.00	UHF AIR BAND	1645.0-1660.0	SATELLITE

NOTE: ALL FREQUENCIES ARE MHz

SHORTWAVE BAND INCLUDES COASTAL,
AERONAUTICAL, BROADCASTING AND
FIXED OPERATIONS

RCC = RADIO COMMON CARRIER
WCC = WIRELINE COMMON CARRIER
RCS = RADIO COMMON SERVICE
AVM = AUTOMATIC VEHICLE MONITOR
ISM = INDUSTRIAL/SCIENTIFIC/MEDICAL
PLM = PRIVATE LAND MOBILE

FREQUENCY ALLOCATION CHART

TELEVISION CHANNELS

054.00-060.00	CHANNEL 2	656.00-662.00	CHANNEL 45
060.00-066.00	CHANNEL 3	662.00-668.00	CHANNEL 46
066.00-072.00	CHANNEL 4	668.00-674.00	CHANNEL 47
076.00-082.00	CHANNEL 5	674.00-680.00	CHANNEL 48
082.00-088.00	CHANNEL 6	680.00-686.00	CHANNEL 49
		686.00-692.00	CHANNEL 50
174.00-180.00	CHANNEL 7	692.00-698.00	CHANNEL 51
180.00-186.00	CHANNEL 8	698.00-704.00	CHANNEL 52
186.00-192.00	CHANNEL 9	704.00-710.00	CHANNEL 53
192.00-198.00	CHANNEL 10	710.00-716.00	CHANNEL 54
198.00-204.00	CHANNEL 11	716.00-722.00	CHANNEL 55
204.00-210.00	CHANNEL 12	722.00-728.00	CHANNEL 56
210.00-216.00	CHANNEL 13	728.00-734.00	CHANNEL 57
		734.00-740.00	CHANNEL 58
470.00-476.00	CHANNEL 14	740.00-746.00	CHANNEL 59
476.00-482.00	CHANNEL 15	746.00-752.00	CHANNEL 60
482.00-488.00	CHANNEL 16	752.00-758.00	CHANNEL 61
488.00-494.00	CHANNEL 17	758.00-764.00	CHANNEL 62
494.00-500.00	CHANNEL 18	764.00-770.00	CHANNEL 63
500.00-506.00	CHANNEL 19	770.00-776.00	CHANNEL 64
506.00-512.00	CHANNEL 20	776.00-782.00	CHANNEL 65
		782.00-788.00	CHANNEL 66
514.00-520.00	CHANNEL 23	788.00-794.00	CHANNEL 67
520.00-526.00	CHANNEL 24	794.00-800.00	CHANNEL 68
526.00-532.00	CHANNEL 25		
532.00-538.00	CHANNEL 26	800.00-806.00	CHANNEL 69
538.00-544.00	CHANNEL 27	806.00-812.00	CHANNEL 70
544.00-560.00	CHANNEL 28	812.00-818.00	CHANNEL 71
560.00-566.00	CHANNEL 29	818.00-824.00	CHANNEL 72
566.00-572.00	CHANNEL 30	824.00-830.00	CHANNEL 73
572.00-578.00	CHANNEL 31	830.00-836.00	CHANNEL 74
578.00-584.00	CHANNEL 32	836.00-842.00	CHANNEL 75
584.00-590.00	CHANNEL 33	842.00-848.00	CHANNEL 76
590.00-596.00	CHANNEL 34	848.00-854.00	CHANNEL 77
596.00-602.00	CHANNEL 35	854.00-860.00	CHANNEL 78
602.00-608.00	CHANNEL 36	860.00-866.00	CHANNEL 79
608.00-614.00	CHANNEL 37	866.00-872.00	CHANNEL 80
614.00-620.00	CHANNEL 38	872.00-878.00	CHANNEL 81
620.00-626.00	CHANNEL 39	878.00-884.00	CHANNEL 82
626.00-632.00	CHANNEL 40	884.00-890.00	CHANNEL 83
632.00-638.00	CHANNEL 41	890.00-896.00	CHANNEL 84
638.00-644.00	CHANNEL 42		
644.00-650.00	CHANNEL 43		
650.00-656.00	CHANNEL 44		

Notes

159150 - Metro Police

FM
* 1625530 - Weather forecast

AM 119.1 } Nat. Airport
   124

KHB 36 NOA- Manassas - Nat weather forecast